The emancipation of Catholics, Jews and Protestants

Manchester University Press

The emancipation of Catholics, Jews and Protestants

Minorities and the nation state in nineteenth-century Europe

edited by
Rainer Liedtke and Stephan Wendehorst

Manchester University Press
Manchester and New York

distributed exclusively in the USA by St. Martin's Press

Copyright © Manchester University Press 1999

While copyright in the volume as a whole is vested in Manchester University Press, copyright in individual chapters belongs to their respective authors, and no chapter may be reproduced wholly or in part without the express permission in writing of both author and publisher.

Published by Manchester University Press
Oxford Road, Manchester M13 9NR, UK
and Room 400, 175 Fifth Avenue, New York, NY 10010, USA
http://www.man.ac.uk/mup

Distributed exclusively in the USA by
St. Martin's Press, Inc., 175 Fifth Avenue, New York,
NY 10010, USA

Distributed exclusively in Canada by
UBC Press, University of British Columbia, 6344 Memorial Road, Vancouver, BC, Canada V6T 1Z2

British Library Cataloguing-in-Publication Data
A catalogue record for this book is available from the British Library

Library of Congress Cataloging-in-Publication Data applied for

ISBN   0 7190 5149 5 hardback

First published 1999
06 05 04 03 02 01 00 99   10 9 8 7 6 5 4 3 2 1

Typeset by Special Edition Pre-press Services, London
Printed in Great Britain by Bookcraft (Bath) Ltd, Midsomer Norton

Contents

	List of contributors	vii
	Preface	ix
1	Introduction *Rainer Liedtke*	1
2	British Catholics *Ian Machin*	11
3	British Jews *David Cesarani*	33
4	French Protestants *André Encrevé*	56
5	French Jews *Frances Malino*	83
6	German Catholics *Wolfgang Altgeld*	100
7	German Jews *Christopher Clark*	122
8	Italian Protestants *Gian Paolo Romagnani*	148
9	Italian Jews *Gadi Luzzatto Voghera*	169
10	Emancipation as path to national integration *Stephan Wendehorst*	188
	Chronology of formal emancipation	207
	Select bibliography	211
	Index	215

List of contributors

Wolfgang Altgeld is Professor of Modern and Contemporary History at the University of Mainz. Among his many publications are *Das politische Italienbild der Deutschen* (1984); *Katholizismus, Protestantismus, Judentum* (1992); *Widerstand in Europa* (1995) and *Kleine Geschichte Italiens* (1998).

David Cesarani is Parkes/Wiener Professor of Twentieth-Century Jewish History and Culture at the University of Southampton and Director of the Institute of Contemporary History and the Wiener Library in London. He has published *The Jewish Chronicle and Anglo-Jewry, 1841–1991* (1993), edited *The making of modern Anglo-Jewry* (1990); *The final solution: Origins and implementation* (1994); *Genocide and rescue: The holocaust in Hungary, 1944* (1997) and co-edited: *The internment of aliens in twentieth century Britain* (1994) and *Citizenship, nationality, and migration in Europe* (1996).

Christopher Clark is Lecturer in History at the University of Cambridge and Fellow of St Catharine's College, Cambridge. He has published widely in the field of Prussian and German history and is the author of *Politics and conversion: Missionary Protestantism and the Jews in Prussia, 1728–1941* (1995).

André Encrevé is Professor of Contemporary History at the University of Paris XII and editor-in-chief of the *Bulletin de la Société de l'histoire du protestantisme français*. His main publications include: *Les Protestants en France de 1800 à nos jours* (1985); *Protestants français au milieu du XIXe siècle: Les réformés de 1848–1870* (1986). He is editor of *Les protestants*, volume 5 of the *Dictionnaire du monde religieux dans la France contemporaine* (1992).

List of contributors

Rainer Liedtke is Research Fellow in Modern History at the Technical University of Berlin. He has published *Jewish welfare in Hamburg and Manchester, c. 1850–1914* (1998) and is co-editor of *Two nations: British and German Jews in comparative perspective* (forthcoming 1999).

Gadi Luzzatto Voghera is a historian living in Venice. He has published *Oltre il Ghetto* (1993), *L'antisemitismo: Domande e risposte* (1994) and *Il prezzo dell'eguaglianza. Il dibattito sull'emancipazione degli ebrei in Italia (1781–1848)* (1998).

Ian Machin is Professor of British History at the University of Dundee. Among his numerous publications are *The Catholic question in English politics* (1964); *Politics and the Churches in Great Britain, 1832–1868* (1977); *Politics and the Churches in Great Britain, 1869–1921* (1987) and *Churches and social issues in twentieth-century Britain* (1998).

Frances Malino is Sophia Moses Robison Professor of Jewish Studies and History at Wellesley College. She has published *The Sephardic Jews of Bordeaux* (1978); *A Jew in the French Revolution: The life of Zalkind Hourwitz* (1996) and co-edited: *Essays in modern Jewish history* (1982); *The Jews in modern France* (1985); *Profiles in diversity: Jews in a changing Europe* (1998), first published in 1990 as *From East and West: Jews in a changing Europe*.

Gian Paolo Romagnani is Professor of Modern History at the University of Verona and a council member of the Società di Studi Valdesi. Among his many publications are: *Storiografia e politica culturale nel Piemonte di Carlo Alberto* (1985) and the two-volume *Prospero Balbo, intelletuale e uomo di Stato (1762–1837)* (1988, 1990).

Stephan Wendehorst is part-time Lecturer in Modern History – Jewish History and Culture – at the University of Munich/Venice International University. He is author of *British Jewry, Zionism and the Jewish state, 1936–1956* (forthcoming).

Preface

A lecture series on Jewish emancipation in eight European states, which the editors organised for the Oxford Centre for Hebrew and Jewish Studies in the autumn of 1994, stands behind this book. Although the event was well received by the Oxford academic community, it did not attract much attention beyond the group of scholars and students of Jewish history who attended the lectures. In order to broaden the scope of the project for the purposes of publication, scholarship on Jewish and Christian emancipation in four core European nation states – Britain, France, Germany and Italy – has been brought together. By its inclusion of Catholic, Jewish and Protestant minorities this study has been able to juxtapose the emancipatory experience of different minorities within one national context and also to contrast the experience of one minority group under the conditions that prevailed in different countries. Of the Oxford lecturers, only David Cesarani is represented here. Seven further contributions have been solicited from experts in the nineteenth-century historical development of a particular European minority group to form the present volume.

The editors wish to thank the individual contributors to this work for what has been a pleasant collaboration and for their willingness to support a novel idea. Each scholar has contributed not only his or her individual style and approach to the study but also a set of convictions about the position of the respective minority, which the editors have respected. Furthermore, this volume would not have been possible without the support and encouragement of several persons to whom the editors would like to express their gratitude. Philip Alexander, formerly president of the Oxford Centre for Hebrew and Jewish Studies, endorsed the lecture series which resulted in this publication. David Sorkin first drew attention to the fact that a comparison of Jewish and Christian minority groups would make a worthwhile intellectual venture. An anonymous reader for Manchester University Press encouraged the

Preface

project and provided valuable criticism. Lionel de Rothschild provided invaluable help with the translation of the chapter by Wolfgang Altgeld. Simone Sartori and Ulrich Wyrwa helped to clarify many Italian language queries.

The chapters by Wolfgang Altgeld, André Encrevé, Gian Paolo Romagnani and Gadi Luzzatto Voghera were translated by Rainer Liedtke, Charlotte Bigg, Lucy Emmett and George Ferzoco, respectively. Vanessa Graham, the history editor at Manchester University Press, has been enthusiastic about the project since it was first proposed to her. She, together with Carolyn Hand and Louise Edwards, has seen to a smooth production process and given every possible support to the editors. Corinne Orde has done an outstanding job as our copy-editor.

R. L.
S. W.

1

Introduction

Rainer Liedtke

The term 'emancipation' denotes a stage in the development of social groups that is characterised by religion, class or gender. The scope of this study is restricted to religious and religiously defined minorities. In the various European nation states, from the late eighteenth century onwards, these groups underwent a process of formal 'equalisation' with regard to their political, civil and legal status. In the late 1800s, the possession of full civil and political rights was usually limited to the members of an Established Church. Adherents of heterodox Christian denominations as well as Jews found themselves on the margins of at least political society. Formal emancipation was generally not paralleled by an equalisation of economic and social opportunities and participation in the cultural and political life of society as a whole.

There is a considerable body of scholarship on the emancipation of various minorities in nineteenth-century Europe and, in particular, on the formal emancipatory processes that led to full civil and political rights. The emancipation of the Jews in Western and Central Europe is a core research area of Jewish historiography.[1] Similarly, there exists significant scholarship on the historical development of Protestant and Catholic minorities. No attempt has yet been made, however, to bring together scholarship on the different religious minorities. By including Catholic, Jewish and Protestant minorities in the same study, we can juxtapose emancipation as it was experienced by different minorities within one national context and the experience of one minority group under the conditions prevailing in different countries. Four core European nation states – Britain, France, Germany and Italy – have been included in the study. The time frame encompasses the period from the 1780s to the First World War.

[1] See Pierre Birnbaum and Ira Katznelson (eds), *Paths of Emancipation: Jews, States and Citizenship* (Princeton, 1995), for a recent comparative presentation of different Jewish emancipation processes.

Rather than summarise the results of the individual studies, I shall make some more general observations that have a bearing on all contributions. Without claiming to be exhaustive, these comments may serve as an informal guideline for the individual essays. They should not be taken for a comparative analysis of the minorities' emancipatory experiences; such an analysis is left for the reader to make. Here the focus is on the problems involved in defining minorities, the terminology of emancipation and the significance of the comparative approach for the understanding of religious minorities.

Defining minorities

How does one define a minority?[2] The minorities under discussion in this volume range from about twenty thousand Protestants in Italy to several million Catholics in Germany constituting more than a third of that country's entire population. Whereas the Protestants in nineteenth-century Italy lived mainly in one small mountain enclave, German Catholics were numerically the dominant population in two German states and several regions. A similar juxtaposition, though in somewhat less extreme measure, could be applied to French Protestants and British Catholics. Although Jews were a quantitatively definable minority in all four countries, they also ranged from being a substantial part of the population in several large cities and regions in Germany and, towards the end of the century, in Britain to constituting only very small groups in France and, in particular, Italy. Clearly, numbers do not wholly explain a minority position. More useful are the evaluation of the social relations that were maintained by the group and, in particular, the questions of whether its members enjoyed fewer privileges and less recognition in these relations than the members of other groups and whether their opportunities in life and their power to assert themselves were more limited than those of a majority group. It does not necessarily follow that this majority presented itself as a monolith without further fragmentation, since all minorities and majority societies under consideration were internally stratified according to class, religious practice and gender, which in turn were dynamic concepts.

Obviously, an essential precondition for the constitution of a minority was the will of the members of that group consciously to retain the characteristics that caused the limitation of their opportunities or, in

---

[2] I am grateful to Wolfgang Altgeld for providing stimulating ideas for the discussion of this point.

Introduction

other words, their discrimination. In nineteenth-century Europe religion was the single most important factor in the constitution and definition of minority groups. Individuals whose religion differed from that of the majority group did not enjoy equal opportunities in their social relations, which excluded them from equal political participation and limited their ability to perform in the economic sphere. It was possible to broaden one's opportunities by converting to a majority faith, but – especially in the case of Jewish apostates – this did not always result in achieving social acceptance.

The condition of being a minority was fundamentally different for Catholics and Protestants on the one side and Jews on the other. In nineteenth-century Europe Jews were a minority everywhere. Catholics and Protestants were minorities only within specific territorial entities, where they encountered, respectively, a dominant population made up of adherents to the other Christian denomination. What should be kept in mind, however, is that territorial changes within one country could bring about a radical redrawing of the map of Christian majority–minority relations. In the nineteenth century this happened during the unification processes in Italy as well as Germany; it had also occurred with the Napoleonic restructuring of the German states. Britain and France did not go through the same experience.

Nevertheless, whereas a Christian group could enter into a minority situation, Jews, even in their densest concentration, remained the classical minority in all places and at all times. Jews thus had a starting-point in their quest for equality which differed from that of Catholics and Protestants in positions of minority. Among other things, this had an effect on the mentalities behind demands for equality, the support lent to a minority from without and, in particular, the potential alliances minorities could form in order to achieve their goals.

Emancipation concepts

'Emancipation' is a historical term that found entry into the vocabulary of majority–minority relations at different times in different countries. It has been used by historical scholarship as a convenient and apparently all-encompassing concept to describe a vital stage in the development of religious minorities, often without further differentiation. The fragmentary nature of emancipation – chronologically, but also with regard to the variety of impacts on different groups within a minority – has not received sufficient scholarly attention. Depending on social status, wealth and income, gender, piety and so forth, emancipation or the lack of equal rights could mean very different things for the various members of a minority: there were driving forces that stood to gain much from emancipation; there were individuals who had no particular interest in advancing equality; and, at least in some cases, there were stern opponents of unconditional equality, who feared that it would cause their groups to erode and eventually disappear.

Moreover, the process itself took place on more than one level. Political emancipation and the granting of full civil rights were often preceded by an equalisation in the religious or even the economic spheres, which was usually termed 'toleration'. Thus, what ultimately distinguished religious minorities from a majority society was generally not so much any disabilities they might suffer in adhering to a different faith as their ineligibility to participate in political processes, limitations on their potential for economic success and prohibitions on their social contacts. Above all, it is vital to realise that a process of emancipation did not end with the removal of disabilities on the political and legal planes.

Emancipation did not happen in a historical vacuum: it must be viewed in the context of the general social and economic development of specific countries. On the one hand, it was a conscious process that required an effort on the part of law-making authorities and generated public debates. But at the same time, the internal modernisation of a society could advance the standing of religious minorities or fuel the debate about civic equality and thus in itself provide a degree of emancipation that was codified later. In the same way, retrogression could mean a setback for emancipationist ambitions. This should also be taken into consideration when making international comparisons. The political, legal, social and economic state of development of each country under consideration, or even in the different regions within one nation, provided not only the background to the progress of formal emancipation of religious minorities but were key factors in the process.[3] The comparison can, however, yield many more results.

The significance of comparison

The individual contributions presented in this volume are not comparative. It would certainly have been desirable to have a comparative analysis of Jewish and Christian emancipatory processes for each country from a single hand, yet historians who are equally at home in both areas of

[3] This also makes an inclusion of most Eastern European countries problematic, since in the sphere of minority–majority relations pre-modern conditions predominated throughout much of the nineteenth century.

Introduction

research are thin on the ground. Thus, it is left to the reader to make comparisons and I can merely draw attention to some useful points to keep in mind while doing so. Two kinds of comparison may be made: between individual minorities and between minority experiences in different national contexts. Emancipation had a different meaning for Catholics, Jews and Protestants. The comparative approach addresses the question as to what importance a different religion and cultural heritage had for the emancipatory process and the shape of majority–minority relations in the various European nation states. Did states adopt general policies to deal with religious minorities? In what way did the treatment of Christian denominations differ from that of the Jews? Is it possible to identify common denominators not only in the treatment of one minority, such as the Jews, but also in the way religious difference generally was regarded in nineteenth century Europe? What may seem typical for one country or one minority may have been common in the wider European context. Conversely, the comparison can draw attention to characteristics that have hitherto not been perceived as being unique to any one minority's experience. In the absence of comparison there will be no challenge to accepted paths of thinking and no test of peculiarities.

Catholics and Protestants were distinguished primarily by their religious beliefs. While this was also the basis for the separation between Jews and Christians, a number of other factors, inevitably tied to religious practice, contributed to their segregation. The most important of these were language, Jewish dietary laws and divergent days of rest and timings of religious festivals, which limited the opportunities for Jews and Christians to socialise with each other. While Catholics and Protestants also often developed specific socio-economic profiles, Jews were distinguished from Christians, at least in most countries, not only by restrictions on their place of settlement, or ghettoisation, and on their necessarily very narrow choice of occupation but also by segregated legal structures relating to their community. These regulated internal Jewish life and represented the minority as a whole to society at large and found no parallel in Christian Church organisations. Thus the barriers Jewish emancipation had to overcome were necessarily higher.

Emancipation rarely came unconditionally but was generally based on a quid pro quo. It was sometimes connected to an educational agenda aimed at 'regenerating' the minority, which ultimately demanded the eradication of all peculiarities. At the very least, it was hoped that the minority would adopt the cultural practices and preferences of the majority society and change its socio-economic profile or its 'moral character'. Likewise, the patriotism and potential for national allegiance of minorities was often in doubt; speculation about their alleged connections to external and sometimes hostile powers was rife. A comparison of what was expected of different minorities in one country can demonstrate how specific the quid pro quo that was applied to one of them really was. A juxtaposition of the regeneration demanded of Jews or of non-dominant Christian groups in different countries shows, on the one hand, whether any overarching grievances and fears underpinned the emancipation of one minority and, on the other, how self-assured and confident the respective European majority societies were when granting equality to outsiders. This can also be seen when one compares the divergent routes and different methods that were employed by the various minorities in order to advance their emancipation. These depended on the sort of restrictions they were subjected to, the kind of resistance they were facing in political circles and the internal organisational structure as well as the socio-economic composition and demography of each minority. All three factors differed from country to country but also from one minority group to another.

Finally, with a focus on a single national context and especially a single minority, claims are easily made that an emancipation occurred 'late' or 'at an early stage'. Such statements must remain meaningless and arbitrary unless a comparison with other emancipatory processes is undertaken. The timing of emancipation depended to a great extent on the condition and development of the respective European nation states. Although religion has always been a criteria for differentiating groups from one another, religious minorities in need of emancipation are a characteristic of the age of the nation state and nationalism. The history of minority experiences provides a key to a better understanding of nineteenth-century state and society. The place that minorities occupied in the development of the nation state informs us about their potential for integration and about the distinct ideological concepts of the particular states and societies under investigation. The treatment of religiously defined minorities was symptomatic of changing notions of citizenship and shifting balances in the perception and reality of relations between the civic and religious spheres. Minorities were agents and objects in the redefinition of citizenship and of the relationship between these two spheres. The concluding essay of this volume will address the implications of nineteenth-century nation building for the emancipation of religious minorities.

The individual contributions have been arranged by country. Ian Machin analyses the emancipatory experience of British Catholics. He draws particular attention to the fact that an understanding of the process

Introduction

is impossible without constant reference to Ireland, the one part of the United Kingdom where Catholics formed the majority. The Emancipation Act of 1829 was mainly the result of Irish pressure. Moreover, the Catholic population resident in Britain was enormously augmented by Irish immigrants, who had already outnumbered the 'old Catholics' by the early nineteenth century. Machin demonstrates that the legislation of 1829 by no means concluded Catholic emancipation: several further Acts were required during the following decades to put Catholics on an equal footing with members of the Established Church. Sectarian riots, constant complaints about the moral and social condition of Irish Catholic immigrants and accusations of ultra-montanism and dual loyalties accompanied the slow and arduous integration process of Catholics into nineteenth-century British society. Nevertheless, by the close of the century, British Catholics still remained inferior in both a formal and an informal social sense.

British Jews began their emancipation campaign after Catholics had achieved political equality. David Cesarani argues persuasively that the received historical account that British Jews had the most benign history of all Jewish populations in Europe and that they experienced a benevolent, if protracted, emancipatory process has only recently been challenged by a younger generation of historians. The 'whiggish' view of British Jewish history has been replaced by a less positive account, which claims that emancipation was such a lengthy process because of, among other factors, the centrality of religion and the concept of the Christian state in nineteenth-century Britain and which demonstrates that Jews were expected to show by their conduct that they deserved emancipation. Jews recognised this 'anti-Semitism of toleration' and feared the consequences of transgression. Cesarani stresses that at the root of this 'emancipation contract' was the issue of whether Jews could belong to the English nation, a question that was itself the product of the search for an English identity.

André Encrevé describes the complicated status of Protestants in pre-Revolutionary France, who were represented in high offices but were forced to keep a low profile as far as their religious affiliation was concerned. In the course of the Revolution Protestants achieved religious equality for the first time, but during the period of the Terror they were also persecuted, even if the conflict was mainly between the state and the Catholic Church. After the Revolution French Protestants strove for civil and religious integration into the national community. However, the Catholic hierarchy and a large part of the Catholic population, although not necessarily hostile to Protestant civil equality, refused to endorse religious emancipation for the minority. There was considerable opposition to freedom of worship outside traditionally Protestant regions, and, particularly after the final defeat of Napoleon, violent anti-Protestant riots took place. The curtailment of religious practice continued to be the norm during the Restoration and under the regime of Napoleon III. The minority's full equality in the religious domain was only confirmed with the legislation of 1879, although in conservative and monarchist circles, which were traditionally allied with the Catholic hierarchy, a mistrust of Protestants prevailed until well into the twentieth century.

French Jews, as Frances Malino writes, also benefited from the Revolution, which granted citizenship and political equality, first to the Sephardic Jews of the southwest and then to the Ashkenazim of Alsace. However, the emancipation of most Jews was partly revoked in 1808 when the Napoleonic administration demanded doctrinal and concrete economic guarantees that they were worthy of citizenship. During the Restoration this legislation was not renewed, and although it took another three decades before the last vestiges of formal inequality had disappeared, a large number of Jews was able to enter the public institutions of French society at large, including the universities and the political parties. Towards the end of the century their equality was again challenged during the Dreyfus affair, which ignited anti-Semitic waves of violence throughout the country.

Wolfgang Altgeld describes how Catholics became a minority in the process of German nation building. With the simultaneous destruction of the Imperial Church and secularisation of Church property at the beginning of the nineteenth century the traditional foundations of Catholic life in Germany were shattered. Although all Christian denominations had been assured equal civic and political rights in the Federal Constitution (*Deutsche Bundesakte*) and the constitutions subsequently created by individual states, Catholics were severely disadvantaged in almost all of the states that were dominated by Protestants, especially in Prussia. The interests of the state and the Catholic Church contradicted each other on a number of occasions and led to a self-identification of Catholics as a denominational and, at the same time, a social and political minority. After the foundation of the Empire in 1871, a permanent Catholic political party was established. Soon afterwards laws were promulgated at the level of either individual states or the Empire as a whole, which were designed to abolish the public influence of the Catholic Church. The resistance of Catholic clergy and lay people called for a variety of legislative and persecutory measures. The so-called *Kulturkampf*, which resulted in a general politicisation of Catholicism, was not only about the demarca-

Introduction

tion of the spheres of the state and the Catholic Church; it was also about the question of which inheritance from pre-national cultures should be woven into the new national culture and which groups would therefore be privileged.

In contrast to the Catholics, German Jews experienced a drawn-out and haphazard emancipatory process in the political, legal and economic spheres. Christopher Clark draws attention to the fragmented nature of the process because responsibility for Jewish policy remained with the individual German states. Jews resident in territories annexed by the French obtained unconditional emancipation, though this was largely rescinded after Napoleon's defeat. The decades preceding the Revolution of 1848 were characterised by the lack of a co-ordinated approach to Jewish legal reform and equality set out in the 'Basic Rights' of the Frankfurt Constitution, which were again annulled when the Revolution had failed. It took another two decades before Jews were guaranteed complete legal and political equality in all German territories in the constitution of the Empire of 1871. Clark points out that during the protracted emancipatory process German Jewry experienced the transition from traditional to modern society through urbanisation, professionalisation and the emergence of an acculturated bourgeoisie, yet its narrow occupational structure remained remarkably stable. Among other factors, this opened avenues for anti-Semitic accusations and the survival of a 'Jewish question' long after Jews had ceased being a minority of second-class citizens.

In his analysis of Italian Protestant emancipation, Gian Paolo Romagnani focuses on the Waldensians of Piedmont who experienced a brief period of toleration and comparative equality when their territory was annexed by Napoleonic France. With the restoration of Piedmontese sovereignty in 1815 Protestants were again subject to legal and economic restrictions, in particular in all areas where they were numerically inferior to Catholics. Only in the aftermath of the 1848 Revolution was legal discrimination against non-Catholic subjects constitutionally prohibited, although Catholicism remained the official state religion. In the second half of the century, though overall numbers remained small, Italian Protestantism diffused throughout the peninsula. A significant number of Protestants were to be found among the political class of post-unification Italy, yet there existed no Protestant middle class comparable to that in other European countries. Protestants continued to be discriminated against by the Catholic population, especially in rural areas, but all in all, the minority experienced a comparatively untroubled integration into the national community.

In his analysis of Italian Jewish emancipation, Gadi Luzzatto Voghera draws attention to the problem of the geographical concentration of Italian Jews in the north of the country and lists a number of potential pitfalls of a purely statistical interpretation of the minority's historical experience. He then documents the protracted emancipation process by combining general observations with a biographical summary of the life of the Venetian Jew Moisé Soave. His experiences demonstrate the efforts of the small Italian Jewish elite, which from the early nineteenth century endeavoured to transform Jewish cultural characteristics and redefine Jewish economic activities with the explicit intention of making them part of Italian society. The adjustment of the Jews to a middle-class model of social and economic life and the adaptation of their religion to Italian middle-class standards gave rise to a wide-ranging programme of re-education and acculturation. In parallel with this regeneration ran the protracted process of Jewish legal and political emancipation, which found its formal termination in the abolition of the Roman ghetto at the time of the completion of the Italian nation state in 1870.

2

British Catholics

Ian Machin

The gradual emancipation of the British Catholic minority took place mainly in the nineteenth century. The term 'emancipation' is taken in the broadest sense to signify the Catholics' release not only from legal restrictions on their political participation and liturgical activities but also, to a large extent, from unofficial social discrimination. Thus both 'formal' emancipation, in the sense of promoting legal equality, and 'informal' emancipation, in the sense of promoting social equality, will be discussed.

It is virtually impossible to address the development of Catholics in Britain without constant reference to Catholics in Ireland. Ireland was the one part of the post-1800 United Kingdom which had a Catholic majority, comprising about three-quarters of the population.[1] Ireland was vulnerable to invasion by France during the wars in the late eighteenth century, and the Catholic majority was given important concessions by the Protestant and aristocratic Irish Parliament. These concessions, however, fell short of admitting Catholics to the Irish Parliament, an aspiration known as Catholic emancipation. William Pitt hoped to carry Catholic emancipation after the Irish Union Act of 1800 so that Catholics could sit in the new United Parliament at Westminster. But King George III thwarted his premier's wishes by adhering to the Protestant exclusiveness of his Coronation Oath, and Pitt resigned. Subsequently the king prevented the passage of other concessions to Catholics. The same attitude was maintained by his successor, George IV, until he reluctantly agreed to the introduction of a bill (the Relief Bill) in 1829, which allowed Catholic entry to Parliament.[2]

---

[1] R. Currie, A. Gilbert and L. Horsley (eds), *Churches and churchgoers: Patterns of Church growth in the British Isles since 1700* (Oxford, 1977), pp. 220–1; F. S. L. Lyons, *Ireland since the Famine* (London, 1973), p. 18.

[2] G. I. T. Machin, *The Catholic question in English politics, 1820 to 1830* (Oxford, 1964), pp. 99–105, 167–72, 177–8; W. Hinde, *Catholic emancipation: A shake to men's minds* (Oxford, 1992), pp. 77–159; G. I. T. Machin, 'The Catholic question and the monarchy, 1827–9', *Parliamentary History*, 16, 2 (1997), 213–18.

From 1772 the penal laws passed against Catholics in Ireland following the Revolution of 1688 were progressively removed. In 1793 the Franchise Bill passed by the Irish Parliament allowed Catholics to vote in parliamentary elections, subject to a minimum qualification of property ownership. Two years later the Irish Parliament sought to transfer more of the training of Catholic priests from the continent to Ireland by bestowing a financial grant, subject to annual renewal, on Maynooth College, not far from Dublin. But the government's refusal to follow the Franchise Act with the concession of Catholic emancipation helped to cause the rebellion of 1798, which involved an unsuccessful French invasion. After the rebellion had been suppressed Pitt's government passed the Union Bill, but Catholic emancipation was still withheld after this measure had come into operation.[3] The combination of partial restriction and partial concession helped to sustain the development in Ireland of

> a powerful fusion of religion and identity unequalled in any other part of the British Isles with the possible exception of Protestantism in Ulster, which in turn drew strength from its implacable opposition to Catholic nationalism.[4]

During the first three decades of the nineteenth century the main political question affecting Catholics in the United Kingdom was that of their political emancipation – their frustrated desire to be accepted as members of the Houses of Lords and Commons at Westminster. There was much dispute and agitation, especially in Ireland, over the conditions on which emancipation might be granted by the United Parliament.[5] Finally the reform succeeded when it was embodied in the Relief Bill, which was prepared and introduced by the Duke of Wellington's government in 1829,

---

[3] J. Ehrman, *The Younger Pitt*, vol. 1 (London, 1983), pp. 424–7; vol. 3 (London, 1996), pp. 158–94; D. Keogh, *The French disease: The Catholic Church and Irish radicalism, 1790–1800* (Dublin, 1993), especially pp. 218–20; K. Whelan, *The tree of liberty: Radicalism, Catholicism, and the construction of Irish identity, 1760–1830* (Cork, 1996); Marianne Elliott, *Partners in revolution: The United Irishmen and France* (New Haven, 1982); H. Senior, *Orangeism in Ireland and Britain, 1795–1836* (London, 1966), pp. 22–137.

[4] D. Hempton, *Religion and political culture in Britain and Ireland: From the Glorious Revolution to the decline of empire* (Cambridge, 1996), p. 72.

[5] Machin, *Catholic question*, pp. 12–15, 19ff.; M. Roberts, *The Whig Party, 1807–12* (London, 1965; first edn 1939), pp. 7–34, 45–57, 81–102; B. Ward, *The eve of Catholic emancipation*, 3 vols (London, 1911–12), vol. 1, p. 49ff.

passed by Parliament, and given the royal assent.[6] This measure, together with the repeal in the previous year of the Test and Corporation Acts, which had officially barred non-Anglicans from government and corporation office, signified the resumption of a policy by British governments to extend civil equality to religious minorities. This tendency was displayed in many ways during the remainder of the nineteenth century, including the admission of Jews to Parliament from 1858 and of atheists from 1886. Catholic emancipation was not only the granting of long-desired liberation for a large minority in the United Kingdom but an important precedent for the concession of similar liberation to smaller religious and non-religious groups.

Catholic emancipation was the main legal advance made by Irish and British Catholics in the nineteenth century. But the act's central feature, admittance to Parliament, was accompanied by restrictions in the same enactment that emphasised the unfavourable status still possessed by Catholics. They could hardly take exception to their exclusion from ecclesiastical office in the Established Churches – such as the post of High Commissioner to the General Assembly of the Church of Scotland – or from posts in universities and schools which were controlled by the Established Churches or in which the latter had privileged status. Nor was it likely that Catholics would object much to the new oath, demanded of Catholic Members of Parliament and civil servants by the emancipation legislation of 1829, whereby they denied civil authority in the United Kingdom to the Pope and disclaimed any intention to subvert the Protestant religion and government. Nor, in the circumstances of the time, were they likely to protest overtly about the act's provisions that a Catholic could not become Sovereign or Regent of the United Kingdom, or Lord Lieutenant (Viceroy) or Lord Chancellor of Ireland, or Lord Chancellor of England. But they were likely to feel more aggrieved about a restriction on their own religious practice under clause twenty-six of the act, which stated that Catholic clerics should not hold public processions in which full liturgical vestments were worn and in which the consecrated Host was carried.[7] There was, in fact, a good deal more legislative

---

[6] Hinde, *Catholic emancipation*, p. 160ff.; Karen A. Noyce, 'The Duke of Wellington and the Catholic question', in N. Gash (ed.), *Wellington: Studies in the military and political career of the first Duke of Wellington* (Manchester, 1990), pp. 139–58; F. O'Ferrall, *Catholic emancipation: Daniel O'Connell and the birth of Irish democracy, 1820–30* (Dublin, 1985); E. Norman, *The English Catholic Church in the nineteenth century* (Oxford, 1984), pp. 29–68.

[7] Hinde, *Catholic emancipation*, pp. 161–2.

concession to be gained before Catholics could feel fully emancipated from an unfavourable legal condition. They have not entirely reached this position in Great Britain today.

I

The emancipation of 1829 was mainly the result of Irish pressure. This was chiefly exerted from 1823 by Daniel O'Connell's Catholic Association, which obtained very wide support from Irish Catholic priests and people.[8] A British Catholic Association was formed with connections to this body, and several local branches of the British association were founded.[9] The 'Papist Returns' of 1767 for England and Wales obtained by the House of Lords had produced a total figure of only 67,928 Catholics. Marked regional differences were shown in these returns, the distribution of Catholics by county ranging from Lancashire (which had a third of the total) to Cambridgeshire which had only seven Catholics.[10] In 1755 there were said to be 16,490 Catholics in Scotland, or just over one per cent of the population; they were resident mostly in Banffshire (in the northeast of the country) and in the western Highlands and Islands. By 1780 the estimated total number of Catholics in England and Wales was about 80,000.[11] Numbers increased substantially from about 1790. This was mainly because of immigration from an overcrowded Ireland and, to some extent, because of an influx of clergy and others in the 1790s seeking asylum from the French Revolution. Catholics in Great Britain by 1840 have been estimated at 305,000.[12] In that year the number of vicars apostolic in England and Wales who had regional supervision in place of territorial bishops was doubled to eight (three vicars apostolic were established in Scotland in 1827). The number of Catholic chapels in England and Wales, said to be only thirty in 1796, grew to 330 in 1821 and 595 in 1851.[13]

[8] O'Ferrall, *Catholic emancipation*, pp. 30–85; J. A. Reynolds, *The Catholic emancipation crisis in Ireland, 1823–9* (New Haven, 1954).

[9] R. W. Linker, 'The English Roman Catholics and emancipation: The politics of persuasion', *Journal of Ecclesiastical History*, 27 (1976), 151–80; Machin, *Catholic question*, pp. 46–7; T. Burke, *Catholic history of Liverpool* (Liverpool, 1910), pp. 41–2.

[10] J.-A.Lesourd, *Les Catholiques dans la société anglaise, 1765–1865*, 2 vols (Lille, 1978), vol. 1, pp. 76–7, 179.

[11] J. Bossy, *The English Catholic community, 1570–1850* (London, 1975), p. 185; T. G. Holt, 'A note on some eighteenth century statistics', *Recusant History*, 10 (1969–70), 4–5. The figure for Scotland in 1755 is quoted in C. Brown, *The social history of religion in Scotland since 1730* (London, 1987), p. 45.

[12] Currie et al., *Churches and churchgoers*, p. 35.

[13] Lesourd, *Les Catholiques*, vol. 1, p. 607 (and pp. 600–9).

The largest nineteenth-century increase in the number of Catholics in Britain took place through Irish immigration following the disastrous potato famine in 1845 and subsequent years. The famine caused large numbers of Catholics and smaller numbers of Protestants, perhaps a quarter of the total, to leave their native shores and seek work and subsistence in Britain, the United States of America, Australia or elsewhere. By 1851 Catholics in Britain had already increased to about 846,000 (including some 150,000 in Scotland) out of a total population of about twenty-one million.[14] By 1900, on account of natural growth and further immigration, Catholics had reached just over two million in a British population of thirty-seven million.[15] Catholics then comprised about 6 per cent of the total population, compared with about 0.8 per cent in 1800 and some nine per cent today.

Catholics in Britain did not have the same numbers, political bargaining strength or nationalist aspirations as those which gained important concessions for the Irish Catholics in the 1790s and in 1829. But, although they were a small and unprivileged minority, British Catholics were allowed to vote in parliamentary elections, unless it was decided to administer certain oaths which they might wish to avoid taking on conscientious grounds.[16] In 1778 Catholics in Britain obtained a minor measure of relief that removed some of the legal restrictions placed on them. For example, it permitted Catholics officially to inherit property. This concession helped, however, to cause the anti-Catholic Gordon Riots in London in 1780. A more significant measure, the Relief Act of 1791, granted freedom of worship and education to Catholics in England and Wales, and a similar measure for Catholics in Scotland was passed in 1793.[17] At this time British Catholics hoped to win concessions not only through the political pressure which their Irish co-religionists were able to exert with moderate success on the British government. They hoped to gain from the sporadic liberal tendencies in British politics that also encouraged the larger minority of Protestant Dissenters in the late 1780s to claim relief from their own restrictions, through repeal of the Test and Corporation Acts. These acts officially denied government office, both

---

[14] Currie *et al.*, *Churches and churchgoers*, p. 35.

[15] *Ibid.*

[16] Machin, *Catholic question*, pp. 78–9; N. Gash, *Politics in the age of Peel: A study in the technique of parliamentary representation* (London, 1953), p. 115.

[17] C. Haydon, *Anti-Catholicism in eighteenth-century England, c. 1714–80* (Manchester, 1993), pp. 204–44, 264–5; Lesourd, *Les Catholiques*, vol. 1, pp. 368–79; C. Johnson, *Developments in the Roman Catholic Church in Scotland, 1789–1829* (Edinburgh, 1983), p. 31; B. Ward, *The dawn of Catholic emancipation in England, 1781–1803*, 2 vols (London, 1909), vol. 1, p. 126ff, 297ff, vol. 2, p. 51ff.

national and local, to non-Anglicans. A British Catholic committee formed in 1787 appeared to try to lessen its own differences with Protestant Dissenters by taking the name 'Protesting Catholic Dissenters' and by emphasising the restrained religion that marked them out from enthusiastic devotees of the papacy. They drew up a 'Protestation', which denied temporal authority to the Pope and rejected papal infallibility. A 'Cisalpine Club' formed by Catholics in 1792 was another clear indication of anti-ultramontane tendencies.[18] Ironically, however, on account of the Irish situation Catholics fared much better than Protestant Dissenters in obtaining concessions in the 1790s. Parliamentary efforts by the Whigs opposing the government failed in 1787, 1789 and 1790 to obtain the repeal of the Test and Corporation Acts. Repeal was not gained until 1828. Some champions of Catholic emancipation then withheld their support from repeal because they feared it would remove a reason for Nonconformists to support emancipation.[19]

The attempt to emphasise a 'native British' or pseudo-Gallican form of Catholicism – and the disputes among Catholics to which such an attempt gave rise – lead to consideration of a notable feature of the Catholic minority in nineteenth-century Britain: its wide social and religious divisions, which created much friction, even perhaps incompatibility, but did not prevent an underlying unity in seeking the removal of legal restrictions. A small group of Catholic landed aristocracy and their families had resisted the temptation to join the Established Church and were regarded by their co-religionists as helping to provide leadership. The *Catholic Year Book* of 1900 listed forty-one Catholic peers of Great Britain and Ireland and fifty-four Catholic baronets.[20] The holder of the dukedom of Norfolk, England's premier peerage, was usually (though not always) Catholic in the nineteenth century and has been Catholic throughout the twentieth. Moreover, there had always been middle- and working-class Catholics, and the majority of Catholics recorded in the Papist Returns of 1767 were agricultural or urban workers.

The number of Catholic labourers greatly increased on account of the Irish immigration. From the early nineteenth century immigrants formed

---

[18] Machin, *Catholic question*, pp. 10–11; Norman, *English Catholic Church*, p. 29ff.

[19] For the difficulties found by some supporters of Catholic emancipation in aiding the cause of repeal of the Test and Corporation Acts, see G. I. T. Machin, 'Resistance to repeal of the Test and Corporation Acts, 1828', *Historical Journal*, 22 (1979), 116–20, 123–4, 127–8, 138–9.

[20] O. Chadwick, *The Victorian Church* (London, 1970), vol. 2, p. 403. For treatment of the 'old Catholics' and the converts, see B. Ward, *The sequel to Catholic emancipation, 1830–50*, 2 vols (London, 1915), vol. 2, pp. 105ff, 236ff.

the majority of the Catholic population of Great Britain. Most immigrants probably belonged to the unskilled labouring class. On coming to Britain they were called on to transfer their attentions from agriculture to industry, though some were already experienced as weavers. Towards the end of the nineteenth century their descendants began to show more social diversity; a few were by then engaging in professional occupations. Ultramontane forms of religious expression – colourful and enthusiastic by nature and showing a marked devotion to the papacy and its pronouncements – were far more characteristic of the immigrants than of the 'old Catholics'. This was a cause of tension between them, not least when the immigrants were confronted by conservative native priests who had to take them into their flocks. The Catholic Archbishop Manning, visiting western Scotland in 1867, noted that 'the [Catholic] clergy of Scotland, being in their home territory, ha[d] held themselves aloof as if affronted by the Irish invasion'.[21] A recent study of nineteenth-century Catholic worship in England, however, has emphasised the similarities as much as the differences between the national and social groups.[22] The Irish Catholic immigrants did not live in ghettos; they shared the cheapest areas of the towns with native unskilled workers. Nevertheless, they maintained a high degree of social cohesion. This arose not only because of where they lived but also because they engaged in similar occupations, forms of recreation and religious practices, and they often had to themselves the newly-built churches and schools for which they had largely paid.[23]

Finally, there was the additional ingredient of a sizeable number of converts. These had usually been led to join the Church of Rome through dissatisfaction with the 'Anglo-Catholic' limitations of the High Church 'Oxford Movement', which commenced in 1833 and which promoted an understanding of the Church of England as an organic, independent body, not a creature of the state. John Henry Newman and Henry Edward Manning, both of whom were later cardinals, were promising

---

[21] Quoted T. Gallagher, *Glasgow, the uneasy peace: Religious tension in modern Scotland* (Manchester, 1987), p. 43. For these tensions see also M. A. G. O'Tuathaigh, 'The Irish in nineteenth-century Britain: Problems of integration', in R. Swift and S.Gilley (eds), *The Irish in the Victorian city* (London, 1985), pp. 27–8; Burke, *Catholic history of Liverpool*, pp. 65–6; P. F. Anson, *Underground Catholicism in Scotland, 1622–1878* (Montrose, 1970), pp. 257–8.

[22] Mary Heimann, *Catholic devotion in Victorian England* (Oxford, 1995), pp. 17–24.

[23] A Catholic congregation consisting mainly of immigrants is studied in T. M. Devine (ed.), *St Mary's, Hamilton: A social history, 1846–1996* (Edinburgh, 1995). Cf. B. Aspinwall, 'The formation of the Catholic community in the west of Scotland', *Innes Review*, 33 (1982), 44–57.

Anglican clergymen who became Roman Catholics through this route. The converts usually belonged to the upper or middle classes. In their converted zeal they tended, though not invariably, to adopt ultramontane enthusiasm. They impressed by their social elevation and their intellectual ability rather than their numbers – though these were not negligible, being estimated at 82,000 in the years up to 1901.[24] Several of the Catholic peers in 1900 were converts, including the marquesses of Bute and Ripon, both notable in different ways as public vindicators of Catholic faith and practice. From the 1860s divisions between 'ultramontane' and liberal Catholics developed strongly over such matters as scriptural interpretation, scientific evidence and papal infallibility.[25] Hopes for the 'conversion of England' expressed by some Catholics, such as Ambrose Phillipps de Lisle, who was himself a convert, were disappointingly slow in realisation, and today little seems to be left of them. Benjamin Disraeli said he would only begin to worry about the possibility of national conversion if the grocers started to turn to Catholicism[26] – and there were no noticeable signs that this central and representative group in the population was succumbing.

Nearly all the Whigs supported Catholic emancipation in 1829. This relief was itself an aspect of parliamentary reform, as it admitted a new minority group to seats in the Legislature. After the Wellington ministry had been ousted in 1830, and the incoming Whig government had passed its more general parliamentary reform scheme two years later, a good deal of the Whigs' reforming efforts for the remainder of the 1830s was focused on Ireland. Seeming to favour the Catholic majority in that country, notably through the Irish Church Temporalities Act of 1833, which sharply reduced the number of bishoprics in the Church of Ireland, the Whigs' policy incurred ultra-Protestant opposition in Great Britain. This had already shown itself in the form of the Brunswick Clubs of 1828–29, which had tried to resist Catholic emancipation.[27] It appeared again in the Protestant Association founded in 1835, in the continuing Orange Lodges, and in Protestant Operative Societies.[28] These small but vociferous ultra-Protestant bodies were supported by anti-Catholic newspapers and pamphlets and rested partly on a pronounced evangelical

---

[24] Lesourd, *Les Catholiques*, vol. 2, p. 739.

[25] Cf. J. L. Altholz, *The Liberal Catholic movement in England: The 'Rambler' and its contributors, 1848–64* (London, 1962); J. D. Holmes, *More Roman than Rome: English Catholicism in the nineteenth century* (London, 1978), pp. 111–97.

[26] Norman, *English Catholic Church*, p. 209.

[27] Machin, *Catholic question*, pp. 131–56.

[28] For these associations and their activities see J. Wolffe, *The Protestant crusade in Great Britain, 1829–60* (Oxford, 1991), especially pp. 1–2, 77–83, 159–60, 247–9.

scriptural basis, being thoroughly suspicious of Catholic 'superstition', 'idolatry' and 'immorality'.[29] The activities of these associations naturally tended to rise and fall in accordance with the appearance and subsidence of political episodes involving Catholic concessions and claims. Thus the Central Anti-Maynooth Committee was formed to resist a much enlarged government grant to the Catholic Maynooth College in Ireland in 1845. The National Club was another Protestant defence body that emerged from the agitation against this grant. The Protestant Alliance and the Scottish Reformation Society were among the associations formed to resist the restoration of a Catholic hierarchy in England and Wales in 1850–51.

In 1838, to counteract such efforts, a Catholic Institute of Great Britain was founded 'for the protection and encouragement of the Catholic religion and the Catholic people'. This organisation had 124 branches by 1843. In opposition to the Ecclesiastical Titles Act of 1851, which officially forbade a restored Catholic hierarchy, a Catholic Defence Association of Great Britain and Ireland was formed.[30] The Protestant defence societies sometimes expressed the wish not only to prevent new concessions to Catholics but also to repeal previous measures of benefit and relief, including the emancipation legislation of 1829 and the Maynooth Act of 1845. A bill to repeal the Maynooth Act indeed came close to success in the House of Commons in 1856.[31]

II

Of the reforms which advanced the interests of Catholics in the period from 1829 to the end of the nineteenth century, I shall deal first with the reforms which, like that of 1829, signified emancipation from legal restrictions. Next will be summarised other policies that, directly or indirectly, were concerned with advancing Catholic interests.

Several of the 'emancipating' reforms were obtained primarily through government acceptance of the demands of Protestant Nonconformists. Catholics were far less active in requesting these concessions, probably because relatively few of them had the vote in parliamentary elections

---

[29] G. F. A. Best, 'Popular Protestantism in Victorian Britain', in R. Robson (ed.), *Ideas and institutions of Victorian Britain* (London, 1967), pp. 115–42; E. R. Norman (ed.), *Anti-Catholicism in Victorian England* (London, 1968), pp. 13–21; S. W. Gilley, 'English attitudes to the Irish in England, 1780–1900', in C. Holmes (ed.), *Immigrants and minorities in British society* (London, 1978), pp. 81–110.

[30] Wolffe, *Protestant crusade*, pp. 167–9.

[31] G. I. T. Machin, *Politics and the Churches in Great Britain, 1832 to 1868* (Oxford, 1977), p. 276 (also pp. 230–3, 263–4, 273–4, 278, 285, 290, 303–4).

until, at least, the Parliamentary Reform Bills of 1867–68 were passed. But on some previous occasions – for example, in the general election of 1847 – organised efforts were made by Catholic associations to advise Catholics on how to give their votes.[32]

Until the 1870s British Catholics maintained a quieter and more obscure political role than the Protestant Nonconformists. But they benefited, like the latter, from the passage of legislation that provided more civil equality in England and Wales. (There was comparatively little of such legal inequality in Scotland.) These measures included an act of 1836 commuting tithes to money payments, and the Marriages Act of the same year, which recognised not only marriages in non-Anglican churches, provided a registrar was present, but also civil marriages as official ceremonies. In the 1850s there was some relaxation of the rule of the exclusion of non-Anglicans from degrees at the universities of Oxford and Cambridge. An act in 1863 enabled non-Anglican prison chaplains to be appointed, and a measure of 1867 allowed non-Anglican workhouse chaplains. An act of 1868 abolished the compulsory payment of church rates to maintain the parish churches of the English Establishment. There was, moreover, a University Tests Act in 1871, which permitted non-Anglicans to take all degrees – except, for the time being, in divinity – at the universities of Oxford, Cambridge and Durham. The only other English university, London, was not subject to these tests, and in 1853 the Scottish universities lost the only tests they had, which limited teaching posts to members of the Church of Scotland. A Burials Act of 1880 allowed non-Anglicans to be interred with their own religious ceremonies in Church of England parish churchyards, and a Marriages Act of 1898 removed the requirement that a civil registrar be present at marriage services in Protestant Nonconformist and Catholic churches.

Apart from these measures, which were passed mainly in order to satisfy the claims of Protestant Nonconformity, several concessions were carried in relation to Catholics alone, mostly with the aim of stabilising the Anglo-Irish Union by pacifying the obstreperous Catholic majority in Ireland. But some were passed partly as measures to establish civil equality for the small and comparatively quiet Catholic minority in Britain. These included an act of 1844 relieving Catholics from various penalties under such old legislative measures as the Acts of Supremacy and Uniformity. Further penalties were removed by an act of 1846. But Catholics remained subject to the restrictions imposed by the 1829

[32] *Ibid.*, pp. 188–9, 191.

emancipation legislation, despite attempts to relieve them of some of these.[33] Some success in this direction, however, was gained in the 1860s. An act of 1866 abolished a special oath in the 1829 act requiring Catholics to promise that they had no intention of subverting the Church Establishment or the Protestant religion and government. After an act of 1867, Catholics no longer had to make a declaration against transubstantiation (required by the 1829 act) before they could take government office. Another act of 1867 removed the ban of 1829 on a Catholic becoming Lord Chancellor of Ireland, although a proposal in the bill to open the Lord Lieutenancy of Ireland to Catholics was removed on amendment.[34] Well before this, in 1848, government grants were first given to Catholic schools in order to improve the training of teachers.[35] From 1863 government money supported Catholic prison chaplains, and from 1866 Catholic chaplains could be appointed in the army and navy. Sustained attempts in the 1870s by C. N. Newdegate, a Conservative MP, and W. H. Whalley, a Liberal MP, to institute inspection of Catholic convents by the government did not result in legislative success.[36] There remained a good deal of anti-Catholic feeling in Parliament at this time. But although Parliament passed a bill in 1874 to try to prevent Ritualist law-breaking in the Church of England, it was not prepared to emulate the Bismarckian *Reichstag* in adopting legislation against Roman Catholicism.

The reforms passed by successive governments with the aim of pacifying the Irish Catholics and making them content with the Union were concerned partly with the reduction of civil inequality, as already indicated, but also with the bestowal of financial aid. The Irish Church Temporalities Act of 1833 encouraged hopes of obtaining religious equality, as, to some extent, did the commutation of Irish tithes in 1838. Two of Robert Peel's reforms for Ireland – the Charitable Trusts Act of 1844 and the Maynooth Act of 1845 – aimed in different ways to increase the financial resources of Irish Catholicism. The Maynooth Act trebled and made permanent the annual government grant to Maynooth College by the Westminster Parliament since the Union in 1801 and,

---

[33] *Ibid.*, pp. 169, 178–9; Wolffe, *Protestant crusade*, pp. 230–1.
[34] Machin, *Politics and the Churches, 1832 to 1868*, p. 348.
[35] S. Gilley, 'Protestant London, No-Popery, and the Irish poor, 1830–60', part I, *Recusant History*, 10 (1969–70), 216, 227 n.6.
[36] Chadwick, *Victorian Church*, vol. 2, p. 406; W. L. Arnstein, *Protestant versus Catholic in mid-Victorian England: Mr Newdegate and the nuns* (Columbia, 1982), pp. 125–62, 174–81, 198–200.

for five years before that, by the Irish Parliament.[37] The disestablishment of the Church of Ireland in 1869 also gratified Irish Catholics, as it gave them the greatest degree of religious equality that they had ever received.[38]

The strong tendency towards concessions to Catholics in Ireland and Britain was not, however, unbroken. The passing of the Ecclesiastical Titles Bill in 1851 was a reminder that even a Liberal government would not necessarily be wholly in favour of Catholic interests. Lord John Russell, Prime Minister from 1846 to 1852, showed his readiness in the late 1840s to make Catholic concessions. But in 1850 he felt affronted by the Pope, who re-established a Catholic hierarchy in England and Wales, consisting of an archbishop of Westminster and twelve bishops, without officially seeking the British government's agreement. Russell's cabinet decided, not without objections from some of its members, to introduce a bill forbidding Catholic clerics to hold territorial titles in the United Kingdom. It was decreed that such titles should be held only by clergy of the Established Church, the only exemptions being clergy of the unestablished Scottish Episcopal Church. The ban applied even to Ireland, where such titles had long been unofficially assumed. This Ecclesiastical Titles Bill was passed by very large majorities in Parliament,[39] but the act itself was scarcely ever applied. It was repealed in 1871, on the one hand so that clergy in the recently disestablished Church of Ireland could continue to use their titles and on the other hand, no doubt, to remove a cause of friction with Catholics. Scotland had been omitted from the restoration of 1850 in spite of having a higher proportion of Catholics than England and Wales. In 1878 Scotland received a restored hierarchy

---

[37] D. A. Kerr, *Peel, priests and politics: Sir Robert Peel's administration and the Roman Catholic Church in Ireland, 1841–6* (Oxford, 1982), pp. 224–89, also p. 110ff. and pp. 290–351; Machin, *Politics and the Churches, 1832 to 1868*, pp. 169–77.

[38] Machin, *Politics and the Churches, 1832 to 1868*, pp. 355–79; G. I. T. Machin, *Politics and the Churches in Great Britain, 1869 to 1921* (Oxford, 1987), pp. 22–30; I. Machin, 'Disestablishment and democracy, c.1840–1930', in E. F. Biagini (ed.), *Citizenship and community: Liberals, radicals and collective identities in the British Isles, 1865–1931* (Cambridge, 1996), pp. 137–8.

[39] Machin, *Politics and the Churches, 1832 to 1868*, pp. 210–28; Robert J. Klaus, *The Pope, the Protestants, and the Irish: Papal aggression and anti-Catholicism in the mid-nineteenth century* (New York, 1987), pp. 65–342; D. G. Paz, *Popular anti-Catholicism in Victorian England* (Stanford, 1992), pp. 8–12; D. A. Kerr, *A nation of beggars?: People, priests and politics in famine Ireland, 1846–52* (Oxford, 1994), pp. 241–81; J. L. Altholz, 'The political behavior of the English Catholics, 1850–67', *Journal of British Studies*, 3 (1964), 89–103; K. T. Hoppen, 'Tories, Catholics, and the general election of 1859', *Historical Journal*, 13 (1970), 48–67.

to serve its estimated 332,600 Catholics, and the opposition was much less than it had been in 1850-51.[40]

III

As well as the activities of anti-Catholic associations, there were outbreaks of anti-Catholic rioting from time to time. The riots, which were directed against the poor Irish Catholic immigrants rather than the Catholic upper and middle classes, continued to erupt after the numerous anti-Catholic associations became less prominent from about 1860.[41] In the riots there was certainly an ingredient of anti-Catholicism, in a religious sense, against the Pope and the priesthood and the evils and dangers for which they were allegedly responsible. But this aspect of the turmoil was probably superficial and to be expected. It is unlikely to have involved, for example, an exact knowledge of the doctrines of transubstantiation or the immaculate conception. It is almost beyond doubt that a more important cause of friction and violence was the economic and social challenge posed to jobs and living standards by the Irish immigrants. This was probably the main underlying cause of rioting against the numerous incomers who gave England and Wales a 2.5 percentage of Irish-born immigrants and Scotland a 7.2 percentage by 1851.[42]

While the Irish Protestant immigrants (on whom little work has yet been done) merged relatively easily with the Protestant and predominantly evangelical native population around them,[43] the Irish Catholic immigrants tended to be much more apart. As a distinct cultural group, they were centred on the Catholic home, church, school and perhaps newspaper.[44] The native Protestant reaction to the Irish Catholic

---

[40] Anson, *Underground Catholicism in Scotland*, pp. 314–39; D. McRoberts, 'The restoration of the Scottish Catholic hierarchy in 1878', in D. McRoberts (ed.), *Modern Scottish Catholicism, 1878–1978* (Glasgow, 1979), pp. 3–29.

[41] Wolffe, *Protestant crusade*, pp. 305–8.

[42] Swift and Gilley, *Irish in the Victorian city*, p. 1–12; Brown, *Social history of religion in Scotland*, p. 46.

[43] E. McFarland, *Protestants first: Orangeism in nineteenth-century Scotland* (Edinburgh, 1990), p. 65. Cf. R. B. McCready, 'The Dundee Irish: Periphery of a periphery?', in *The core and periphery* (Glasgow, 1994), pp. 12, 17; Gallagher, *Glasgow: The uneasy peace*, p. 27.

[44] W. M. Walker, 'Irish immigrants in Scotland: Their priests, politics and parochial life', *Historical Journal*, 15 (1972), 649–67; R. Samuel, 'The Roman Catholic Church and the Irish poor', in Swift and Gilley (eds), *Irish in the Victorian City*, pp. 267–300; M. J. Mitchell, 'The establishment and early years of the Hamilton mission', in Devine (ed.), *St Mary's, Hamilton*, pp. 37–42. On Catholic newspapers see G. A. Beck (ed.), *The English Catholics, 1850–1950: Essays to commemorate the centenary of the restoration of the hierarchy of England and Wales* (London, 1950), p. 475ff.

immigrants was, if not usually hostile, certainly often unfriendly. It has been said that they were subjected to the application of 'racial' stereotypes which branded them as inferior.[45] 'There abides he', wrote Thomas Carlyle in 1839, 'in his squalor and unreason, in his falsity and drunken violence, as the ready made nucleus of degradation and disorder'.[46] In 1836 Disraeli had written in no less decided and uncomplimentary terms:

> This wild, reckless, indolent, uncertain and superstitious race have no sympathy with the English character. Their fair ideal of human felicity is an alternation of clannish broils and coarse idolatry. Their history describes an unbroken circle of bigotry and blood.[47]

Friedrich Engels was sympathetic to the immigrant Irish and saw them, over-optimistically, as potential material for initiating social revolution. But he wrote about them, from his own observations in Manchester, in a vein that advertised their social peculiarities and physical dangers:

> The Irish have brought with them the habit of building pigsties immediately adjacent to their houses. If that is not possible, the Irishman allows the pig to share his own sleeping quarters. This new, abnormal method of rearing livestock in the large towns is entirely of Irish origin ... The Irishman eats and sleeps with his pig, the children play with the pig, ride on its back and roll about in the filth with it. Thousands of examples of this may be seen in all the big cities of England ... The Irish are not used to furniture ... The kitchen also serves as a living room and bedroom ... Why should an Irishman want anything more than the minimum accommodation? At home, in Ireland, he lived in a mud cabin where a single room sufficed for all purposes. In England, too, his family needs no more than one room.[48]

This can be taken as an eloquent comment on the vast social distinctions that marked British Catholicism. The conditions described could hardly have been further removed from the genteel, secluded luxury of the aristocracy or the ample comfort of the middle-class converts. The emigrants from the famine indeed, often ill and debilitated when they entered

---

[45] See the discussion in O'Tuathaigh, 'The Irish in nineteenth-century Britain', pp. 20–3.

[46] Quoted F. Engels, *The condition of the working class in England in 1844*, trans. and ed. W. O. Henderson and W. Chaloner (Oxford, 1958), p. 105.

[47] Quoted I. Machin, *Disraeli* (London, 1995), p. 29; and R. Swift, *The Irish in Britain, 1815–1914: Perspectives and sources* (Oxford, 1990), p. 28.

[48] Engels, *Condition of the working class*, p. 106; see also pp. 77, 89–90. Cf. J. E. Handley, *The Irish in Scotland* (one-volume edn, Glasgow, 1964), pp. 180–82; for attitudes to the Irish immigrants at the start of the twentieth century see, R. Roberts, *The classic slum: Salford life in the first quarter of the* [twentieth] *century* (London, 1973), pp. 22–3.

Britain and thereafter living in poor and squalid conditions, were seen as notable spreaders of disease. The number of Irish settlers showed wide differences between one part of the country and another. Rural areas and small towns had hardly any settlers, but in some urban areas – Liverpool, Manchester, Birmingham, parts of London, Glasgow, Edinburgh and Dundee – they formed sizeable minorities.[49] In Liverpool, one of the chief receiving ports, the Irish-born ingredient had grown by 1851 to 83,813 out of a total population of 375,955.[50] A district registrar in this city wrote in his quarterly report of November 1847:

> The return shows a great increase in the mortality of this district, which is without doubt solely attributable to the many thousands of Irish paupers who have landed here within the last three months, bringing with them a malignant fever, which is very appropriately called the 'Irish fever' ... many hundreds of them were suffering from diarrhoea and syphilis when they arrived, which will account for so many deaths from those causes ... so many thousands of Irish are continually pouring in, and their habits are so disgustingly filthy, that little can be done as yet to stay the great mortality among them.[51]

The Irish Catholic immigrants, therefore, suffered from their religious disadvantages (in a mainly Protestant country) and from their destitution. They were also under a third disadvantage – unpopularity with the native workers, who feared that they might be displaced from their own work because of Irish willingness to accept lower wages. But this fear was reduced, though by no means eliminated, by the prosperity boom and the wide opportunities for employment which benefited Great Britain in the third quarter of the nineteenth century.

The unpopularity of the immigrants on these grounds explains why they were sometimes discriminated against and victimised in their daily lives. They could not feel fully emancipated until they had rid themselves of their inferior and despised material state and the hostile tensions and physical attacks which this helped to cause. They had almost succeeded in doing so, not by the late nineteenth century but by the late twentieth, perhaps partly because in the second half of the twentieth century non-white immigration superimposed itself on the Irish as a fresh exemplar of many of the same ills, accusations, discrimination and attacks.

---

[49] See the comparative table of immigrant numbers in F. Neal, *Sectarian violence: The Liverpool experience, 1819–1914* (Manchester, 1988), p. 9; also, for instance, L. H. Lees, *Exiles of Erin: Irish immigrants in Victorian London* (Manchester, 1979).
[50] Neal, *Sectarian violence*, p. 9.
[51] Quoted *ibid.*, p. 91 (see also pp. 81, 94, 99, 109).

Rioting against the Irish Catholics was the most direct example of hostility to them. It had occurred in the Gordon Riots in London in 1780,[52] but this example was not repeated for a considerable time. The strongly Protestant Orange Lodges, which commenced in Ireland in 1795, began to appear in Britain three years later.[53] As the British lodges spread, Irish Protestant immigrants were often found among their members. Rioting between Orangemen and Catholics frequently took place after the annual Orange processions on 12 July, held to commemorate the Protestant victory at the Battle of the Boyne in Ulster in 1690. The holding of St Patrick's Day parades by the Irish Catholic immigrants similarly helped to stimulate rivalry and conflict.

The first Orange–Catholic riot in Manchester followed the procession of 12 July in 1807; the first Orange–Catholic riot in Liverpool followed the procession of 12 July 1819; and in 1822 there were the first Orange–Catholic riots in Glasgow, again following the procession of 12 July.[54] Such occasions of sectarian display and the consequent physical clashes became part of British nineteenth-century urban culture. As examples of popular ritual the demonstrations were similar to the annual Guy Fawkes bonfire celebrations on 5 November. These were also originally an anti-Catholic commemoration of the failure of the Gunpowder Plot of 1605.[55]

Glasgow and Liverpool and their environs, where there were notably large Irish Catholic minorities, were particular centres of sporadic rioting. It has been noted that a tradition of sectarian violence had become firmly established in the working-class life of these two cities by the middle of the nineteenth century. They experienced a particularly intense sectarianism not usually paralleled in other British towns which had large numbers of Irish Catholic immigrants.[56] From 1835 Liverpool also saw constant sectarian struggles for control of the city council; Catholics frequently gained election to the council and to other official positions.[57] If Liver-

---

[52] Haydon, *Anti-Catholicism*, pp. 204–44. Cf. R. K. Donovan, *No Popery and radicalism: Opposition to Roman Catholic relief in Scotland, 1778–82* (New York, 1987).

[53] Senior, *Orangeism*, p. 151ff.

[54] Neal, *Sectarian violence*, pp. 15–16, 21, 30.

[55] Paz, *Popular anti-Catholicism*, pp. 228–47.

[56] Neal, *Sectarian violence*, p. 40; Handley, *Irish in Scotland*, pp. 253–9; J. F. McCaffrey, 'Roman Catholicism in Scotland in the nineteenth and twentieth centuries', *Records of the Scottish Church History Society*, 21 (1983), 291; R. Swift, 'The Irish in nineteenth century Britain: Towards a definitive history?', *Labour History Review*, 57, 3 (1992), 10.

[57] Neal, *Sectarian violence*, pp. 37–8, 44–8. See also the comparative denominational table of council members in major provincial cities, in E. P. Hennock, *Fit and proper persons: Ideal and reality in nineteenth-century urban government* (London, 1973), p. 357.

pool became the leading centre of sectarian conflict (and some towns reflected it on a smaller scale in this respect), there were other towns with large Irish Catholic minorities, such as Dundee, which were far less severely affected by physical clashes.[58]

Apart from the rioting which accompanied the ritual processions, physical conflict between Catholics and Protestants also tended to erupt, especially at times of national political tension concerning Catholic issues. Thus there was sectarian rioting at Airdrie, near Glasgow, in 1835 – a time when policies of concession to Catholics had recently been prominent and when the Protestant Association was founded.[59] After the restoration of the Catholic hierarchy in 1850 there was more popular disturbance.[60] There were riots at Greenock, a port near Glasgow, in 1851–52, and at Wigan, located between Liverpool and Manchester, in 1852. One of the worst cases of sectarian conflict was the Stockport Riots of June 1852. In retaliation for an alleged attack on an Anglican Sunday school, two Catholic chapels were wrecked, a Catholic was killed, and many people were injured.[61] In the early 1850s much tension was also caused by the inflammatory addresses of anti-Catholic lecturers, some of whom, such as Alessandro Gavazzi and 'Father' Achilli, were converts from Catholicism.[62]

In 1862 a fresh ingredient made its contribution to sectarian rioting. The 'Garibaldi riots' broke out in London and in Birkenhead, near Liverpool, over the question of supporting Italian unification against the temporal interests of the papacy.[63] In 1867 and 1868 there were anti-Catholic riots in the Birmingham region and in several towns in south Lancashire and Cheshire. These were stirred up by an itinerant Irish Protestant speaker, William Murphy, a convert from Catholicism. Murphy's audiences, which included both Protestants and Catholics, were so excited by his denunciations that violence and destruction repeatedly followed in his wake. This uproar was probably a reaction to recent

---

[58] W. M. Walker, *Juteopolis: Dundee and its textile workers, 1885–1923* (Edinburgh, 1979), pp. 120–1.

[59] Gallagher, *Glasgow*, p. 29.

[60] Neal, pp. 130–46 and ff.

[61] Pauline Millward, 'The Stockport riots of 1852: A study of anti-Catholicism and anti-Irish sentiment', in Swift and Gilley, *Irish in the Victorian City*, pp. 207–24; Machin, *Politics and the Churches, 1832 to 1868*, pp. 238–9, 241.

[62] Handley, *Irish in Scotland*, pp. 252–7.

[63] S. Gilley, 'The Garibaldi riots of 1862', *Historical Journal*, 16 (1973), 698–732; F. Neal, 'The Birkenhead Garibaldi riots of 1862', *Transactions of the Historic Society of Lancashire and Cheshire*, 31 (1982), 87–111; Burke, *Catholic history of Liverpool*, pp. 154–5. Cf. C. T. McIntire, *England against the Papacy, 1858–61: Tories, Liberals, and the overthrow of papal temporal power during the Italian Risorgimento* (Cambridge, 1983).

terrorist activities in Britain by members of the Irish Republican Brotherhood; it also illustrated current fears of the disestablishment of the Church of Ireland and of other concessions that might be made to the Irish Catholics.[64] Irish disestablishment did happen in 1869 and involved not only the withdrawal of official state support from the Church of Ireland but also the ending of the Maynooth grant to the Catholics and of a government grant to Irish Presbyterians. But Gladstone, who carried this policy, showed his dislike of the definition of papal infallibility by the Vatican Council of 1870 when he published a celebrated attack on the doctrine, *The Vatican Decrees,* in 1874. Murphy continued to harangue audiences until he died from injuries received in an assault on him by immigrant Catholic coal-miners at Whitehaven, Cumberland, in 1871.

Rioting between Catholics and Protestants tended to die down in Britain, though not in Ireland, from the mid-1870s. But there were still outbreaks of rioting, sometimes sparked off by opposition to Irish nationalist terrorism, as for example at Camborne (Cornwall), Brighouse (Yorkshire), and Tredegar (Monmouthshire), in 1882.[65] In Scotland the tension continued, especially in the late 1870s and the early 1880s. Liverpool was the scene of repeated outbursts of rioting in the first decade of the twentieth century, against both Ritualist activities in the Church of England and the Romanism to which it was feared these activities were leading.[66]

IV

From the 1870s Catholics in Britain were gradually ceasing to be a beleaguered, barely tolerated body and were becoming more settled and confident. They were, on the whole, allowed by their Protestant neighbours to live in greater peace. Following the Parliamentary Reform Acts of 1867–68, they had rather more voting power and played a greater part in politics, both locally and nationally, in support of Catholic schools and

---

[64] W. L. Arnstein, 'The Murphy Riots: A Victorian dilemma', *Victorian Studies*, 19 (1975), 51–81; H. J. Hanham, *Elections and party management: Politics in the time of Disraeli and Gladstone* (London, 1959), pp. 303–7; Machin, *Politics and the Churches, 1832 to 1868*, pp. 355–72; P. Joyce, *Work, society and politics: The culture of the factory in later Victorian England* (London, 1982), pp. 257–61; Gallagher, *Glasgow*, pp. 25–6.

[65] Machin, *Politics and the Churches, 1869 to 1921*, p. 125; L. Miskell, 'Custom, conflict and community: A study of the Irish in Cornwall and South Wales, 1861–91' (unpublished Ph.D. thesis, University of Wales Aberystwyth, 1996).

[66] Machin, *Politics and the Churches, 1869 to 1921*, pp. 234–55; P. J. Waller, *Democracy and sectarianism: A political and social history of Liverpool, 1868–1939* (Liverpool, 1981), p. 172–248; Neal, *Sectarian violence*, pp. 202, 207.

Irish Home Rule.[67] These interests emphasised their religious identity and, in the case of the Irish immigrants, their national identity. But the interests were uncomfortably two-sided. In regard to education Catholics looked to Conservative support, but over Home Rule they looked, if sometimes indirectly, to the Liberals. Their educational aims included attempts to influence policy by obtaining election to the School Boards, which were established by the Education Acts of 1870 for England and Wales) and 1872 (for Scotland). Catholics were urged to support candidates of their own Church in these elections to ensure that state support of Catholic schools would be continued and that the option given to School Boards to provide money from the local rates to support needy children at voluntary (i.e. denominational) schools would be maintained. Catholics also desired that their own schools should have the right to receive money from rates on the same basis as the state schools. This was granted under the Education Acts of 1902 (for England and Wales) and 1918 (for Scotland).[68] The Voluntary Schools Association was formed in 1884 by Bishop Herbert Vaughan to defend the interests of Catholic schools, and a National Catholic Conservative Association was founded in 1882.

The support of these educational aims united Catholics in Britain but weakened the alliance of Catholics with Liberal Nonconformists, which had been strong over the question of Irish disestablishment. Many Nonconformists were against maintaining the voluntary schools. As Irish Home Rule became a prominent political issue by the 1880s, however, Catholics became partially allied again with Nonconformists over this question. But many British Catholics did not support their Irish co-religionists – whether in Ireland or Britain – over the issue of Home Rule. Cardinal Manning was a strong supporter of the cause, but some non-Irish Catholics took a Conservative line in opposition to it.[69] Organisations formed in Britain to aid the cause of Home Rule were supported mainly by the Irish Catholic immigrants. The Home Rule Confederation of Great Britain, formed in 1871, had many local associations. It was replaced in 1883 by the Irish National League of Great Britain. This organisation had 630 branches by 1890 and was itself replaced by the United Irish League of Great Britain in 1899.

[67] Cf. D. Quinn, *Patronage and piety: The politics of English Roman Catholicism, 1850–1900* (Basingstoke, 1993), p. 71ff.
[68] Machin, *Politics and the Churches, 1869 to 1921*, pp. 37–9; Norman, *English Catholic Church*, pp. 174–83.
[69] S. Fielding, *Class and ethnicity: Irish Catholics in England, 1880–1939* (Buckingham, 1993), p. 79–82.

In a determined effort to persuade one or other of the main British parties to adopt a policy of Irish Home Rule, Charles Stewart Parnell, leader of the Home Rule party, supported by the British Catholic bishops, urged the Irish in Britain to vote Conservative in the general election of 1885.[70] There were still only some 150,000 Catholic electors in Britain, but the recent adoption of mainly single-member constituencies in the British electoral system had given greater concentration to the strength of immigrant votes. Although by no means all Irish Catholic electors in Britain obeyed Parnell's injunction, it was claimed that, as a result of his appeal, twenty seats were transferred from Liberal to Conservative. The issue of Home Rule had suddenly thrust the small immigrant Irish Catholic electorate into a crucial position, although the number of Catholics returned for British constituencies remained very small – only four in 1885, compared with eighty-three from Ireland.[71] Despite Parnell's action, the Liberals won the 1885 election, and soon after the contest it was revealed that Gladstone, the Liberal leader, had become converted to Home Rule. Bills to establish a separate Irish Parliament were defeated in 1886 and 1893, and the Irish constitutional issue remained prominent until a solution was reached in 1921–22.

In addition to their increased political importance, British Catholics had a more secure and confident role in society in other ways by the late nineteenth century. Some had been advanced to august secular positions. Sir John Acton, a hereditary Catholic and one of the leading British historians, became a peer in 1869. The Marquess of Ripon, a Catholic convert and the son of a Prime Minister, became Viceroy of India in 1880; and another Catholic, Lord Kenmare, became chamberlain of the Queen's household in that year. The first Catholic to become a cabinet minister, Lord Llandaff, took office in a Conservative government in 1886; and in 1894 Lord Russell of Killowen, also a Catholic, became Lord Chief Justice of England.[72] Catholics were also being welcomed as dignitaries at important national events. A papal envoy was present at Queen Victoria's jubilee ceremony in 1887, and messages of goodwill were exchanged between the Queen and the Pope.[73] Two leading

---

[70] Machin, *Politics and the Churches, 1869 to 1921*, pp. 53, 124, 160–1, 178–9, 221, 248, 276; I. S. Wood, 'Irish immigrants and Scottish radicalism, 1880–1906', in I. Mac-Dougall (ed.), *Essays in Scottish Labour history* (Edinburgh, 1978), pp. 70, 83–4; J. F. McCaffrey, 'Politics and the Catholic community [in Scotland] since 1878', *Innes Review*, 29 (1978), 140–55.

[71] Chadwick, *Victorian Church*, vol. 2, p. 405.

[72] *Ibid.*, p. 406.

[73] *Ibid.*

Catholic converts, Newman and Manning, became celebrated Cardinals; they died in 1890 and 1892 respectively.[74] In 1903 a splendid new Catholic cathedral in the Byzantine style was opened at Westminster.

On the other hand, although the number of Catholics continued to increase rapidly, many were lost on account of lapsing. It was claimed in 1885 that perhaps as many as 750,000 had lapsed from Catholic practice since 1841.[75] Moreover, even if the Catholics had obtained emancipation from most of their legal inequalities, there still existed three notable ones at the end of the century. These were the debarment from the offices of Lord Lieutenant of Ireland and Lord Chancellor of England (a bill of 1891 to remove these exclusions had failed to pass); the ineligibility to hold the position of monarch (which remains in force today); and the prohibition of holding outdoor processions in which full eucharistic vestments were worn and the consecrated Host was carried. The third restriction was sharply underlined in 1908. The culminating event of a large international eucharistic congress held in London in September that year was to be an outdoor procession in full ecclesiastical vestments, issuing from Westminster cathedral and carrying the consecrated Host through the streets. But the intended procession – even though a similar one had been held in 1899 – was against the letter of the law, namely section 26 of the 1829 Relief Act. Ultra-Protestant attack on the procession was threatened. After intervention by the government to try to eliminate any religious action which might provoke rioting, the outdoor procession took place in plainer vestments and without the Host, which was displayed in a monstrance on the cathedral's balcony.[76] After the banning of a similar procession at Carfin, Lanarkshire, in 1924, a Catholic Relief Act of 1926 removed the legal restriction on these ceremonies.[77]

In 1900 the small Catholic minority was more secure in British society and less subject to legal constraint and physical attack than it had been formerly. But Catholics remained socially inferior in both a formal and an informal sense. The liberal British state had given them a series of important concessions relating to civil equality and financial assistance, but it had not removed all the disadvantages. Opposition to the growth of

---

[74] D. Newsome, *The convert cardinals: John Henry Newman and Henry Edward Manning* (London, 1993).

[75] K. S. Inglis, *Churches and the working classes in Victorian England* (London, 1963), p. 122ff. But see also O'Tuathaigh, 'The Irish in nineteenth-century Britain', p. 25.

[76] G. I. T. Machin, 'The Liberal Government and the eucharistic procession of 1908', *Journal of Ecclesiastical History*, 34 (1983), 559–83.

[77] Machin, *Politics and the Churches, 1869 to 1921*, pp. 329–30; Susan McGhee, 'Carfin and the Roman Catholic Relief Act of 1926', *Innes Review*, 16 (1965), 56–78.

Ritualism in the Church of England was at a high pitch in 1900. In the turbulence over this question, which affected particularly Liverpool in the first decade of the twentieth century, Roman Catholics were often involved and sometimes attacked.[78] In political matters most Catholics remained separated from the majority of the population by their direct involvement in Irish nationalist politics, which was shown by the attachment of many of them to the United Irish League of Great Britain and later to Sinn Fein Clubs. It was only after the Irish constitutional problem was at least partially resolved in 1922 that Catholics of Irish descent played more of a mainstream role in British politics. By this time, too, social mobility was more clearly affecting the Catholics of Irish descent. This was taking some of them into professional and business occupations, where they often had to surmount traditional prejudice against them. Discrimination against Catholics seeking appointment to 'white-collar' jobs continued until at least the middle of the twentieth century.[79] Despite the continued removal of legal inhibitions, as indicated by the Relief Act of 1926, anti-Catholicism still manifested itself openly in the 1920s and 1930s. This was especially the case in Scotland where the much higher proportion of Irish Catholic settlement had created, with the exception of Liverpool, a tougher and more consistent Protestant resistance.[80] Nevertheless, the general tendency had become one of greater Catholic integration into British society.

---

[78] Waller, *Democracy and sectarianism*, pp. 207–10.
[79] Gallagher, *Glasgow*, pp. 250–1.
[80] S. J. Brown, 'The campaign for the Christian Commonwealth in Scotland, 1919–39', in W. M. Jacob and N. Yates (eds), *Crown and mitre: Religion and society in northern Europe since the Reformation* (Woodbridge, 1993), pp. 209–10; T. Gallagher, 'Protestant extremism in urban Scotland, 1930–9: Its growth and contraction', *Scottish Historical Review*, 64 (1985), 143–67; T. Gallagher, *Edinburgh divided: John Cormack and No Popery in the 1930s* (Edinburgh, 1987); Waller, *Democracy and sectarianism*, pp. 285–7, 323–7, 339–44; Wolffe, *Protestant crusade*, pp. 306–7.

3

British Jews

David Cesarani

The Jewish experience in Britain has been generally regarded as more benign than that of any other Jewish population in Europe. This happy history has usually been attributed to the stability of British politics and settled British national identity. However, over the past twenty years historians have reconsidered the unalloyed optimism of the British Jewish saga.[1] This reappraisal has been closely related to a more qualified appreciation of British national identity and the political stability of the British Isles. Thanks to the work of Hugh Kearney, Linda Colley and Keith Robbins, among others, 'Britishness' increasingly appears as an artful fabrication of recent provenance. The notion that the British Isles constituted a united polity of great antiquity has been replaced by the concept of English hegemony over a 'domestic empire' acquired and patched together no earlier than the 1700s. Even the idea of England, once treated as the oldest centralised nation state in Europe, is being questioned as the persistence of regional identities well into the nineteenth century is being rediscovered.[2]

If credence is given to these claims for the late development of British national identity and the fragility of the British polity, then the course of British history appears less exceptional in a European context. By extension, the British Jewish experience ceases to be automatically unique. Features of emancipation that were once marginalised in British Jewish

---

[1] For useful historiographical surveys, see T. Endelman, 'English Jewish history', *Modern Judaism*, 11 (1991), 91–109 and *ibid*., 'Writing English Jewish history', *Albion*, 27 (1995), 623–36; T. Kushner (ed.), *The Jewish heritage in British history: Englishness and Jewishness* (London, 1992), pp. 1–27; editor's introduction to D. Cesarani (ed.), *The making of modern Anglo-Jewry* (Oxford, 1990), pp. 1–11; L. P. Gartner, 'A quarter-century of Anglo-Jewish historiography', *Jewish Social Studies*, 48 (1986), 123–40.

[2] H. Kearney, *The British Isles* (Cambridge, 1989); L. Colley, *Britons: Forging the nation* (London, 1992); K. Robbins, *Nineteenth-century Britain: England, Scotland, and Wales: The making of a nation* (Oxford 1989).

historiography because they did not fit with the 'alembic of tolerance', in the words of Cecil Roth, have assumed a more central relevance since they can now be seen to register previously neglected aspects of British national history.

I

According to Cecil Roth and his followers, Jews advanced steadily towards civil and political equality as British society shrugged off medieval habits of thought and embarked on the road of progress towards creating a modern, liberal, democratic nation. Anti-Jewish sentiment withered along with religious fanaticism, while discriminatory barriers were dismantled until membership of Parliament remained as the last significant office of state to be prised open to Jewish entry. Only reactionary and clerical opponents of the Jews entrenched in the House of Lords prevented the speedy achievement of full equality. After British Jews had won the right to sit in Parliament in 1858, they enjoyed a period of unrivalled security and prosperity that was interrupted only by the rather unwelcome arrival of East European Jews. It was these newcomers who provided ammunition for those who wished to revive native anti-Jewish traditions or import 'modern anti-Semitism' from the continent.[3]

This long-held view of Jewish emancipation as a benevolent, if protracted, process has been challenged through a careful re-examination of its antecedents and its consequences. Historians of late-Victorian Anglo-Jewry have long noted the timid character of Jewish culture in Britain, the high degree of Anglicisation (sometimes verging on the absurd), the exaggerated patriotism of British Jews and their ambivalent response to the mass immigration of Jews from Eastern Europe. However, since the 1980s, Israel Finestein, Bill Williams, Geoffrey Alderman, David Englander and others have explicitly traced these qualities back to the pressure of the dominant liberal culture and the legacy of emancipation – the conviction among Jews that they were expected to show that they deserved emancipation by living up to the highest standards of conduct and constantly affirming their attachment to British civilisation. While these scholars differ over the extent to which British Jews believed in the existence of a putative 'emancipation contract' which delineated permissible Jewish behaviour in the public sphere, and explain Jewish conduct in

[3] C. Roth, *A history of the Jews in England* (Oxford, 1964) [first edn 1941].

a variety of ways, they have all challenged the roseate and untroubled version which prevailed for nearly a century.[4]

More recently, Frank Felsenstein has drawn attention to the extent of hostility towards Jews and Judaism evinced in British popular culture during the century and a half that preceded emancipation. Much of this animosity derived from Christianity, the resilience of which in England has been greatly underestimated. Michael Ragusis has argued powerfully that a Protestant mission to convert Jews and infidels lay at the core of Englishness in the eighteenth and nineteenth centuries.[5] Indeed, British historiography has for some time been veering away from the view of Georgian and early-Victorian Britain as being lackadaisical in spirit. J. C. D. Clark, G. F. A. Best, Brian Harrison, Ian Machin and John Wolffe, to name a few, have reasserted the vitality of Anglicanism and popular Protestantism. The consolidation of British Jewry and the struggle for admission to the legislature appears in a very different light when religion is credited with a central place in British national identity and political life.[6]

The 'whiggish' view of British Jewish history, typified by the work of Cecil Roth, that hinged on the attainment of emancipation and its fulfilment has been supplanted by a more fractured and less positive account, which stresses the extent to which British society was animated by Christianity and helps to explain why emancipation took so long. Asserting the centrality of religion also compels closer attention to the

[4] See, for example, B. Williams, 'The anti-Semitism of tolerance: Middle-class Manchester and the Jews, 1870–1900', in A. J. Kidd and K. W. Roberts (eds), *City, class and culture* (Manchester, 1985), pp. 74–102; I. Finestein, 'Post-emancipation Jewry: The Anglo-Jewish experience', in Finestein, *Jewish society in Victorian England* (London, 1993), pp. 154–81; D. Englander, 'Anglicised not Anglican: Jews and Judaism in Victorian Britain', in G. Parsons (ed.), *Religion in Victorian Britain*, vol. 1 *Traditions* (Manchester, 1988), pp. 253–73; the various contributions to Cesarani (ed.) *Making of modern Anglo-Jewry*; G. Alderman, 'English Jews or Jews of the English persuasion? Reflections on the emancipation of Anglo-Jewry', in P. Birnbaum and I. Katznelson (eds), *Paths of emancipation: Jews, states, and citizenship* (Princeton, 1995), pp. 128–56; D. Feldman, *Englishmen and Jews: Social relations and political culture, 1840–1914* (New Haven, 1994); D. Cesarani, *The 'Jewish Chronicle' and Anglo-Jewry, 1841–1991* (Cambridge, 1994).

[5] F. Felsenstein, *Anti-Semitic stereotypes: A paradigm of otherness in English popular culture, 1660–1830* (Baltimore, 1995); M. Ragusis, *Figures of conversion: 'The Jewish question' and English national identity* (Durham, N.C., 1995). See also J. Shapiro, *Shakespeare and the Jews* (New York, 1996).

[6] J. C. D. Clark, *English society, 1688–1832* (Cambridge, 1985), G. F. A. Best, 'Popular Protestantism in Victorian Britain', in R. Robertson (ed.), *Ideas and institutions of Victorian Britain* (London, 1967); B. Harrison, *Drink and the Victorians: The temperance question in England, 1815–1872* (London, 1971); G. I. T. Machin, *Politics and the Churches in Great Britain, 1832 to 1868,* (Oxford, 1977); J. Wolffe, *The Protestant crusade in Great Britain, 1829–1860* (Oxford, 1991).

opponents of Jewish emancipation who were once dismissed as mere fanatics. In addition, it promotes awareness of the contradictions within the emancipatory process and the conflicts that ensued from the implicit contract between the Jews and Christian society. This more nuanced record reveals the years 1858–80 to be not so much a golden era rudely ended by the immigrants as a period in which all the problems that would appear in the 1880s were latent or already evident. The total impression is of a trajectory that is much closer to the continental European Jewish experience, while mercifully being spared its ghastly dénouement in the middle of the twentieth century.

Needless to say, this re-evaluation of British Jewish history is not uncontested. Todd Endelman, David Katz and William D. Rubinstein, for example, defend the notion that the Jewish experience in Britain was singular and unusually favourable. They acknowledge anti-Jewish currents in the pre-emancipation era, but contrast these eddies to the tide of progress carrying the Jews towards prosperity and social acceptance. In their view, while the post-emancipation Jewish communities in Britain faced questions of adjustment, none were of existential significance. On the contrary, British Jews felt secure enough to play a leading role in national affairs and to act forcefully on behalf of Jews in other countries. The ambivalent response to the newcomers after 1880 has its own aetiology, which is not to be found predominantly, if at all, in any notion of an 'emancipation contract' or the legacy of the struggle for emancipation.[7]

It is my contention in this chapter that such a positive assessment of the British Jewish experience cannot easily be sustained in the light of the latest research on the depth of animosity towards the Jews in eighteenth-century England, the centrality of Protestantism and the conversionist ethos to English national identity, and the pressure on British Jews to conform to an ideal of Britishness that was applied with increasing stringency as the English/British struggled to define themselves against centrifugal forces at home and rivalry from abroad during the last three decades of the Victorian era. This chapter draws on and refers to detailed empirical studies, but space permits only the groundwork of an argument to be laid out. Those interested in this contentious topic are urged to

---

[7] T. Endelman, *The Jews of Georgian England, 1714–1830* (Philadelphia, 1979); D. Katz, *The Jews in the history of England, 1485–1850* (Oxford, 1994); W. D. Rubinstein, *A history of the Jews in the English-speaking world: Great Britain* (London, 1996). Feldman, *Englishmen and Jews* is a subtle exploration of all these issues and cannot be reductively placed in any one category. His sinuous reading of British Jewish history is a salutary warning against the flattening effects of polemic, although polemic has its place, too.

follow the references to the relevant primary and secondary sources, and they should always be aware that this is a hotly contested issue in a field that is among the liveliest in modern Jewish historiography.

II

Britain is a recent construction that began to disintegrate almost as soon as it was completed. The upsurge of nationalism in Ireland, Scotland and Wales in the 1970s and the 'threat' to the Union alerted historians like Tom Nairn to the essential artificiality of the United Kingdom and its precarious origins.[8] The relevance of this for Jewish history should be clear. In answer to the question of his essay title, 'Why was there a Jewish Question in Imperial Germany?', Peter Pulzer says: 'The concept of nationality ... is central to our whole subject, for the nineteenth century was characterised by the struggle to create and define a German national consciousness'. A 'Jewish question' developed in Germany because

> with the creation of the Empire, *Volk* [people] as defined in the earlier decades of the century, merged with *Staat,* as defined in these decades. Ethnic and civic criteria now coincided. Nationality could no longer be defined without citizenship, nor citizenship without nationality. In the non-national state, the citizen had been defined by his loyalty: there was therefore a strong incentive to minimise the number of outsiders and to integrate the Jews into the state ... In the national state there was a temptation to define loyalty by nationality: this created an incentive to maintain a distinction with outsiders and therefore to exclude Jews, or at least to treat them with suspicion.[9]

I would contend that this argument applies with equal force to Britain. Running through the emancipation debate between 1830 and 1858 was a deep preoccupation with the nature of Britishness and the relationship between citizenship and nationality. However, in Britain this relationship was expressed chiefly in religious terms and refracted through confessional allegiances. This was most clearly evident in the defence of the Anglican supremacy, and the notion of the Church of England as being commensurate with the political nation.[10]

---

[8] T. Nairn, *The break-up of Britain* (London, 1977) and *The enchanted glass: Britain and its monarchy* (London, 1988), pp. 127–89; J. Osmond, *The divided kingdom* (London, 1988), ch. 7.

[9] P. Pulzer, *Jews and the German State: The political history of a minority, 1848–1933* (Oxford, 1992), pp. 30, 33.

[10] This is the predominant theme of Feldman, *Englishmen and Jews*, part 1.

In *Britons,* Linda Colley demonstrates how, after the Act of Union brought England and Scotland together on a statutory rather than a dynastic basis, an identity was constructed around Protestantism to serve the British Isles as a whole:

> Protestantism was able to become a unifying and distinguishing bond as never before. More than anything else, it was this shared religious allegiance combined with recurrent wars that permitted a sense of British national identity to emerge alongside of, and not necessarily in competition with older, more organic attachments to England, Wales or Scotland, or to county or village. Protestantism was the dominant component of British religious life. Protestantism coloured the way that Britons approached and interpreted their material life. Protestantism determined how most Britons viewed their politics. And an uncompromising Protestantism was the foundation on which their state was explicitly and unapologetically based.[11]

Even after Catholic emancipation, Christianity remained the touchstone of national identity. Indeed, precisely because the linkage between Protestantism and British national identity was ruptured in 1829, a new cement had to be found to unite the disparate ethnic and religious units that comprised Great Britain. Colley maintains that the national crusade against slavery embodied this new unity of creed and purpose. The rapid and successful campaign to emancipate Black slaves, which culminated in the Emancipation Act of 1833, enabled the British elite to maintain its reputation for supporting the cause of liberty and project it as an ingredient of national identity. Curiously, Colley does not pass any observation on the comparatively slow emancipation of the Jews, which actually overlapped with the manumission of the slaves. Yet it would be curious if the same dynamic did not apply to the debate over the future of the Jews in Britain. The defence of the Christian polity through the exclusion of the Jews, as much as the termination of slavery, was an issue on which Protestants and Catholics could find common ground: the two campaigns ought to be associated. But while the abolition of slavery could be supported by all sections of the populace because it reaffirmed Britishness and Christian values and because it had no tangible cost (since the objects of the campaign were far away), the emancipation of the Jews challenged Britishness at home, affronted Christianity and threatened to have an immediate impact upon domestic interests.[12]

---

[11] Colley, *Britons*, p. 19.
[12] *Ibid.*, pp. 358–9.

The young, conservative politician William Ewart Gladstone, for one, was tormented by the rupturing of the national religion consequent upon the admission of Catholics, and later Jews, into the political nation.[13] As Israel Finestein has noted, the resistance to Jewish emancipation mounted by Anglican stalwarts such as Sir Robert Inglis and Lord Derby was based on the notion of the state as being Christian. According to this concept, England was a Christian country governed by a Christian legislature, and it was held to be virtually inconceivable that non-Christians could be admitted into full citizenship; nationality, religion and citizenship were interdependent.[14]

The profound reservations concerning Jewish emancipation did not end in 1858. Nor did they suddenly re-emerge in the late 1870s after a period in which Jews were harmoniously integrated into the state. Rather, as Jews were gradually granted full civic rights they brushed up against the state in a variety of ways that exposed and underlined their particularity. The key to understanding this friction lies in the myth of the neutral liberal state. Politicians like Gladstone may have superficially abandoned the notion of the confessional state and self-consciously begun to espouse a liberal, even utilitarian, definition of its character. Yet the values that they invested in the state were those of the Christian majority.[15] The apparently value-free, utilitarian notion of the state as guarantor of 'the greatest happiness for the greatest number' was implicitly inimical to minorities. By virtue of the doctrine of majoritarianism both liberalism and universalism were Christianity secularised and camouflaged. As G. M. Young observed in his classic portrait of Victorian England, 'the evangelical discipline, secularised as respectability, was the strongest binding force' in the nation. The 'parallel operation of Evangelicalism and Utilitarianism cannot be ignored'.[16]

The majoritarian Christian, utilitarian ethos marked out the Jews as different. When the state acted in accordance with these values, there was inevitably friction between it and the Jews. In more concrete terms, from the Factory Acts of the mid-1860s onwards the state began to interfere more and more in the life of its citizens. In several critical areas of activity this interference conflicted with the way in which Jews lived or wished to live and dictated that they were going to have to defend what it was that

---

[13] H. C. G. Matthew, *Gladstone, 1809–1974* (Oxford, 1988), pp. 59–73.

[14] I. Finestein, 'Some modern themes in the emancipation debate in early Victorian England', in J. Sacks (ed.), *Tradition and transition* (London, 1988), pp. 135–40.

[15] J. P. Parry, *Religion and democracy: Gladstone and the Liberal Party, 1867–1875* (Cambridge, 1988).

[16] G. M. Young, *Portrait of an age: Victorian England* (Oxford, 1986), pp. 5–11.

rendered them different. Even though these differences were usually negotiated and managed, they served to define the Jew as different and 'other'. The foundations for the accusation that Jews were guilty of communalism and possessed a dual loyalty, which Liberals were to level at them in the late 1870s during the Bulgarian agitation, had been laid decades earlier.

III

The question of whether a Jew could ever be a member of the English, Christian nation lay at the heart of the emancipation debate. It was a central tenet of the opposition to Jewish emancipation in England, no less than in Germany, that the nation and the state were Christian in character. Moreover, advocates of emancipation had to overcome deeply embedded prejudices and stereotypes concerning the Jews. On the basis of a minute examination of all forms of popular literature Frank Felsenstein has shattered the notion that English society in the eighteenth century was open, tolerant, secularised and welcoming of Jews. From 1660 to 1830, he writes, 'their position in English society was viewed as at least anomalous and sometimes pernicious by the majority of the indigenous population'.[17] Jews were tolerated but never accepted:

> Whether considering them as objects of pity or as seasoned enemies, eighteenth century English commentators on the Jews largely concur in viewing their survival as having a validity that can be measured only by reference to the Christian cosmos ... The closed minded treatment of these Jews in English popular culture mirrors the assumption that they are to be deemed a fallen people.[18]

Jews were tolerated precisely because they were despised: they necessarily served as a foil for Christian triumphalism and as objects for missionary activity. Those who welcomed them into English society and promoted their cause did not do so out of love for the Jews or Judaism but in expectation of their eventual demise. Philo-Semitism, often adduced as a chief cause of the readmission of the Jews to England and their favourable treatment thereafter, actually confirmed and reinforced negative images of the Jew:

> The *idée fixe* of messianist thought towards the Jews is that, despised though they may be, and whether they wish it or not, they are ... but ripe plums for conversion to Christianity. Almost no legitimate strategy or argu-

---

[17] Felsenstein, *Anti-Semitic stereotypes*, p. 21.
[18] *Ibid.*, pp. 69–70.

ment is too mean if it will help to bring about an end that can only be to the greater glory of the Christian faith. If eighteenth century English philo-Semitism is in many ways less blinkered than traditional anti-Semitism, its rhetoric is hardly less insistent in its acceleration of certain stereotypical attitudes that are made to imbue Christian behaviour toward the Jews.[19]

Felsenstein demonstrates that the 'Jew Bill' of 1753 – the act to enable the naturalisation of foreign-born Jews by Parliament – became a lightening conductor for popular notions that the Jews were ineradicably different and unassimilable unless converted. The increasing strength of rationalist and secular thought in England in the half-century after the 'Jew Bill' furore eroded some of the grosser calumnies against the Jewish people but never completely eliminated them. They recur in the writings of William Cobbett and Charles Dickens, which were published on the cusp of the emancipation campaign.[20]

The maltreatment of Jews and the disparagement of Judaism were not confined to popular representations: they were enshrined in English law until the mid-nineteenth century. Writing at the turn of the century, the Anglo-Jewish lawyer H. S. Q. Henriques noted that 'it was not until 1846 that Jewish religious endowments were made valid'. As a consequence of the 1698 Blasphemy Act any bequest to the benefit of religious views that were not officially tolerated by law were deemed illegitimate. This provision was repeatedly enforced by English courts, to the detriment of the Jews. According to that judicious commentator, 'it would follow that before 1846 Judaism was not a religion recognised by law and that a Jewish synagogue was an illegal establishment'.[21]

Henriques's account of the relation of the Jews to the law is bleak, but he stood closer to the events in question than many later historians who sponged out his jaundiced appraisal and replaced it with the 'alembic of tolerance'. More remarkably, his commentaries, which had first appeared in the *Jewish Quarterly Review,* were republished at the instigation of the Jewish Historical Society of England in 1908, in celebration of the fiftieth anniversary of the admission of the Jews to Parliament! There must then have been a measure of agreement with the astonishing, bitter sentiments that he expressed before embarking on his chronicle and analysis of the struggle for emancipation:

When considering the acquisition of political rights by the Jews, credit is often given to our legislators for never having enacted laws with the

---

[19] *Ibid.*, p. 95.
[20] *Ibid.*, pp. 187–212, 232–43.
[21] H. S. Q. Henriques, *The Jews and the English law* (London, 1908), pp. 18–19, 32.

express object of depriving the Jews of all share of political power. The gratitude for this mercy need not be excessive, for, without any special legislation, the Jews were effectually excluded from such power under the law as it existed at the time of their return, nor were the governing classes at all hasty in removing the disabilities which, if not intentionally imposed, were at least deliberately maintained.[22]

This near-contemporary assessment runs counter to the view of the many historians who have seen the Jews as the inadvertent victims of discrimination that was in fact aimed against Roman Catholics and Protestant Nonconformists.[23] Henriques, like others of his contemporaries, was keenly aware of just how recently Jews and Judaism had been almost universally held in contempt by English society and how English Christians had deliberately sought to penalise the Jews for their beliefs.

Paradoxically, this contempt was the motor force for conversionism which, in turn, sustained toleration of the Jew. It was a salient feature of English society. Michael Ragusis has documented the 'remarkable role that the idea of Jewish conversionism played in Protestant England from the 1790s throughout the 1870s'.[24] The English habitually ranked countries according to the toleration they displayed towards the Jews, but not for the love of Jews *per se*. Catholic nations were relegated to the lower rungs because their persecution of the Jews deterred the latter from accepting the validity of Christian doctrine. Protestant England, which was the bearer of the true form of Christianity, would welcome the Jews and, by exposing them to pure Christian forms, would win them over. The conversion of the Jews was a necessary precursor to the conversion of the heathens and the salvation of the entire planet.[25] These currents did not dissipate with the advent of the nineteenth century. Ragusis maintains that 'the question of Jewish conversion, which had been primarily a matter of scriptural exegesis in the decades immediately following the French Revolution, became situated from the 1830s through the 1850s at the centre of political debate over Jewish emancipation'. Polemicists and pamphleteers inquired: Could unconverted Jews enter Parliament? Should the promise of equality be withheld as an enticement to convert?[26]

Lest it be thought fanciful to invoke such theories with respect to the period of emancipation, it may be worth recalling Lord Palmerston's argument in 1857 in favour of admitting Jews to Parliament. Palmerston,

[22] *Ibid.*, p. 221.
[23] See for example Rubinstein, *History of the Jews*, pp. 48–9.
[24] Ragusis, *Figures of conversion*, p. 1.
[25] *Ibid.*, pp. 2–6.
[26] *Ibid.*, p. 23.

that avatar of secularism, rationalism and liberalism, proclaimed to the House of Commons that he had often heard of Jews becoming Christians but never of Christians becoming Jews: 'The progress of mankind is governed by laws which admit of no retrogression. The Old Testament prepared the way for the New Testament, but the New will never lead us back to the Old'.[27]

Throughout the debates on Jewish emancipation, conversionist arguments were heard for and against, buttressing the alien nature of the Jews and the conviction that they were inherently inferior. Opponents of emancipation were mobilised by the felt need to protect a Christian legislature from contamination by this foreign and ungodly tribe. In his famous House of Commons speech supporting the bill to remove the civil disabilities of the Jews in 1833, Thomas Macaulay addressed directly the claim that 'the constitution [was] essentially Christian; and therefore to admit the Jew [was] to destroy the constitution'. His caricature of the argument made by Inglis and others is instructive. They suggested 'it would be monstrous ... that a Jew should legislate for a Christian community'; that a Jew could not be permitted to sit in judgement on a Christian; that it was offensive to contemplate the prospect of Jewish privy councillors giving advice to a Christian monarch. Mocking these arguments, Macaulay modestly proposed that if those who made them really believed in their veracity, they should drive the Jews out of the country since the Jews already wielded considerable political power via their financial influence.[28]

Although Macaulay and the advocates of emancipation eventually overwhelmed the defenders of the Christian state, they were not routed and simply regrouped elsewhere. To illustrate this it is worth examining the House of Lords' response to the compromise that was put forward by a committee of both Houses of Parliament for resolving the deadlock over the 1858 Oaths Bill (the bill was intended to relieve Jewish disabilities). The fourth reason the Lords gave for rejecting the bill was that:

> Because, without imputing any disloyalty or disaffection to Her Majesty's subjects of the Jewish persuasion, the Lords consider that the denial and rejection of that Saviour, in whose name each House of

---

[27] *Hansard* 145, cols. 323–4 (15 May 1857), quoted in E. D. Steele, *Palmerston and Liberalism, 1855–1865* (Cambridge, 1991), p. 143. See also the paraphrase in Henriques, *Jews and the English law*, p. 282.

[28] Excerpts from the speech can be conveniently accessed in T. Macaulay, 'Civil disabilities of the Jews (1831)', in P. Mendes-Flohr and J. Reinharz, *The Jew in the modern world: A documentary history* (Oxford, 2nd edn 1995), pp. 146–50.

Parliament daily offers up its collective prayers for the divine blessing on its councils, constitutes a moral unfitness to take part in the legislation of a professedly Christian community.[29]

The Upper House thus explicitly and unapologetically endorsed the inferior status of the Jews and the notion of the Christian state, making it clear that it bowed only to irresistible pressure.[30] It is also important to recall that emancipation in 1858 was partial and provisional. Jews were not permitted to enter the House of Lords. Technically, Jews could only sit in the Commons on sufferance of a majority of MPs and not by right. The oath enabling Jews to sit in the House only became a permanent standing order in 1860. It was not until 1866 that the haphazard and provisional nature of the oaths for dissenting Christian and Jews was finally ended.[31]

While emancipation was generally welcomed among English Jews, it left some Jewish observers feeling less than euphoric. Abraham Benisch, editor of the *Jewish Chronicle,* commented in a leading article on 11 June 1858 that a

> great contest is worthy [of] a solemn issue. Nothing but a solemn deed insuring the wronged Jews the restitution [sic] of the rights withheld from them, signed, sealed and delivered by both houses in the presence of the whole world can satisfy the demands of justice.

In April 1860 he reflected bitterly that the interim arrangement had the effect of 'making the appearance of the Jew in the House marked, as though he were still wearing the yellow patch which, during the Middle Ages, singled him out for universal scorn'.[32] The initially equivocal form taken by emancipation meant that English Jewry still felt itself to be on trial and extraordinarily sensitive to the competing demands of Jewish tradition and English citizenship.

IV

These dilemmas revealed themselves with bewildering speed. During 1859–60 a war scare in England led to volunteers being summoned to

---

[29] Henriques, *Jews and the English law*, p. 295.
[30] M. C. N. Salbstein, *The emancipation of the Jews in Britain: The question of the admission of the Jews to Parliament* (East Brunswick, N.J., 1982), p. 236.
[31] Ibid., p. 241.
[32] *Jewish Chronicle* (*JC*), 27 April 1860, 4. One correspondent was so incensed that he asked: 'Will Rothschild take his seat with this insult to his faith thrown in his teeth?' See *JC*, 23 July 1858, 253.

repel a possible French invasion. Jewish enrolment in the volunteer movement was small, precipitating adverse comment. One reason for the small Jewish turnout was the choice of Saturday as the day for drilling the units. Jews eager to demonstrate their patriotism were thereby placed in a quandary. As a solution, the *Jewish Chronicle*'s editor, Benisch, favoured the formation of a Jewish unit that would drill on weekdays or Sundays. But there were trenchant objections to this proposal by those who argued that Jews should be fully integrated into English society and share civic duties equally with other citizens.[33]

Notwithstanding emancipation, Jews and Protestant Nonconformists still suffered from official discrimination that called attention to their particularity. Jews, like other Dissenters, resented the obligation to pay church rates for the upkeep of the Anglican Establishment. Benisch argued that 'to be consistent, the state must either support church and synagogue, as in France, or altogether exempt Jews from church-rates, as in Austria'. He counselled Jewish MPs to vote for the abolition of church rates.[34] Jews and Nonconformists also objected to the legislation which prohibited a man's marriage to his deceased wife's sister.[35] On all these issues Jews and Nonconformists shared common ground and worked together. Jewish particularity was happily blurred and the claims which Jews were making against the state could be justified by a classical appeal to liberal nostrums of freedom of conscience.

However, Jews and Nonconformists were at loggerheads over the question of Sunday trading, which bulked ever larger in the mid- and late nineteenth century. In 1867 Parliament extended the 1853 and 1864 Factory Acts to workshops employing more than fifty workers. The act enforced the closure of workshops on the Christian Sabbath, at a stroke endangering the livelihood of the many Jews among the small masters in the tailoring trade. The extension was a typically liberal, utilitarian measure, but it was equally an act of Christian piety and one that was insensitive to Jewish needs. The Sunday question became even more serious for the Jews when the number of Evangelical MPs in the House of Commons increased following the general election of 1868.[36]

---

[33] Letters and 'Gossip', *JC*, 18 November 1859, 7; 29 June 1860, 6; 13 July 1860, 7; 21 September 1860, 2. H. Pollins, *A history of the Jewish Working Men's Club and Institute, 1874–1912* (Oxford, 1981), p. 5.

[34] *JC*, 4 February 1859, 4. Machin, *Politics and the Churches*, pp. 299–301, 306–8.

[35] *JC*, 22 February 1867, 4–5; 10 July 1868, 4. Machin, *Politics and the Churches*, pp. 272–3, 294, 439.

[36] O. Chadwick, *The Victorian Church* (London, 1966), vol. 1, pp. 455–68; J. Wigley, *The rise and fall of the Victorian Sunday* (Manchester, 1980), 68–9; B. Harrison, 'The Sunday trading riots of 1855', *Historical Journal*, 6 (1965), 219–45.

Partly as a result of such contradictions, the attitude of Jews towards the Church of England changed fundamentally. Up to 1860, the Anglican Establishment was regarded as one of the strongest barriers to Jewish equality and as being fundamentally antagonistic to Jewish interests. But when the Nonconformists renewed their battle against the church rates in the late 1860s, the *Jewish Chronicle* held aloof. It lauded the state Church as 'an invaluable protection to so weak a community as the Jews, sure to be the first to be attacked in religious commotion'.[37] The withdrawal of Jews from the Nonconformist alliance, which had reached its apogee in the campaign to free Edgar Mortara in 1859–60,[38] left the Protestant sects feeling betrayed. While they continued to co-operate on certain issues, such as the ending of tests for entering the universities of Oxford and Cambridge, there were more points of disagreement. Friction with the Protestant Nonconformists who were the backbone of the Liberal Party contributed to the political realignment of Anglo-Jewry in the 1860s.

During the ten-month period in which Disraeli was the Prime Minister in 1868, the Liberal press indulged in anti-Jewish innuendo against him. Anti-Jewish themes recurred during the general election held at the end of the year when Liberals beheld the spectacle of Jews in the Tory ranks. Henry de Worms, the first professing Jewish Conservative parliamentary candidate, selected for Sandwich, was the object of particularly shameful attacks by the local Liberal press and Liberal party candidate. The *Jewish Chronicle* commented ruefully that 'these zealous friends have injured the Liberal cause far more than its avowed enemies'.[39] More damage was done when the Liberals in Tower Hamlets selected a converted Jew, Joseph d'Aguilar Samuda, to stand as their candidate in the same election. Tower Hamlets had a large Jewish population, which was the constant focus of missionary work; against this background the choice of an apostate was a grotesque miscalculation. When Lionel de Rothschild was drafted in to assist Samuda, this damaged his own support among Jews in the City of London and contributed to his defeat. The Samuda affair was typical of the behaviour of Liberals who could not understand Jewish sensitivities or were not willing to try to comprehend them. It echoes uncannily the attitudes of German Liberals towards the status of converted Jews, about which Marjorie Lamberti has written. The matter was a thorn in the side of relations between German Jews and Liberal

---

[37] *JC*, 1 March 1867, 4–5. See also 5 August 1864, 4.
[38] See D. I. Kertzer, *The kidnapping of Edgardo Mortara* (New York, 1997).
[39] *JC*, 9 October, 1868, 5.

politicians and revealed the Janus face of liberalism. However, the phenomenon was not confined to Germany: it was foreshadowed in a small but significant way in England.[40]

Gladstone's reforming ministry of 1868–74 was crucial for unsettling relations between Jews and the liberal state and for instigating the reassessment of liberal dogma which underpinned the tacit emancipation contract.[41] For Jews the single most sensitive issue was the form of popular education. Under the terms of the 1870 Education Act, wherein voluntary (i.e. religious) schools were deemed inadequate, schools financed from rates levied locally would be built and run by elected school boards. Voluntary schools could gain financial support if they submitted to government inspection. To circumvent the opposition of the various denominations, religious education in 'Board schools' was made compulsory but was void of any particular denominational bias. Under a 'conscience clause' children could be withdrawn from religious education and given specific denominational instruction provided on a voluntary basis. Michael Henry, the new editor of the *Jewish Chronicle*, vehemently objected to the idea that Jewish schools should be placed under state supervision and either be denied the right to transmit Judaism or even be compelled to teach Christianity. He deplored the idea of compulsory mixed schooling, stating that 'the blending of Jewish children of the lower and lower-middle classes with Christian children of the same social calibre is dangerous – frightfully, fatally dangerous'.[42] True to his principles and blind to the contradictory position in which he placed himself, Henry clamoured for the repeal of the University Tests but at the same time advocated the exclusion of Christian children from the Jews' Deaf and Dumb Home.[43] He thus adopted a separatist position on education barely a dozen years after Jews had fought for emancipation on the grounds that they were being excluded from full civil rights.

But who would pay for independent, separate and exclusive Jewish schools? In a leading article on 29 April 1870, Henry argued that since Protestant and Roman Catholic schools were state aided, then Jews should benefit from state funding, too; but if the state would not pay for Jewish schools, then the Jews themselves would have to do so. This was

---

[40] Geoffrey Alderman, *The Jewish community in British politics* (Oxford, 1982), 35–6; See M. Lamberti, *Jewish activism in Imperial Germany: The struggle for civil equality* (New Haven, 1978) pp. 94–104, on the 'Mugdan Affair', 1908–9, a similar issue in which German Liberals thoughtlessly endorsed a Jewish convert.

[41] E. J. Feuchtwanger, *Gladstone* (rev. edn, London, 1989), pp. 150–68.

[42] *JC*, 15 April 1870, 6–7.

[43] *Ibid.*, 9–23 July 1869.

tantamount to adopting what would today be called a pluralistic position, which was fundamentally at odds with classical liberalism. It certainly did not meet with the approval of Protestant Nonconformists like Joseph Chamberlain, who held that state schooling should be wholly 'universal, compulsory and secular.'[44] When it appeared clear that the state would not pay for Jewish schools, Henry reiterated the separatist position. In an extraordinary editorial on 18 November 1870 he addressed the parents of Jewish school-age children. 'We urge them', he wrote,

> before it is too late, to shun the government schools, to shun government interference, and to manage and support their own schools just as they manage and support their own synagogues and their own burial grounds. If they do otherwise they will regret their decision. The Jews are essentially, irrefutably, inevitably divided from their Christian fellow-countrymen in the sphere of juvenile instruction.[45]

Henry hoped that the Education Act would prove unworkable and in his newspaper he chronicled every difficulty it encountered. But, after two years it was clear that compulsory state schooling had come to stay, while there was no burst of school building on the part of the Jewish communities. Moreover, there was pressure from within Anglo-Jewry to abandon the separatist position repeated endlessly in the columns of the *Jewish Chronicle*. Baron Henry de Worms, who became the second Jewish Conservative MP, was also the president of the Borough Jewish School in 1873 when it considered submitting to state supervision in order to qualify for a grant. At public meetings Worms argued that the 'conscience clause' ensured that Jewish pupils would receive a Jewish education. More important, to reject state aid would send a signal to the rest of the country: 'I say that if the Jews show themselves averse to taking advantage of the facilities offered to them by the Education Acts of the country, they are justifying the great educational establishments of Rugby, Harrow, Eton in excluding Jewish children therefrom'.[46]

The Education Act of 1870 was the most fundamental collectivist measure of this period, signalling that the state was now willing and able to enter into areas of life once deemed the sovereign domain of the individual. But it was not the only one. Jews were afflicted by a host of regulations that highlighted their differences from the majority. Thus, the provision of kosher meat was endangered in 1873 by new regulations

---

[44] Feuchtwanger, *Gladstone*, p. 157.
[45] *JC*, 18 November 1870, 7.
[46] *JC*, 30 January 1874, 741–2.

governing slaughterhouses.[47] In the same year several Jews were prosecuted under the Lord's Day Observance Act as a result of efforts by zealous Evangelicals.[48] In 1869 the *Jewish Chronicle* compared the 1867 Factory (Extension) Act to the penal legislation passed by Robert Castlereagh. The paper later cheered the amendment of the act by Sir David Salomons in 1871.[49]

The implications of collectivism, or state intervention, were not lost on British Jews. The mood of anxiety it provoked was expressed by the *Jewish Chronicle*. In an editorial on 3 November 1871, Henry explained,

> all we desire to maintain is this: that it is not sensible or advisable to imagine that our community stands on the same footing as other denominations; or that arrangements which can be readily adapted to those can be as easily adapted, or in some cases adapted at all, to our Anglo-Jewish body ... We trust that in all we have said we have not manifested any ungracious consideration of the indulgence shown our community by parliament and by the administration of parliamentary statutes; but it is natural that we should be anxious for the intact maintenance of Jewish requirements, even more than of Jewish material interests.[50]

In consequence, the *Jewish Chronicle* welcomed the fall of Gladstone's government in 1874 and the election of a Conservative ministry under Disraeli. For the first time, a significant portion of the Jewish vote went to the Conservatives and the first Jewish Tory MP was elected. When in the course of the election campaign Gladstone proclaimed that Jews in the City were bound to support the Liberal Party, the paper insisted that since there were no Jewish issues at stake, consequently, no party could lay claim to their votes as Jews.[51]

Jews had discovered that liberalism was at best ambivalent towards, and at worst intolerant of, their interests. Their attempts to find political salvation in the lee of the Church of England and the Tory party only antagonised the Liberals still further. At issue was the defence of Jewish particularity in defiance of the blurring of differences between Jews and Christians that was silently expected, by Christians at least, to issue from emancipation. Liberals implicitly held the Jews to a contract which entailed their merging into the mainstream of English Christian society

---

[47] *Ibid.*, 4 April 1874, 8–10.
[48] *Ibid.*, 28 February 1873, 696.
[49] *Ibid.*, 21 April 1871, 6.
[50] *Ibid.*, 3 November 1871.
[51] *Ibid.*, 30 January 1874, 730, 732–3; Alderman, *Jewish community*, p. 39.

and berated them when they deviated from it. On a succession of issues – marriage laws, education, Sunday trading, dietary regulations – the Jews pleaded for exemption from universal legislation. The pent-up frustration of the Liberals with the persistence of Jewish particularism was to surface explosively during the 'Bulgarian agitation'.

V

The uneven experience of the Jews in the newly independent Christian states of the Balkans predisposed western Jewish opinion to favour Turkey whenever its empire was faced by external aggression or insurrection among its subject nationalities.[52] In August 1875 the Christian population of Herzegovina and Bosnia revolted against the Turks. The events in Bosnia triggered an insurrection by the Christian population in Bulgaria, whereupon Turkish troops sent to suppress the nationalist forces massacred thousands of innocent Christians. When the *Daily News* transmitted this story to England there was uproar. It was an issue that was bound to take a religious form, and it placed English Jews in an appalling dilemma.[53]

Abraham Benisch, who had resumed editorship of the *Jewish Chronicle*, tried to justify continued Jewish support for Turkey at a time when English Christian opinion was aflame with anti-Muslim feeling. He told readers on 28 July 1876 that 'the horrors committed upon the Bulgars [were] merely incidental to the mode of warfare in those regions', where slavery and massacre were common. 'We are not apologizing for Mohametan atrocities,' he wrote, 'we wish only for matters to be placed in the proper light'. Benisch repeated that he and all other Jews felt repulsion at the spectre of massacred Christians, but he refused to condone the Slav cause and forcefully maintained that its supporters were helping into power a national movement that was as intolerant as the foreign rule it was fighting to overturn. He confessed a week later:

> it is not without hesitation that we have given expression to these views. Not that we believe we are wrong, but we fear we may be judged wrongly. It is not pleasant to go against the stream. But we have duty to perform to the thousands of brethren-in-faith scattered all over the dominions of the Crescent.[54]

[52] See for example *JC*, 18 December 1868, 4: 'As matters now stand, the Turks are the real protectors of the Jews in the East'.
[53] J. McCarthy and J. Robinson, *The 'Daily News' jubilee* (London, 1896), pp. xv–xvi; R. Shannon, *Gladstone and the Bulgarian agitation* (London, 1964).
[54] *JC*, 4 August 1876, 280–1.

Benisch illustrated the awkwardness of the Jewish position when he urged those who supported the Bulgarians to do so for reasons other than religious feeling. This was clearly at odds with the dominant stance of English Jews, which was based on the pre-eminence of Jewish allegiances. By the beginning of September, the *Jewish Chronicle* had given up any pretence of universalist motives: 'Blood is thicker than water', Benisch editorialised;

> And if the sympathy of the Northern Sclavs [sic] with their Southern kinsmen is justified simply because they are of the same race, surely the Jews in the free countries of the West have a right to espouse the cause of their downtrodden coreligionists in the centres of the East.[55]

Others did not see things in the same light. Gladstone came out of semi-retirement from politics to lead a crusade on behalf of the eastern Christians. This set him on a collision course with Disraeli's government and its pro-Turkish policy. Gladstone's pamphlet *The Bulgarian Horrors and the Question of the East* (published in September 1876), ensured that religion, politics and attitudes towards Disraeli's government would be irretrievably, explosively mixed.[56] It was Gladstone's stated belief that because of their loyalty to foreign Jews, English Jews were anti-Slav and tolerated the massacre of Christians. He was convinced that Disraeli's Jewish origins were an influence on the premier's conduct of policy. In a letter to Leopold Gluckstein, reproduced in the *Jewish Chronicle* on 13 October 1876, Gladstone explained:

> I have always had occasion to admire the conduct of the English Jews in the discharge of their civil duties; but I deeply deplore the manner in which, what I may call Judaic sympathies, beyond as well as within the circle of professed Judaism, are now acting on the question of the East; while I am aware that as regards the Jews themselves, there may be much to account for it.[57]

Gladstone was joined in the war of words by A. E. Freeman, a prominent Oxford historian and fellow Liberal. Letters filled the columns of the *Daily News* and *The Times*, asserting the merits of Christian government.

---

[55] D. Cesarani, *The Jewish Chronicle and Anglo-Jewry, 1841–1991* (Cambridge, 1993), p. 62.
[56] Feuchtwanger, *Gladstone* pp. 181–4; Alderman, *Jewish community*, pp. 36–40.
[57] *JC*, 13 October 1876, 438.

Many were abusive towards the Jews and attributed their sympathies to alleged investments in Turkey.[58]

The agitation placed Benisch in a double dilemma, as a Jew who was both an Englishman and a Liberal. Worried that the Liberal Party was alienating Jewish support, on 18 October 1876 he wrote to Gladstone explaining Jewish motives. He pleaded with the Liberal leader to issue a condemnation of Christian atrocities against the Jews to balance his rousing calls to support oppressed Christians. The two men met a few days later. In the course of the interview, Gladstone said he believed that the Jews should have equal rights under Christian rule; but he reiterated his critique of 'Judaic sympathies'.[59] In May 1877, Benisch again corresponded with Gladstone to elicit a message of support for Jewish claims against the insurgent Bulgarians and their allies. The two men met on 3 May, but Gladstone remained unmoved. He wrote the following to Benisch, in a letter published in the *Jewish Chronicle* on 11 May:

> I cannot disguise from myself the fact that of the Jews, apparently a large majority are among the supporters of Turkey and the opponents of effectual relief to Christians. The Christians will be delivered and at no very distant date ... If I am alive, and in politics, I shall strongly plead for their allowing free equality of civil rights to the Jews. But I cannot do this upon the grounds that the conduct of the Jews has deserved their gratitude.[60]

The accusation that Jews, from Disraeli downwards, were motivated by dual loyalty gained in volume. In *The Ottoman Power in Europe* (1877) and numerous articles A. E. Freeman attributed Disraeli's policy to his Jewish and 'Asian' origins. The Eastern Question thus revived the arguments about Jewish emancipation which had been widespread only twenty years previously. The *Jewish Chronicle* highlighted the double standards of Liberal parliamentarians and the Liberal press when it attributed the vehemence of the opposition to 'religious antipathy'. It argued that while English Christians expressed solidarity with Bulgarian Christians,

---

[58] H. C. G. Matthew (ed.), *The Gladstone diaries*, vol. 9, *January 1875–December 1880* (Oxford, 1986), 161; Shannon, *Gladstone*, pp. 202–11; Lord Burnham, *Peterborough Court: The story of the 'Daily Telegraph'* (London, 1955), pp. 20–3; W. Hindle, *The Morning Post, 1772–1837* (London, 1837), pp. 220, 225–6.

[59] *JC*, 3 November 1876, 486; Matthew (ed.), *Gladstone diaries*, vol. 9, p. 164.

[60] *JC*, 11 May 1877, 10; 18 May 1877, 3–4; Matthew (ed.), *Gladstone diaries*, vol. 9, p. 216.

they yet undisguisedly blame[d] the Jews in semi-mercenary language, because the majority of these, impelled both by the ties of community, race, as well as faith, sympathise[d] more with the Turks, the protectors of the Eastern Jews, than the Eastern Christians, the persecutors of their people, and demand[ed] from the Hebrews of the West an abnegation of which they themselves fail[ed] to set an example.[61]

Jews were further dismayed when Goldwin Smith, professor of history at Oxford University and a well-known Liberal, launched an explicit attack on them in the course of an article in the *Contemporary Review*. Smith held that the Eastern Question exposed the political tendencies of the Jews and showed emancipation to have been a mistake. Jews were not like other Nonconformists: theirs was a primitive religion in which tribal exclusivity and race mixed with religion. The 'nobler part' of the ancient Hebrews had become Christians: the rest wandered the earth where they excelled at money-making. Jews gained control of the press and exploited the guilt which Christians felt towards them because of the earlier oppression they had endured at the hands of the Church. Yet it was now plain that they could not be good patriots: 'their only country is their race; which is one with their religion'.[62] Jews were astonished as much by the origin as by the vehemence of this outburst. How could such a great exponent of liberalism be so illiberal in his attitude towards the Jews? It was difficult to believe that Gladstone countenanced such propaganda, but the Liberal leader did nothing to remove himself from such company. In an article in *Nineteenth Century,* he actually reiterated his opinion that the majority of Jews were pro-Turk. However, as much as the Jews might accuse Gladstone of 'illogical reasoning', there was truth in the latter's assertions. Jews wanted to have their cake and eat it: they wanted to defend the rights of Jews to have a special sympathy for fellow Jews abroad, while rejecting any criticism of that right and they wanted to trumpet Jewish solidarity, then claim that it did not really exist.[63]

VI

The exchanges between Jews and non-Jews during the Bulgarian agitation show that an implicit 'emancipation contract' did exist in Victorian Britain. A significant number of Christian statesmen, politicians and polemicists expected certain standards of behaviour from the Jews and

[61] *JC*, 10 August 1877, 9–10.
[62] *JC*, 15 February 1878, 3–4; 22 February 1878, 12.
[63] *JC*, 15 March 1878, 3; 5 April 1878, 3.

were reproachful when they deviated from them. Jews recognised this 'anti-Semitism of toleration' and feared the consequences of transgression. Their apprehension accounts in some measure for the ritualised affirmations of fealty, the anglicising strategies that were put in place with regard to the East European immigrants even in the 1870s, and their desperate efforts to eradicate Jewish poverty and criminality.[64] Yet the implicit emancipation contract was not merely about liberal dogma and the paradoxes of universalism. As David Feldman has noted, underlying the Bulgarian agitation was the old issue of whether Jews could belong to the English nation. This issue was, itself, a product of the quest for an English identity.[65] Nor had the matter been lying dormant: the arguments and the party allegiances were not new. In the years between 1858 and 1876 Jewish particularity had remained a visible problem in English society and politics. Emancipation had not provided a solution to the accommodation of Jewish differences; it had only altered the emphasis on how Jews were to be regulated and in what ways their differences would be defined.

The question was, itself, a product of the search for an English and a British identity, which, by the last quarter of the century had become acute. The jingoism and the imperialism fostered by Disraeli's government and the counter-crusade mounted by the Liberals were signs of a narrowing, exclusive definition of Englishness. From the late 1870s the monarchy was brought into prominence as a unifying institution and a greater emphasis was placed on English culture, embracing the constitution, history, literature and music.[66] Historians like James Froude, J. R. Greene and Sir John Seeley played a particular role in supplying unifying myths of an Anglo-Saxon race.[67] These invented traditions do not differ

---

[64] Williams, 'Anti-Semitism', and B. Williams, '"East and West": Class and community in Manchester Jewry, 1850–1914', *Studia Rosenthaliana*, special issue published together with vol. 23, no. 2 (1989), 88–106; E. C. Black, *The social politics of Anglo-Jewry, 1880–1920* (Oxford, 1988), ch. 2–6. Feldman, *Englishmen and Jews*, part 3, offers a more variegated and complex account of the response to the immigrants and the immigrants' responses to their reception.

[65] D. Feldman, 'The Jews in London, 1880–1914', in R. Samuel (ed.), *Patriotism: The making and unmaking of British national identity*, vol. 2, *Minorities and outsiders* (London, 1989), pp. 208–12, which presents in a nutshell the argument of *Englishmen and Jews*, pp. 94–137.

[66] D. Cannadine, 'The British monarchy, c. 1820–1977', in E. Hobsbawm and T. Ranger (eds), *The invention of tradition* (Cambridge, 1992), pp. 120–38; R. Colls and P. Dodd (eds), *Englishness, politics and culture, 1880–1920* (London, 1986); Robbins, *Nineteenth-century Britain*, ch. 1–2.

[67] J. W. Burrow, *A liberal descent: Victorian historians and the English past* (Cambridge, 1981), pp. 108, 204–5, 267–72; H. A. MacDougall, *Racial myth in English history*

in substance from the equally spurious notions of *Volk*, *Heimat*, *Blut und Boden*. The Jewish question that emerged in Britain after 1876, first in the course of the Bulgarian agitation and then in response to mass immigration, was parallel to that on the continent. Whereas the latter built upon romantic nationalism and the reaction to liberalism, the other grew out of the intolerance of liberalism towards particularism. In effect, both were the same and their outcomes were similar until the fateful parting of the ways in 1914. And yet in Britain, too, emancipation continued to have repercussions precisely because the prosperity and security of the Jews in that country seemed to validate the arrangements reached in the middle of the nineteenth century.[68] Had the contradictions unravelled as horribly as they did across the English Channel, the mid-Victorian settlement might have appeared less of a triumph. Instead, the dead hand of Victorian Judaism – Victorian institutions and attitudes – remained dominant in British Jewry for at least another half century. British Jews have yet to emancipate fully themselves from their emancipation.[69]

(Hanover, 1982), *passim*; P. Levine, *The amateur and the professional: Antiquarians, historians and archaeologists in Victorian England, 1838–1886* (Cambridge, 1986), pp. 83–7, 162–2, 175–6; R. Soffer, 'Nation, duty, character and confidence: History at Oxford, 1830–1914', *Historical Journal*, 30 (1987), 77–104; B. Melman, 'Claiming the nation's past: The invention of an Anglo-Saxon tradition', *Journal of Contemporary History*, 26 (1991), 575–95.

[68] See for example the baneful effect of Victorian attitudes on the capacity of British Jews to respond to Nazi persecution of the Jews in Europe, as documented in R. Bolchover, *British Jewry and the Holocaust* (Cambridge, 1993).

[69] For the contemporary traces of Victorianism, see D. Englander, 'Integrated but insecure: A portrait of Anglo-Jewry at the close of the twentieth century', in G. Parsons (ed.), *The growth of religious diversity: Britain from 1845*, vol. 1 *Traditions* (London, 1993), pp. 97–131; Alderman, *Modern British Jewry*, ch. 7; and S. Brook, *The club: The Jews of modern Britain* (London, 1989).

4

French Protestants

André Encrevé

In 1840 the Huguenot[1] François Guizot, ambassador in London, wrote to a family member: 'Today a Protestant representing France in London finds there in this very house of Commons, powerful Catholics who were persecuted a hundred and fifty years ago. All this, my dear daughter, is the fruit of a more enlightened reason, of a religion better understood.'[2] This is certainly an interesting account, but one which should not be generalised or lead us to believe that, fifty years after the 1787 Edict of Tolerance, French Protestants had become the equal of their Catholic counterparts, especially since Guizot, despite being strongly attached to Protestantism, was far less hostile towards Catholicism than most of his co-religionists.[3] The following description, published in 1925 in a small Protestant journal of everyday life in the area around Albi (Tarn) at the end of the nineteenth century is probably closer to reality:

> [*c.* 1880] it was said that Protestants had an eye in the middle of their foreheads and thus people would stare at us in the streets to verify this physical peculiarity. As we walked by, the women would quickly close their doors so as not to receive the curses that we were supposed to have put on them. After us the ground would be carefully swept behind our heels as if we carried at our feet an eminently contagious evil.[4]

Other texts show that even until the beginning of the twentieth century certain characteristics, more or less monstrous, were attributed to Protes-

---

[1] In this chapter the terms 'Huguenot' and 'Protestant' have been used interchangeably.
[2] Mme de Witt, *née* Guizot, *Monsieur Guizot dans sa famille et avec ses amis, 1787–1874* (Paris, 1880), p. 218, quoted in M.-E. Richard, *Notables protestants en France dans la première moitié du XIXe siècle* (Caen, 1996), p. 141.
[3] In 1861, for instance, Guizot argued in favour of the pope's temporal powers.
[4] Article published in *Le lien albigeois* (monthly bulletin of the Albi Reformed Church), quoted in J. Faury, *Cléricalisme et anticléricalisme dans le Tarn (1848–1900)* (Toulouse 1980), p.360.

tants in some regions: they were said to have black or even hairy tongues or to pursue extravagant practices, such as the worship of trees. And yet, their 'emancipation', from a strictly legal point of view, was rapid between 1787 and 1791. However, a decision taken by the government in Paris has much ground to cover before it is implemented by the local administration and before it is finally endorsed by society at large. In the middle of the twentieth century in the little town of Pignan, near Montpellier, where Protestants constituted nearly half of the population, it was not unusual to say in Catholic circles when the death knell sounded, 'Who has died? Nobody ... a Huguenot!'[5]

The reintegration of the Protestants in the national community took place very slowly. The reasons for this are manifold: they include the small number of Protestants, the tenacity of the religious struggles in the sixteenth and seventeenth centuries, the violence of the persecutions and the traces they left in the collective memory. Furthermore, the circumstances of their legal emancipation (mainly during the Revolution) played a role, as did the bitterness of the political struggles in France in the nineteenth century between the supporters and the opponents of the principles of 1789, which for the first time introduced the idea of equality between men, whatever Church they belonged to. But those who were against the political achievements of the Revolution also tended to be against its religious achievements.

I

The term 'emancipation' is not ideally suited to the experience of French Protestants. Before 1787, except in Alsace, the Huguenots were not even second-class citizens (or rather subjects). They were not recognised in law. Louis XIV, relying on the fiction of the 'conversion' of Protestants to Catholicism, even though it had often been obtained by violence, notably through the *dragonnades,* revoked the Edict of Nantes in 1685[6] and

---

[5] Quoted in G. Cholvy, 'Une minorité religieuse dans le Midi au XIXe siècle: Les protestants de l'Hérault', *Bulletin de la société de l'histoire du protestantisme français (BSHPF)*, 121 (1975), 50.

[6] The text of the Edict states: 'we see presently ... that our efforts have had the effect which we had foreseen, since the best and the greatest part of our subjects of the so-called R.P.R. [*religion prétendue réformée*] have embraced the Catholic one: ... everything which has been ordered in favour of the above-mentioned R.P.R. remains useless [and] we have decided that we could do no better than ... to revoque entirely the Edict of Nantes'. Quoted in L. Pilatte, *Edits, déclarations et arrests concernant la religion prétendue réformée...* (Paris, 1885), p. 241. (The *dragonnades* refer to the practice of billeting dragons on Protestants whose only chance to save themselves from maltreatment and torture by the military was to convert to Catholicism.)

imposed the Catholic sacraments on the Protestants. The Court clung to the illusion of an 'entirely Catholic France', despite the numerous accounts testifying to the invalidity of such a claim,[7] until 1787. The illusion was shattered, however, first by the reports of the officials in the regions where the Edict of Nantes had been in force and second by the lawful existence of a Protestant minority in Alsace, to whom, for obvious political and diplomatic reasons, no statesman could deny the status of being French subjects.[8]

Even those who regarded Protestants as 'heretics' did not deny them a Christian status. For this reason, their presence was tolerated in Alsace, as they were not considered foreigners, in contrast to the Jews. Furthermore a significant part of the French aristocracy, starting with King Henry IV, had become Protestant in the sixteenth century. The king had to convert to the religion practised by the majority of his subjects in 1593 in order to be recognised by the nation as a whole, but this did not necessarily mean that Catholicism was the national religion of the French. Indeed it was not, although the Edict of Nantes did not amount to religious freedom. It allowed Protestant public worship in approximately one thousand towns and villages and thus established beyond doubt that it was possible to be French without being Catholic. Protestants had access to all forms of civil and military employment. They made full use of this new right, starting with Sully, who held the post of director of finances from 1599 to 1611 and was made Marshal of France by Cardinal Richelieu. Other examples include Valentin Conrad, the founder of and permanent secretary to the Académie française, and Admiral Abraham Duquesne. The Edict of Nantes thus made France a unique nation, both Catholic and Protestant. For this very reason it was impossible to base the cohesion of society on allegiance to the Catholic Church. The substitute was loyalty to the Sovereign.

This state of affairs changed dramatically with the revocation of the Edict of Nantes in 1685. Louis XIV denied Protestants the freedom of

---

[7] The authorities hoped that children who were born after 1685, and who therefore did not have the opportunity of being taught by ministers, would become good Catholics; soon, however, the local officials explained to the Court that this was not the case. At the beginning of the eigteenth century a general who was a commander in the Cévennes during the war of the 'Camisards' thus wrote: 'All the children who were in the crib at the time of the general conversions [1680–85] ... are presently more Huguenot than their fathers and mothers ever were ...', P. Joutard, 'La résistance protestante' in *L'histoire*, April 1985, 66.

[8] As there were Reformed Churches in Alsace which enjoyed the freedom of public worship while the Lutheran Church in Paris was clandestine, it is, however, impossible to maintain that, in contrast to Reformed Protestantism, Lutheran Protestantism was allowed in France.

conscience, forced the sick 'newly converted' to receive the Catholic last rites, ordered that children between the ages of five and sixteen be taken away from parents who persisted in their Protestantism and sentenced to death those 'who [were] caught ... at assemblies or at any other practice of a religion other than the Catholic one'.[9] To bury the bodies of Protestants who had refused the last sacraments was prohibited. Protestants who wished to marry were forced to do so in the presence of a priest and had to participate in the three Catholic sacraments of penitence, eucharist and marriage; otherwise their children would be illegitimate in the eyes of the law and, therefore, unable to inherit property.[10] Thus, both in theory and from a strictly legal point of view, the Huguenots' existence was not recognised in the seventeenth century and could, therefore, not be 'emancipated'.

Between 1685 and 1787 the only French Protestants who had any hope of being emancipated were the Alsatians. During this time the king and the Catholic Church attempted to convert them by inundating the province with Jesuits and Capuchins, who 'promised numerous advantages to those who converted ... , limited the prerogatives of the Protestants and subjected them to continuous harassment'.[11] The pressure sometimes bordered on outright persecution, but the complex status of the Alsatian territories, with their numerous ties to the often Protestant nobility of the Holy Roman Empire, put the authorities in a difficult position. In fact, after a decade of intense pressure the state would content itself with conferring an inferior status on the Protestants. For example, they would have to grant the Catholic minority equal representation on municipal councils, even in cities where it was very small; their lords would be obliged to employ Catholic bailiffs and provosts; and they would be required to bring up all illegitimate children as Catholics. At the same time, a number of administrative positions were closed to Protes-

---

[9] Article 9 of the Edict of Revocation allowed the freedom of private worship to those Protestants who were not yet converted (but not to the next generation, since all children were to be brought up as Catholics) on condition that 'they [did] not assemble to pray in this above-named religion, in any possible way' (Pilatte, *Edits*, p. 245); but since some of the Huguenots used this article to avoid participating in the ceremonies of the Roman Church, it was not put into practice. The edict was accompanied by a series of royal declarations, in particular those of 11 December 1685, 29 April 1686 and 1 July 1686, which explicitly rejected any freedom of conscience. By demanding the conversion of the Protestants, while refusing them the right to emigrate, Louis XIV in practice denied the freedom of conscience. On these matters see E. Labrousse, *Une foi, une loi, un roi, la révocation de l'Edit de Nantes* (Paris and Geneva, 1985).

[10] J. Carbonnier, 'L'amour sans loi...', *BSHPF*, 125 (1979), 59. The royal declarations of 13 December 1698 and 14 May 1724 explicitly required the Catholic marriage.

[11] H. Strohl, *Le protestantisme en Alsace* (Strasbourg, 1950), p. 196.

tants, which led some of them to turn to industry, trade or banking. Therefore, in spite of a receding level of persecution in the eighteenth century,[12] Alsatian Protestants were confined to a second-class status.

For other Protestants in the kingdom[13] the eighteenth century was one of clandestine activity and passive resistance. At first they naturally hoped for the re-establishment of the Edict of Nantes. But since Crown and Church stubbornly refused to consider this, they resorted to a successful subterfuge: while they outwardly performed a minimum of Catholic rites – baptism of children to ensure their legitimate status and marriage to ensure their right of inheritance – they remained resolutely attached to their Protestant beliefs, which were passed on at home from generation to generation. From the early eighteenth century Protestants secretly rebuilt their churches. Some went as far as abandoning the pretence of Catholic practices despite the great dangers this entailed, especially in the rural areas. Baptisms and marriages that were performed clandestinely by itinerant ministers posed particular problems for the authorities, since they were not legally valid. This century of clandestine activity gave the Protestant community a specific social profile, for not all social strata were able to play this double game. Before 1685 the Huguenots were represented at all levels of society, from the aristocracy and the bourgeoisie to the peasantry. By the end of the eighteenth century, however, the Protestant aristocracy had almost completely disappeared, except for a few regions. In the cities Protestant communities experienced great difficulty where they did not constitute a significant proportion of the population. As a result the great majority – at least eighty per cent – of the Huguenots lived in rural areas. In a few cities a rich business-oriented bourgeoisie existed, which played an important economic role. The Protestant bourgeoisie was not allowed to buy positions in the service of the Crown, and all but the least prudent avoided investing in land, which they would easily lose in the event of renewed persecutions. Thus, they often turned to commerce, industry and banking.[14] Although they had a high social profile, they were few in number. For the most part Huguenots were craftsmen, village shopkeepers and peasants, who were

---

[12] This is exemplified by the funeral of Marshall Maurice of Saxony – a Lutheran general of German extraction in the service of the king of France – in 1751, which was held in the largest Lutheran church in Strasbourg but was nevertheless attended by representatives of the civil authorities.

[13] It has been shown that despite the ban on emigration and the great dangers involved, about 250,000 Huguenots left the kingdom for countries of refuge like Britain, Germany and Switzerland.

[14] For more details on these questions, consult H. Lüthy, *La banque protestante en France de la révocation de l'Edit de Nantes à la Révolution*, 2 vols (Paris, 1952).

usually poor because many of the regions where Protestantism had survived were mountainous or infertile, like the Cévennes, the Vivarais and the Dauphiné. These Protestants did not, as far as one can tell, aspire to be 'emancipated'. Instead they wanted to regain the rights that had been theirs before the revocation of the Edict of Nantes. To them, this appeared to be the most practical solution since it did not presuppose a fundamental modification of the concept of the Christian monarchy which formed the basis of the structure of the French state. They believed that what had been possible between 1598 and 1685 should be possible in 1787: a Christian state in which social cohesion was based on loyalty to the Sovereign rather than on belonging to a single Church.

From the 1760s the authorities found it increasingly difficult to continue to impose the arsenal of repressive measures that had accumulated since 1685. This did not mean, however, that their recourse to violence came to a complete halt. The last Protestant minister hanged for the sole crime of his religion was François Rochette in 1762.[15] The last *galériens pour la foi* (Protestants who had been condemned to the galleys on account of their faith) were only released in 1775. Nevertheless, the intellectual evolution in these years allowed a rethinking of the legislation, not in the direction of a reintegration of the Huguenots but rather in the direction of their partial emancipation – that is to say, the abolition of some of the restrictions imposed on them.

From about 1765 some local authorities chose to ignore the opening of Protestant 'houses of prayer'. Moreover, the problem of Protestant marriages and the legitimisation of their children became more and more difficult to handle. From 1769 the courts recognised the *de facto* existence of clandestine marriages on several occasions.[16] The magistrates who took such decisions did so above all out of concern for public order, but it is self-evident that, without the progress of the Enlightenment ideology, it would have been much more difficult to make such judgements. The state thus failed to enforce its persecutionary legislation, since those who were in charge of implementing it no longer believed in its legitimacy.

---

[15] Also in 1762 Calas was tortured on the wheel. He was rehabilitated in 1765. The last minister to be martyred was François Charmuzy, who was arrested in 1771 while he was presiding over a religious ceremony. He subsequently died in prison as a result of ill-treatment by his jailers.

[16] Usually in the case of litigation between related individuals. Catholic collaterals sometimes attempted to expropriate the goods of minors on the death of their parents, or of widows married clandestinely by arguing that such marriages were legally non-existent, as happened in the Marie Roubel-Pourrat affair. See J.-B. Dubedat, *Histoire du Parlement de Toulouse* (Paris, 1885), vol. 2, pp. 665–6.

Accordingly, from the beginning of the reign of Louis XVI, some of the king's ministers became more open to a partial emancipation of the Huguenots. After much hesitation Louis relented and signed an Edict to this effect on 17 November 1787. The new edict failed, however, to restore the rights which Protestants had enjoyed under the terms of the Edict of Nantes. It denied them the ability to practise their religion. They were not allowed freedom of worship and were forbidden to reorganise their Churches. In addition, they were forced to respect the Public Holidays established by the Catholic Church and were not permitted to display the slightest disrespect for its ceremonies.[17] The text of the new edict was written in such terms as to show that France remained a Catholic state. Consequently, access to certain positions, such as teaching posts and royal or municipal offices, remained closed to Protestants. The edict was limited to civil matters. It tolerated the existence of non-Catholic individuals, but not of groups. By recognising the legality of their marriages, and therefore the legitimacy of children born from those marriages, it effectively granted them a civil status.

For the king, as a descendent of Louis XIV, the edict no doubt represented the limits of what he was prepared to concede, especially since the Catholic Church was hostile even to mere civil tolerance. Some Catholic dignitaries voiced their discontent, such as the Archbishop of Paris, who declared: 'the king will eternally carry the responsibility for the evils which might result from this edict'. The Assembly of the clergy in 1788 demanded that the legislation be modified in a more restrictive sense. At the opening session one of the members of the parliament of Paris turned to the crucifix and declared that Jesus Christ was being crucified a second time.[18] According to the Geneva publicist Mallet du Pan 'comments [could] be heard everywhere which remind[ed] one of the *Ligue*' among the people of Paris, who resented the return of the Huguenots' social visibility and who seemed not to have forgotten St Bartholomew's Eve.[19]

The partial emancipation of the Huguenots was thus very badly received by the Catholic hierarchy and by a section of the population in the big cities. It also disappointed the Huguenots themselves, because it did not grant them their freedom of worship. As the minister Rabaut

---

[17] Thus Article 30 stipulated that during the funerals of Protestants 'the parents and friends of the deceased [were] allowed to follow the convoy, but it [was] not permitted to sing or to recite prayers in a loud voice'.

[18] Quoted in H. Dubief, 'La réception de l'Edit du 17 novembre 1787 par les Parlements', *Actes des journées d'études sur l'Edit de 1787*, BSHPF, 134 (1988), 284–5.

[19] Quoted in P. Joutard, *Histoire de la France religieuse* [under the direction of J. Le Goff and R. Rémond], Vol. 3, *Du Roi très Chrétien à la laïcité républicaine* (Paris, 1991), p. 59.

Saint-Etienne remarked, 'the [Protestant] class is largely unhappy. Its members do not believe that this law grants them anything more than they have already had for many years.'[20] Nevertheless, a few of the more lucid Protestants realised that since the edict acknowledged the existence of non-Catholic individuals, the king would ultimately be unable to refuse them religious rights. On the whole, however, the Catholic population voiced little opposition to the edict. It did not undermine the privileged position of the Catholic Church, it did not make Protestants the equals of Catholics, and it did not cause a dramatic change in the social position of the French Protestants, who remained largely in the industrial and commercial bourgeoisie, in the crafts and in the peasantry.

II

Thanks to the events of the Revolution, the Protestants were, within a few years, truly reintegrated into the national community, both in a civic and in a religious sense. The French Revolutionaries sought to reform the state and to base social cohesion no longer on allegiance to a Catholic, 'Most Christian' King but on the adoption of the principles of 1789, that is, the values of the Enlightenment. This was not problematic for the Huguenots, who saw no contradiction between these values and the Christian faith. Many representatives of the Enlightenment were themselves Protestants, from John Locke to Jean-Jacques Rousseau. Since the Revolution would reintegrate the Protestants into the national community, they rapidly saw themselves as its instigators and its heirs. Thus, they associated themselves with the supporters of the Revolution – in effect, with the emerging political left wing. While a large part of the French population joined them in this, a significant faction, as well as the Catholic hierarchy, remained opposed to the principles of the Revolution throughout the nineteenth century. As a result, they refused absolutely to accept the achievements of the Revolution with regard to the emancipation of Protestants, if they did not simply take the Revolution as the product of a Protestant conspiracy. This is what the German Johann Georg Heinzmann described in 1800:

> The counter-revolutionaries say that the Protestants are the cause of the Revolution and that they degraded the clergy and disseminated free ideas, which are those of foreigners, not of the French ... The republican

---

[20] Quoted in J. Poujol, 'Aux sources de l'Edit de 1787...', *BSHPF*, 133 (1987), 347.

French value Protestants and give them credit for the first victory of light over dark. The true revolutionary ... is a friend of the Protestants.[21]

To understand the difficulties encountered by the Protestants throughout the period of their reintegration, it is necessary to distinguish between the religious and the civic spheres. As far as one can tell, in 1787 the Catholic Church was opposed to a limited degree of tolerance towards Protestants, whereas the majority of the French people was ready to grant them a number of civil rights. The acknowledgement of civil and religious equality was much more problematic, even if it was a logical consequence of the Enlightenment. A study of the *Cahiers de doléances* (petitions of grievances) shows that thirty-five per cent of them, 152 out of 438, mentioned Protestants. As could be expected, the clergy was opposed to freedom of worship for Protestants. Sixty-four out of the eighty-five *Cahiers* which dealt with this question refused to recognise the rights of non-Catholics; nine even demanded the repression of Protestant religious assemblies, twenty-nine accepted the edict of 1787 with restrictions and three asked for its abolition. The nobility, on the other hand, seemed more liberal: fourteen *Cahiers* approved of the edict and ten asked for its improvement. In general the Third Estate tacitly approved it: three *Cahiers* asked for a general law on the freedom of conscience and six for the return to the Edict of Nantes.[22] All this shows that a civil and religious emancipation of Protestants would have had a good chance of being strongly opposed by the clergy, while the population merely wished for Catholicism to remain the religion of the state.

And yet, at the beginning, things were not going too badly for the Huguenots. The electoral regulations – devised by the Genevese Protestant Jacques Necker, acting as the king's Prime Minister – made no distinction between Catholics and non-Catholics. The Protestants thus freely participated in the writing of the *Cahiers de doléances* and there were seventeen Protestant deputies out of a total of twelve hundred.[23] This means that, for the most part, the Catholic nobility, bourgeoisie and peasantry took for granted the civil equality of the Protestants in the

---

[21] Quoted in J. Poujol, 'Le changement d'image des protestants pendant la Révolution', *BSHPF*, 135 (1989), 501. Heinzmann, who had travelled in France in 1799, published in 1800 his *Voyage d'un Allemand à Paris et retour par la Suisse*.

[22] These figures come from L. Mazoyer's article 'La question protestante dans les cahiers des Etats Généraux', *BSHPF*, 80 (1931), 40–73.

[23] See B. Poland, *French Protestantism and the French Revolution: A study in Church and state thought and religion, 1685–1815* (Princeton, 1957); and Poujol, 'Le changement d'image'.

political arena. But this did not affect their attitude towards the latter's religious rights.

The Protestant community felt justified in making at least two demands. They asked for complete civil equality and, thus, free access to all public offices, real freedom of conscience and public worship, guaranteed by law rather than by a precarious tolerance; and, as a result, they demanded the reconstruction of the Protestant churches destroyed by Louis XIV. As a group, owing to their small numbers, the Protestants did not play a decisive role in the transformation from the Estates General into the National Assembly. Yet, although thanks to it they were reintegrated into the national community within just a few years and acquired an unprecedented degree of religious freedom, their status remained ambivalent. In the summer of 1789, the National Assembly decided to discuss the Declaration of the Rights of Man. When it came to religious rights, the Count of Castellane put forward a simple and clearcut formula: 'no one must be troubled for his opinion or in the practice of his religion'.[24] This wording, however, met with considerable resistance. The minister Rabaut Saint-Etienne, a member of the National Assembly, made a long speech in which he explained:

> It is not just tolerance which I am demanding, it is freedom ... Tolerance! I demand that ... this unfair term be proscribed, which presents us as ... guilty men who are pardoned ... I demand, therefore, for all French Protestants, for all non-Catholics of the kingdom, what you demand for yourselves: freedom, equality of rights ... , that all French non-Catholics be assimilated in every respect and without any reservations to all other citizens, for they are citizens too ... All men are free to express their opinions; all citizens have the right to profess their faith freely, and no one must be troubled because of his religion.[25]

Such were the wishes of Protestants then. However, they did not succeed in making themselves heard. After a long debate in which several Catholic dignitaries[26] participated, the Assembly agreed on a much more

---

[24] S. Mours and D. Robert, *Le Protestantisme en France du XVIIIe siècle à nos jours* (Paris, 1972), p. 192.

[25] 'Opinion de M. Rabaut de Saint-Etienne [sic]...'. In this speech Rabaut Saint-Etienne demanded freedom for the Jews also: 'I demand it for this people separated from Asia, always erring, always chased, always persecuted, for nearly eighteen centuries. It would adopt our habits and customs, if it was incorporated through our laws. It should not be blamed for its morals which are the fruit of our cruelty and the humiliation to which we have unjustly condemned it', *Revue chrétienne* (1889), 587–8.

[26] See on this topic the article by N. Weiss, 'Les séances des 22 et 23 août 1789 à l'Assemblée nationale', *BSHPF*, 38 (1889), 561–75.

restrictive proposal which allowed freedom of conscience but tolerated public worship only reluctantly: 'No one should be troubled for their opinions, even religious ones, as long as their expression does not disrupt the public order as outlined by the law.'[27] The acknowledgement of religious rights was thus difficult, even in a text which aspired to carry universal significance.

In the following months Protestants nevertheless obtained a series of political rights. In December 1789 a decree proclaimed that non-Catholics would gain access to all offices, and in the definition of the voting rights no reference was made to the voter's religion. In July 1790 the Assembly decided to return the confiscated property to the heirs of the Huguenots who had fled after 1685. It subsequently voted for a kind of law or return: the Constitution of 1791 stated that 'those born abroad who had either a French father or a French mother who had left France after 1685 for religious reasons, and who had settled in France and who swore an oath of allegiance' would be declared French citizens. Other measures completed these laws, granting civil equality to Protestants and some compensation for all losses incurred between 1685 and 1787.

As for religious life, the Assembly for a long time refused to acknowledge the freedom of worship. It was explicitly refused on 21 December 1789. The constitution adopted in September 1791 recognised the freedom 'to practise the religion to which one belongs' as a natural and civic right. Yet the term 'public worship' was not used. Not until December 1791 did the new Legislative Assembly decide that the citizens 'attached to a particular cult' would be able to use churches, temples and chapels which the administration judged to be useless for 'the cult maintained at the cost of the nation'. In May 1791, for instance, Parisian Protestants rented a former Catholic church, Saint Louis du Louvre and worshipped there. The inscription on the façade, which read: 'Building consecrated for the use of religious worship by a private society', still had the air of subterfuge about it.[28] It can be said that, from December 1791, Protestants had obtained civil and religious equality, even though the Catholic clergy continued to be paid out of public funds, unlike Protestant ministers.

There remained difficulties on the practical plane. Protestants might have appeared emancipated in the eyes of the largest section of the political class, but they did not appear so to the Catholic hierarchy and to society as a whole. Some indication of the Protestants' smooth

---

[27] Mours and Robert, *Le Protestantisme en France*, p. 192.
[28] See F. Garrisson, 'Genèse de l'Église réformée de Paris (1788–1791), *BSHPF*, 137 (1991), 51.

integration into the Parisian political class is shown by the Protestants who held official positions in the Revolutionary assemblies: the Constituent Assembly (1789–95) elected a Protestant president (bearing in mind that the presidents held their posts for fifteen days only). The Legislative Assembly (1791–92) elected two Protestant presidents (and two secretaries) and the Convention (1792–95) elected eight presidents (and six secretaries). Protestants gained important positions in the Public Safety Committee and the General Security Committee. They were also elected to the local assemblies in the regions where they made up a large part of the population, for example in the Cévennes and Poitou. One may also observe that many of the important actors in the public life of the time were sympathetic to the Huguenots. During a debate on the Declaration of the Rights of Man on 23 August 1789, Mirabeau exclaimed: 'Do not forget that tomorrow is St Bartholomew's Eve'.[29] When the Assembly discussed a proposal aimed at making Catholicism the state religion, Mirabeau intervened again:

> I will beg you not to forget that from this chair, from this tribune from which I am addressing you, one can see the window from which the hand of a French monarch, armed against his subjects by detestable rioters who confused temporal interests with the sacred interests of religion, shot the arquebus which was the starting signal of the massacre on St Bartholomew's Eve.[30]

Although Mirabeau's account of the event was fictitious, in 1793 the president of the Paris Commune had a commemorative plaque put under the window where it was supposed to have happened. This plaque stayed in place for years thereafter. Should one see this as a sign of sympathy towards Protestantism? It should perhaps rather be taken as a sign of an all-out attack against the monarchy.

During the first years of the Revolution the Huguenots, knowing that many of the French were none too favourably inclined towards them, remained cautious. At first, they avoided identifying themselves publicly as Protestants: none of the seventeen elected Protestants revealed his religious identity in 1789. It was not until a year later that one of them, Christophe-Philippe baron de Rathsamhausen, dared to do so; and it is no surprise that he was from Alsace. Later, in the Legislative Assembly, only one of the twenty elected Protestants (out of a total of 745 members)

---

[29] Quoted, among others, by Poujol, 'Le changement d'image', 525.

[30] Note that the legendary account of Charles IX shooting at Protestants from a window of the Louvre on 24 August 1552 goes back to Pierre de Boudeilles Brantôme. See Poujol, 'Le changement d'image', 525.

identified himself as such, the minister Marc David Alba-Lasource. Moreover, the Protestant deputies wisely kept out of the debates when the Assembly decided to reform the Catholic Church and discussed the Civil Constitution of the clergy.[31]

This attitude did not protect them from hostility. As soon as the Assembly started to debate religious questions, many voices were raised against the diversity of worship. Because they held that France was a Catholic nation, they thought that Protestants were therefore not to be considered part of it, though they were against their persecution. The book by abbot Claude Fauchet is representative in this respect. An advocate of the new ideas, he did not hesitate to participate in the taking of the Bastille on 14 July 1789 before becoming a member of the Paris Commune and later a Constitutional bishop. Nevertheless, in a book entitled *De la religion nationale,* which was published at the end of 1789, he wrote that although he entertained excellent relations with several Protestant ministers, '[the Protestants] are not and cannot be *part of* the family, although they are *in* the family and should be loved. They are not and cannot be *part of* the Fatherland, but they are *in* the Fatherland and should be, if I dare say, tenderly taken care of'.[32]

These words are all the more significant because they came from a strong supporter of the Revolution. It is not surprising that in the areas where Protestants were numerous and where the memory of centuries-old conflicts was not forgotten, many Catholics adopted a hostile attitude towards the religious reintegration of Protestants and towards the freedom of public worship – all the more since they thought that the majority of the Assembly wanted to remove the Catholic Church from what they considered to be its rightful place.

In drawing up the Civil Constitution of the clergy the Assembly established a system of remuneration from public funds for the Catholic clergy only, which supported the idea that the Catholic religion was the sole cult of the nation. When in April 1790 Dom Gerle,[33] a cleric who was also an advocate of the new ideas, suggested declaring the Catholic religion the 'national religion', passions ran high. So much so, that on the day of the vote, on 13 April, troops had to guard the premises of the Assembly. But Dom Gerle's proposal was not a new one.[34] As early as 28 August 1789

---

[31] Only one Protestant deputy, Barnave, made an intervention, but that was only in 1791 concerning the implementation of the civil constitution of the clergy, not its preparation.

[32] Quoted in Poujol, 'Le changement d'image', p. 529.

[33] In June 1789 he was the first to swear the Oath of the Jeu de Paume and he is represented on David's famous painting commemorating the event.

[34] On this question consult T. Tackett, *Religion, revolution and regional culture in eighteenth-century France: The ecclesiastical oath of 1791* (Princeton, 1986), pp. 229–49.

an Alsatian priest had made a similar proposal and on 7 February 1790 the Bishop of Nancy repeated it. Eventually, after a long debate in April, the Assembly rejected it following a passionate intervention by Mirabeau. Only the lack of a strong Protestant presence in Paris prevented a conflict in the capital. The Assembly's decision nevertheless provoked strong reactions. A protest note, written by the Assembly's minority on 19 April, was circulated in France and met with wide approval, especially in the regions with a strong Protestant presence.[35] The protesting minority was unhappy with the emancipation of the Huguenots and thought that the latter wanted to eradicate Catholicism. They also feared that the authorisation of public Protestant worship would lead to a return to the civil wars of the sixteenth century. These fears were reinforced by rumours of the sale of possessions of the clergy and by the alleged intention of the Assembly to reform the Catholic cult. In Alsace, a pamphlet maintained:

> The league is formed ... Witness how in the southern provinces Calvinism directs committees, writes speeches, appropriates itself public power with the help of the national guards, and propagates with fury ... the feelings of hatred, intolerance and vengeance which animated Calvin, its founder.[36]

In other places, this led to direct conflict. This was the case in Montauban and Nîmes, for example, where two 'brawls' (as they were described at the time) took place, in which religious and socio-economic discontent merged. In both towns a Protestant commercial and industrial bourgeoisie played a dominant role in the local economy.[37] A considerable part of Catholic opinion was convinced that the Protestants wanted to take over every place or even to massacre the Catholics. After several months of tension and virulent polemic a riot broke out on 10 May in Montauban: five supporters of the Revolution (four Protestants and one Catholic) were massacred by the populace and fifty-five were imprisoned. In Nîmes the troubles were worse. From April onwards there was Catholic agitation. In May bloody brawls broke out which in mid-June turned into a civil war between Protestant supporters of the Revolution, who controlled the national guard, and armed Catholic counter-revolutionaries. The result of several days of fighting and the

---

[35] On this topic, see, for instance, A. Benoist, 'Protestants et Catholiques poitevins sous la Révolution', *BSHPF*, 135 (1989), 593.

[36] Quoted in Tackett, *Religion*, p. 241.

[37] See D. Ligou, 'Les protestants de Montauban et la Révolution', *BSHPF*, 135 (1989), 733–61.

intervention of Montpellier's national guard were 300 casualties on the Catholic side and ninety on the Protestant side.[38]

In 1791 the Protestants recovered their religious rights. The same year the Assembly introduced the Civil Constitution of the clergy, even though it had been condemned by the pope. The 'civic oath' that the clergy was obliged to take according to the Civil Constitution provoked a schism between the 'constitutional clergy', which accepted it, and the 'non-juring clergy', which refused it. Many Catholics saw incorrectly (but this is not the issue here) the hand of the Protestants at play, not least because according to the law all citizens, including non-Catholics, were to participate in the election of 'constitutional' priests and bishops.[39] In certain regions, such as Alsace, Protestant ministers were to take the same oath, a step that many Catholics saw as a prelude to their demand for a salary drawn from public funds. The result was new unrest, which was less extensive than in 1790, but nevertheless very real. Besides, in the Midi Protestants were often accused of avenging themselves for the persecution of Protestant ministers in 1685 by pressing for the strict application of the law and by assisting in the expulsion of 'non-juring' priests. It is fair to say that this conflict was caused not so much by the reintegration of the Huguenots into the national community as by the alleged role of Huguenots in what was perceived as the persecution of the Catholics by the new regime. The result was the deterioration of the relationship between Catholics and Protestants.

In the following years the Revolution took on a more radical course. In the period of the Terror (1793–94), it is readily apparent that Protestants played no significant role in the politics of de-Christianisation. They were by no means spared the closure of their churches, and priests and ministers were forced to resign in equal measure. However, attacks against Protestants were less spectacular than those aimed at Catholics. For example, it was not possible to compel ministers to give up their vows of celibacy, since they could marry anyway. It was also impossible to transform the Protestant temples into 'temples of reason' in the same way that Catholic churches had been transformed, since the Protestant buildings had been destroyed in 1685. Even though the Terror at its worst did not spare Protestants, some Catholics still regarded them as persecutors.

Furthermore, on a theoretical level, those opponents of the Revolution who were also Catholic persisted in thinking that it was abnormal to grant Protestants anything else beyond civil rights. The 'Proclamation

---

[38] See *Histoire de Nîmes* (Aix-en-Provence, 1982), pp. 220–1.

[39] In Alsace there were districts with a Protestant majority. If Protestants were allowed to participate in these elections, they might decide their outcome.

against [sic] those who do not practise the Catholic religion' of 15 July 1793 issued by the superior Council of the 'Catholic and royal' Vendée army, which fought against the Republic, reveals this attitude. In the text, which was written by the leaders of the insurrection to reassure the Protestants, they perceived themselves as being particularly generous when they promised the Huguenots a return to a status that was slightly inferior to that which they had been granted by the edict of 1787:

> considering furthermore that the Catholic status of our armies ... does not exclude the tolerance pronounced in the edict of 1787, but only public worship in any religion other than the Catholic one ... the following is resolved: Article I: the Catholic, Apostolic and Roman religion is and remains the only dominant religion in France, and the only one which may be practised in public. Article II: nevertheless, all those following a different religion, or any other cult or sect, will be tolerated and given a civil status in compliance with the spirit of the edict of November 1787 ... save that the king should decide in favour of alternative statutes following the recommendations made to the late king by the clergy on a few articles of the above-mentioned edict.[40]

It is likely that militant Catholic opponents of the Revolution agreed with this text. Without going as far as contesting the civil tolerance and asking for the return of the persecutions, they were opposed to the concession of religious rights as well as the granting of civil and religious equality to Protestants. However, from September 1794, and later with the Directory, a regime began to take shape which resembled the American separation of state and Church in certain respects and which pleased the Protestants:[41] no denomination was to have a link with the state, and the freedom and equality of the different religious cults was guaranteed. One can understand why the Protestants were satisfied: for the first time in history they enjoyed equality with Catholics in the religious as well as in the civil domain. But these years also saw the birth of a new kind of literature, which denounced the Protestants, Protestantism or the Protestant spirit as the real cause of the Revolution. It would spread successfully from the pens of several writers, from Abbot Barruel and Charles Maurras to Joseph de Maistre and Léon Daudet. For these reasons, the rapid emancipation of the Protestants by the Revolution could not avoid provoking a strong opposition within French society and politics.

[40] Quoted in P. Romane-Musculus, 'Les protestants du bocage vendéen pendant la Révolution', *BSHPF*, 121 (1975), 258–60.
[41] The situation was obviously not identical, since in the USA the Christian religion was honoured without reference to any particular denomination.

III

The attempt of the Directory to stabilise French political life between 1795 and 1799 was cut short by General Bonaparte on 18 *Brumaire* VIII (9 November 1799). This was the end of the attempt to base social cohesion solely on the acceptance of the principles of 1789 and, thus, on civic and personal morals that originated in the Enlightenment but did not depend on any particular denomination or precise religious doctrine. Napoleon Bonaparte was intent on pacifying France and considered the support of the Catholic Church indispensable for this, so he negotiated a concordat with the Pope, which was ratified on 15 August 1801. However, if Napoleon wanted to put an end to the Revolution, he also wished to preserve its main achievements and he had no intention of returning to the pre-1789 union of Church and state. Despite the efforts of the Holy See, he refused to make Catholicism the religion of the state. The Concordat contented itself with acknowledging that the Catholic religion was 'the religion of the vast majority of the French people'.[42] This was an incontestable fact, but it did not result in any privileges for Catholicism. Moreover, the Pope recognised the existence of the French Republic and did not demand that the 'Christian monarchy' be re-established. He confined himself to putting on record the 'Consuls' private practice [of the Catholic religion]',[43] without insisting that such practice should remain in the future. The possibility of a non-Catholic head of state was even mentioned explicitly. Thus, social cohesion was no longer defined in purely secular terms, as it had been between 1794 and 1799; but neither did France revert to being a Catholic nation.

The situation was clarified by the Organic Articles added to the Concordat by Bonaparte in April 1802. They concerned the implementation of the Concordat, but they also defined the status of the Protestant cults, which exemplifies Bonaparte's wish to preserve part of the Revolutionary legacy. From the vantage point of the state a religious marriage had no bearing on the civil sphere – the Catholic Church no longer held the registers of baptisms, marriages and deaths. Furthermore, priests were no longer allowed to bless a marriage unless it was preceded by a civil ceremony. Divorce, which was forbidden by the Catholic Church, remained allowed by the state. In order to avoid renewed civil discord, Article 45 also stipulated: 'no [Catholic] religious ceremony will take place outside buildings devoted to Catholic worship in those cities where there are temples dedicated to other cults', and priests 'will not be

---

[42] A. Lods, *La législation et le régime juridique des cultes protestants* (Paris, 1887), p. 35.
[43] *Ibid.*, p. 37.

allowed to make ... any direct or indirect accusation against people or religions authorised by the state'.[44] These provisions were not fully implemented until 1879, but they nevertheless indicate Bonaparte's will not to make France a Catholic nation.

Moreover, the Organic Articles on the Protestant denominations granted official recognition to the Lutheran and Reformed Churches. Just like priests, their ministers were to be paid by the state, which also assigned a number of former Catholic churches to the Protestants in 'compensation' for the destruction under Louis XIV. This in turn embittered certain Catholics. The Articles were imposed by Bonaparte rather than negotiated with representatives of the Protestant Churches. They did not respect the fundamental principles of the reformed ecclesiology.[45] Nevertheless, for the first time in history, ministers gained official recognition, were invited to public ceremonies (a delegation of twenty ministers was present at the imperial coronation) and were paid by the state, while the legislation promised freedom and equality to all authorised religions. France had officially become a multi-confessional state – especially after the 'Israelite cult' became publicly recognised. Moreover, Bonaparte's dictatorial regime temporarily eased the denominational conflicts.

Protestants enjoyed the same civil and religious rights as Catholics, even if the Catholic clergy naturally took precedence in official ceremonies. From the state's point of view, the Protestants were emancipated. Nevertheless, few Protestants could be found in the highest political echelons during this period. There was only one Protestant minister of state between 1799 and 1814, five senators (out of a total of eighty), twenty members of the *corps législatif* (out of 300) and nine members of the *tribunat* (out of 114).[46] Napoleon, who was probably an agnostic himself, did not discriminate against Protestants. When he quarrelled with prominent Protestants, such as Mme de Staël or Benjamen Constant, it was because of their liberal political ideas, not because of their religious convictions. In the regions where Protestants were numerous the state did not hesitate to grant them important responsibilities. In Nîmes, for instance, the mayor was Protestant and the municipal council was composed of twenty Protestants and ten Catholics, although the Protestants constituted only a quarter of the population). Thus, until 1814 Protestants considered themselves to be emancipated and reintegrated into the national community.

[44] *Ibid.*, p. 44.
[45] See on this topic D. Robert, *Les Églises réformées en France (1800–1830)* (Paris, 1961).
[46] For more details, see Richard, *Notables*.

There was, however, a gap between the law and social reality. Towards the end of the Napoleonic regime Protestants understood that they were not yet considered the equal of Catholics in every respect. It was not civil equality that was at issue, but rather religious equality, which a large part of Catholic opinion refused to accept. These Catholics were prepared to allow Protestant worship in the traditionally Protestant areas – the Cévennes, Poitou, etc. – and in the regions where royal persecution had not succeeded in eliminating it. But they were of the opinion that the state had an obligation to protect only the Catholic cult throughout France, that it owed a particular and exclusive respect to it and that it should be forthcoming in meeting its demands. In their eyes, Protestantism should be allowed where it already existed but should not extend its sphere of influence. These Catholics believed in freedom of conscience but rejected freedom of public worship and religious equality. They based their claims on the concept of 'Christian (meaning Catholic) civilisation', that is, on the idea of a civilisation in which the institutions are blessed and controlled by the Catholic hierarchy. In principle, their position was the same as that set out in the edict of 1787, except that they allowed freedom of worship in the traditionally Protestant regions. But they put up determined opposition to the equality of the religious cults and especially to the opening of new Protestant churches in places where there was not a traditional Protestant presence. By analogy with the North American Indian reservations, these Catholics might be described as adherents of a 'theory of the Protestant reservation'. They let Protestants live undisturbed in their 'reservations', as long as they remained there and did not attempt to influence society at large through their religious beliefs or their political and social preferences (usually favourable to the Enlightenment and, thus, to liberalism and democracy), which were all considered foreign to the French tradition.

Yet it was impossible to eliminate twenty-five years of history. Above all, even if the Revolution proved incapable of creating a stable system of government (the French political instability of the nineteenth century being a consequence of this), it did not fail to create a new society which its opponents were unable to destroy. Religious freedom was on the verge of becoming a social and political reality. This resulted in the above-mentioned uncertainties and ultimately in the victory of religious freedom, which followed from the political victory of the Third Republic. The latter was founded on the principles of 1789 against the proponents of a monarchy on the model of the *ancien régime*.

The 1814 Charter stated in Article 5: 'Each person is free to practise his religion with equal freedom and enjoys the same protection for his worship.' This could not but satisfy Protestants and appears to be an acknowledgement of the religious achievements of the Revolution. However, Article 6 stated: 'Nevertheless the Catholic, Apostolic and Roman religion is the religion of the State', which definitely sounded like the *ancien régime*. There is no better illustration of the ambiguities of the Restoration, which was an attempt to reconcile two opposing principles. The Huguenots noticed that two Protestants had taken part in the commission which drafted the Charter, that a Protestant (the Marquis of Jaucourt), was made Minister for Foreign Affairs in September 1814 and that in Nîmes the Protestant mayor, nominated by Napoleon, was replaced by another Protestant. There were few changes in the religious legislation. The new government contented itself with allowing Catholic processions in all towns and villages. Thus, the return of the Bourbons did not provoke any fears among Protestants.

However, the situation deteriorated in the regions where the relations between Protestants and Catholics were strained. In Nîmes memories of the 1790 brawls were still fresh, especially since the Catholic side had lost. From the beginning of 1815 groups of royalists chanted in the streets that they were going to 'make black pudding with the blood of Calvin', and 'wash their hands in the blood of Protestants'.[47] After Waterloo royalist gangs spread 'White Terror' in the Gard. They burned and pillaged Protestant churches and attacked Protestant individuals, while women, in particular, were the victims of sadistic violence. Incidents of arson, murder (one to two hundred people killed and many more injured, according to the sources) and extortion multiplied. This led many Protestants to flee towards the Cévennes, to Geneva, to Paris and to other big cities. In the Gard, where the religious (Catholic) and civilian (royalist) authorities did not hurry to their protection, Protestants were terrorised, while in other areas they were alarmed by rumours of a new St Bartholomew's Eve, which fortunately did not materialise. Religion was not the only cause of these events. As earlier, social and political elements played a role. Many Protestants believed that Catholics wanted to push them to revolt against the king, who would then, they supposed, revert to the situation of 1787. Whether such an interpretation is justified or not,[48] this particularly violent and bloody episode had serious consequences. Henceforth there was bad blood between Protestants and monarchists. The result was that Protestants became opponents of the Bourbons, whereas earlier they had sided indiscriminately

---

[47] D. Robert, *Histoire des protestants en France* (Toulouse, 1977), p. 341.

[48] In *Les Églises réformées en France*. Robert, who wrote at length on the topic of the White Terror, argued that it was a plausible hypothesis (see pp. 269–85).

with any regime that had assured them civil equality and freedom of worship. The attitude of the government, which grew more and more sympathetic to the desires of the Catholic hierarchy, confirmed them in their choice. Neither Louis XVIII nor Charles X wished to abolish the civil equality or the freedom of worship of the old Protestant communities. But even in its most liberal phase (1817–21) the government never put the Protestant and the Catholic cults on an equal footing, because it saw itself as the protector of the Catholic Church. For instance, when a small group of Catholics decided to convert to Protestantism, the government strongly advised it not to do so. From 1822 the government did not prevent the construction of Protestant churches in traditionally Protestant areas. On the other hand, it demanded that the new churches be erected on the outskirts, as if to demonstrate that the Protestants were only tolerated; they should disturb Catholic worship as little as possible. To obtain the authorisation for placing a bell in a church tower and ringing it usually took several years. If Protestants failed to decorate their houses for the Corpus Christi procession they were fined. As time went on, the political powers drew nearer to the Roman Church. The 'law of sacrilege' of 1825 introduced capital punishment for anyone caught stealing an object belonging to the Catholic cult, especially if that object was the Eucharistic Host. A similar law for the protection of the Protestant cult did not exist. Protestants also noted that during the reign of Louis XVIII only two Protestants were in the cabinet and eight in the upper house, while Charles X did not make any Protestant either a minister of state or a peer. Following the government's example, the local authorities in the provinces, under the pressure of the ruling class (Catholic hierarchy, aristocracy and bourgeoisie), showed no goodwill towards Protestants. This period of the Restoration was, thus, seen by Protestants as a step back on the road to their reintegration into the national community. They felt barely tolerated in the regions where they had been living for centuries, and they believed that their religious rights were not being respected. In July 1830 they were delighted to see Charles X leave France forever.

The July Monarchy, which attempted to apply the principles of liberalism, appeared to the Huguenots to be favouring their emancipation. If in 1848, when the regime fell from power, the Huguenots did not yet feel truly part of the French national community, it was largely due to the provincial authorities, which were responsive to the opinions of the Catholic clergy rather than to the central government's intentions. This can be seen in the new constitution, which recognised Catholicism merely as the religion of the majority of the French and which promised equality of the cults, without restrictions.[49] Protestants were also aware of a 'Protestant presence' in positions of power, which was reminiscent of the times of Henri IV. During the reign of Louis-Philippe, François Guizot played a prominent role as Prime Minister from 1840 until 1848. In addition there were four Huguenot ministers of state and one under-secretary of state between 1830 and 1848 and several prefects and ambassadors. The king also married several of his children to Protestants and had a Protestant oratory built in the Tuileries Palace for his Protestant daughter-in-law.[50] When the Archbishop of Paris refused to invite François Guizot to the ceremony commemorating the death of Pope Gregory XVI, all the other ministers, in support of Guizot, boycotted the event.[51] At the political centre, therefore, matters appeared to be settled.

Nevertheless, the Huguenots would feel truly emancipated only when their religious rights were fully acknowledged. This would happen when they were allowed to establish Protestant churches throughout France – that is to say, when they could teach the Gospel, as they understood it, in all communities. Taking advantage of the climate of liberalism, they started missionary activities in the 1840s. They quickly encountered the hostility of the local authorities, which only tolerated conversion to Protestantism if it was confined to individual cases. The provincial ruling classes often did not progress beyond the stage of tolerance, believing that Protestants should not go outside their 'reservations'. The result was a series of conflicts, because Protestants could not accept an inferior status to that of the Catholic cult, which had no such geographical constraints.[52] However, when Protestants who were harassed by the local authorities succeeded in alerting the central administration, it usually decided in favour of religious liberty. There were, however, exceptions. On 6 May 1844, for example, following several incidents that threatened the freedom of worship of several neo-Protestant groups, the Minister of the Interior gave the following instructions, which he thought conciliatory, to the prefects: 'One has to establish to what extent their [the Protestants'] demand is earnest and if it be the case, one has to allow them [to open a new place of worship] provided there are no overriding

---

[49] There remained only one formal distinction in favour of Catholicism in Article 6: 'The ministers of the Apostolic, Roman and Catholic religion, practised by the majority of the French, and those of the other Christian religions, will receive payment from the State.'

[50] In 1832 his daughter Louise married the king of the Belgians, a Lutheran. In 1837 his second daughter Marie married the Duke of Würtemberg, also a Lutheran. In May 1837 the Crown Prince married a Lutheran princess, Helen of Mecklenburg, who would have become the first Lutheran French Queen.

[51] See Richard, *Notables*, p. 147.

[52] *Ibid.*

considerations'.[53] Since the minister gave the prefects the power to veto the opening of a Protestant church, if they saw fit to do so, the freedom of public worship was not fully established. Moreover, bureaucratic practice often made a distinction between the denominations acknowledged by the Organic Articles (Reformed and Lutheran) and the independent Protestant Churches (Baptist, Methodist, etc.) that had appeared since 1830. The latter encountered serious difficulties in their attempts to open new places of worship.

There were also many aspects of everyday life where Protestants were not treated in the same way as Catholics. The circular issued by the Ministry of Justice on 26 January 1839, for example, forbade Protestant ministers free access to military hospitals. The administration also often prevented converted Catholic priests from becoming ministers in the regions where they had previously preached. A Protestant deputy remarked that 'In England no one would dare to say that Mr Newman should not preach the Catholic religion in the very place where he was a Protestant minister'.[54] One could refer to numerous other examples of such administrative bias. Sometimes it was society itself which expressed its rejection of equality. This was the case in Strasbourg in 1840, when the town decided to honour Gutenberg by a statue with four bas-reliefs. It proved impossible to have Luther figure on one of them, even though he would have been surrounded by thirty-five other characters, because the Catholics of the city could not bear the presence of a 'heretic' on a public monument.

The conclusions to be drawn are that the greatest part of the Parisian bourgeoisie, which controlled the government and the central administration, was ready to accept the complete emancipation of the Protestants. This was not yet the case for the provincial bourgeoisie and the Catholic hierarchy. The question that must therefore be asked is whether this attitude was representative of the French people, which was overwhelmingly Catholic.

The revolution of 1848 introduced universal suffrage and a series of liberal reforms, including the freedom of association. This could only please the Protestants. Furthermore, the new constitution adopted the liberal wording of the 1830 Charter, withdrawing the slight bias in favour of Catholicism and making no distinction between the different cults, whether or not they had previously been recognised.[55] In 1848

---

[53] Quoted in S. Mours and D. Robert, *Le protestantisme en France du XVIIIe siècle à nos jours* (Paris, 1972), p. 263.
[54] Quoted in Richard, *Notables*, p. 158.
[55] Article 7: 'All are free to practise their religion and will receive from the State an equal

Protestants had the feeling that they had finally become citizens enjoying the same rights as Catholics. Only the introduction of universal franchise had made such a result possible, which seemed to correspond well with the wishes of the French people, as far as it could express them freely.

This remained so for several years. For example, when the government decided to curtail the freedom of meeting for political purposes, the decree of 28 July 1848 explicitly exempted religious meetings. From 1849 the freedom of assembly became less respected when the decree of 22 June made it possible to ban meetings if they might disrupt public order. However, the government's intention to defend religious freedom remained incontestable. The Minister for Religious Cults wrote to the Minister of Justice on 29 July 1850:

> Today everyone can, without previous authorisation, practise any worship and arrange meetings with the sole aim of practising this religion ... Should it not be said that controversy does not really form an integral part of worship? And that if controversy becomes the main or the sole purpose of a religious meeting, this very meeting must no longer be regarded as a religious one? To say this would be to forget that in most Protestant sects public worship consists of prayer, singing and above all of discourses on religion and morals ... and that in Catholic worship, the sermons and reunions are very often devoted to religious polemics.[56]

The state clearly defended the religious freedom and placed the Protestant cults, whether they were publicly recognised or not, on an equal footing with the Catholic. After centuries of difficulties the Huguenots thought that they had finally achieved their goal of religious equality, which was all the more valuable as it had been achieved on the basis of universal suffrage.

What the Protestants did not take into account was the rejection of this type of society, which was based on the Enlightenment, by a large part of the French bourgeoisie and by the Catholic hierarchy. These two sectors approved of the coup of 2 December 1851, whose main function was to spare France the free elections scheduled for 1852. Napoleon III, although not a clerical himself, was tied by his political and social alliances and created the most dictatorial regime of nineteenth century France. As might be expected, the emancipation of the Protestants suffered. From early 1852 the local authorities, backed by the Catholic

---

protection in this practice. The ministers of the religious cults already recognized by the law, or those which will be recognized in the future, are entitled to a salary from the State'.

[56] Quoted in André Encrevé, *Les protestants en France de 1800 à nos jours* (Paris, 1985), p. 81.

hierarchy, attacked the more recent Protestant assemblies (those which dated from the 1840s). Their main instrument was the decree of 25 March 1852, which again made prior authorisation of all assemblies, 'whatever their nature', obligatory.

The Huguenots, surprised to have their religious meetings banned, went to court. When the courts upheld the limitation of their religious freedom, they turned to the government, which confirmed the decisions of the local authorities. On 24 August 1854 the Minister for Religious Cults wrote a letter to the Minister of Justice, the tenor of which was diametrically opposed to what was written on the same topic in 1850:

> I, therefore, regard the three following points as unequivocal: 1) Freedom of conscience is absolute and everyone can practise their religion as long as it is only personal or domestic worship. 2) The 1852 constitution does not endorse the unlimited freedom of religious cults. 3) The freedom of the religions, even if recognised, does not exclude a right of supervision by the State.[57]

In 1854 the Minister for Religious Cults maintained that in France, the very country that liked to present itself as the upholder of the rights of humanity, freedom of *public* worship did not exist! This was not quite a reversal to the situation of 1787, since civil equality was not brought into question. However, the state acknowledged only the freedom of private worship. Just as during the first years of the Restoration, the Huguenots felt they had taken a step backward on the road to emancipation. It is true that this only concerned about one thousand recently converted Huguenots and that the state did not threaten the freedom of worship of the older Protestant communities. Many Protestants did not accept these decisions, even though they had been taken by secular powers. In these years several Protestant ministers were imprisoned for having led unauthorised meetings, just like before 1789.[58] They had to appeal to foreign protectors. In 1856, for example, Protestants turned to the British Foreign Minister, Lord Clarendon, who had come to Paris to negotiate the end of the Crimean war, to intervene with the emperor on their behalf. There is no better example of the Protestants' lack of emancipation.

The social and political alliances of Napoleon III explain this situation. In order to come to power in December 1851 he was forced to make an alliance with the most conservative sections of French society and with

---

[57] Encrevé, *Les protestants*, pp. 83–4.
[58] For more details on these problems, see André Encrevé, *Protestants français au milieu du XIXe siècle: Les réformés de 1848 à 1870* (Geneva, 1986), pp. 811–908.

the Catholic hierarchy. These groups, who felt nostalgia for the *ancien régime*, had no intention of going beyond mere toleration of the traditional Huguenot communities as long as they stayed within their 'reserves'. These policies, however, did not last very long. The Bonapartist ideology had its origins in the Enlightenment and had some modernising components. Napoleon's co-operation with the most conservative elements of French society was a product of the circumstances of French political life in the 1850s. When, from the 1860s, his Italian policy brought Napoleon III into conflict with these forces, the problem of the Huguenots was gradually laid to rest.

Protestants nevertheless had to wait until the victory of the secular and anticlerical Republicans, from 1879, before they could fully regain a position in the religious domain which equalled that of the Catholics. Only then could a prefect reply to a bishop that the opening of a Protestant place of worship was no concern of his. On 4 July 1879 the Prefect of Nièvre wrote to the Bishop of Nevers:

> I cannot help but point out to you, your Grace, that this does not concern the administrative interests of the Catholic Church ... and that from the point of view of the spiritual interests of Protestant cults, it is out of question that they should be subjected to your judgement ... I could limit myself to reminding you that all religious cults recognised in France are equal before the law and that there is no privilege in favour of this or that religion, allowing the representatives of the Catholic Church, however prominent, to make themselves the arbiters of the religious needs of non-Catholics.

When the bishop appealed to the minister, the latter supported the prefect: 'The representatives of one denomination are not entitled to intrude in the relations between the civil authority and the other religious cults'.[59]

And since the Republicans won all the elections until 1914, Protestants continued to be treated on an equal footing with Catholics by the state. There are several possible explanations for this. For example, the strong Protestant presence among the leaders of the Republican party and the government. In the first government, constituted in 1879, half the cabinet consisted of Protestants, a record unsurpassed to this day! More fundamentally, the victory of the Republicans was the victory of a group of men who wanted to complete the achievements of the Revolution and implement the principles that guided their precursors, in particular, Article 1 of the Declaration of the Rights of Man: 'Men are born and

---

[59] Encrevé, *Protestants français*, pp. 905–6.

remain free and equal in rights'. Although the Concordat remained in force until 1905, the Republicans, as earlier on the Directory, were determined to base social cohesion on acceptance of the principles of 1789 and on civic and personal morals that were independent of any particular Church. The application of the principles of 1789 was facilitated for the Huguenots by their unreserved acceptance of those principles, which for them (in contrast to the Catholics of that time) did not pose contradictions with Christianity. This also shows the deep attachment of the French people to those principles, since it was the implementation of universal suffrage which had made possible the emancipation of the Protestants. Previously, the restricted franchise had led to a mere toleration of Huguenots.

For the state, Protestants were considered to be emancipated from 1879 onwards. This, however, was not altogether true for society as a whole. Minority groups remained opposed to the principles of 1789 and to the equality of citizens regardless of their religious affiliation – something that became clear on several occasions.[60] At the end of the century the conservative press launched a vehemently anti-Protestant campaign on the pretext, for example, of the colonial rivalries between (Catholic) France and (Protestant) Britain.[61] Later Charles Maurras and the Action française were openly hostile towards Protestants. In 1914 Catholic publicists again accused Protestantism of being responsible for German nationalism and pan-Germanism. For the state and, therefore, for the majority of the French, since the Republic was based on universal suffrage, matters were settled from 1879 – except, admittedly, under the Vichy regime, which was at least in part suspicious of Protestants.[62] The *Etat français,* which existed from 1940 to 1944, was no longer a republic, enjoyed no democratic legitimacy and openly rejected the principles of 1789.

---

[60] Already in 1870 during the Franco-Prussian war some groups accused Protestants of being traitors in the pay of their German co-religionists.

[61] See on this topic J. Baubérot, *Le retour des huguenots* (Paris and Geneva, 1985), pp. 91–109.

[62] See on this topic the memoirs of the minister M. Boegner (who presided over the Eglise Réformée de France and the Fédération Protestante de France from 1929 to 1960), entitled *L'exigence œcuménique* (Paris, 1968). He mentions there the 'secret circular sent to certain police brigades ... asking them to supervise the activities of Protestant ministers, especially in the Drôme, the Ardèche, the Gard, and to collect the information together with mayors ... and priests.' (pp. 143–4). It is true that the Huguenots were largely opposed to the Vichy regime.

5

French Jews

Frances Malino

On 12 May 1889 prayers of gratitude could be heard in the synagogues of France and Algeria as rabbis honoured the Central Consistory's mandate to celebrate the centenary of the Revolution.

> Behold my brothers, what was begun in 1789 and behold what was solemnly proclaimed on 21 of September 1791 by the Constituent Assembly. And do you know who in this Assembly defended the Israélite cause with the most vigour? ... The *abbé* Grégoire, whose name merits being inscribed in gold letters in the book of our benefactors ... After the abbé Grégoire it was Mirabeau and Clermont Tonnerre who took upon themselves our cause, and the National Assembly, conforming to the immortal principles of the Revolution, voted our civil and political emancipation enthusiastically and unanimously.[1]

Rabbi Félix Meyer was not a historian and thus may be excused his error in chronology (the Constituent Assembly took its decision on 27 and not on 21 September 1791). But his description of the voting of civil and political emancipation as 'enthusiastic' and 'unanimous' can neither be relegated to mere homiletics nor be said to be unique to him. On the contrary. A century after the formal granting of citizenship to the Jews of France, a process that had in fact been torturous and protracted had successfully given way to myths, heroes and blessings.

I

The Jews formed a tiny minority in France – perhaps two in one thousand by the end of the eighteenth century. But numbers alone are deceptive, for Jews did not live in evenly dispersed locations throughout the land but

---

[1] *Discours prononcé à l'occasion du centenaire de la Révolution française au Temple israélite de Valenciennes, le 12 Mai 1889 par M. Félix Meyer Rabbin* (published by the Administrative Committee of the Jewish Community).

rather in officially recognised autonomous communities in southwestern and eastern France. Within these communities they established charitable institutions, elected a governing body, defined the curriculum of their schools, registered their births, marriages and deaths and adjudicated cases in their own courts. Punishment of recalcitrant members of the community was left to the rabbis and syndics (lay leaders), and only rarely were local authorities called upon to intervene in Jewish matters. In spite of the similar internal dynamics of their several communities, however, the daily lives of the Jews differed radically from one community to another. The most striking differences were those between the privileged Sephardim, often referred to as *portugais*, whose culture and religious traditions testified to an Iberian past, and the majority population of Ashkenazim, or *allemands,* whose centuries of cultural and linguistic development took place within small German towns and villages. The conditions, moreover, by which the Sephardim and Ashkenazim entered and remained in France served only to exaggerate these differences.

Examples abound of the humiliations the Ashkenazim faced during the last quarter of the eighteenth century: the affair of the counterfeit receipts in Alsace, in which peasants, brandishing receipts signed in Hebrew, refused to pay their debts; the numerous restrictions, economic, geographic and sartorial; the onerous taxes paid by the community of Metz; and, finally, the tentative 'reforms' of 1784, which required a census of the Alsatian Jewish population in order to facilitate the expulsion of illegally resident Jews. Yet there was another side to the France of the *ancien régime*: one which saw an impoverished foreign-born Jew corresponding with and befriending such influential members of state as Chrétien Lamoigon de Malesherbes, Jean Lenoir, former *lieutenant général* of police, and the minister Henri Léonard Bertin, and which permitted that same Jew to share a highly coveted prize offered by the Metz Academy of Arts and Sciences for an essay competition on 'how to make the Jews more useful and happy in France'.[2] Yet would the *ancien régime*, with its 1787 edict of toleration for non-Catholics and its reform-minded ministers, have ultimately granted the Jews equal rights? Without the Revolution, would the Jews have found themselves integrated into the body politic? Indeed, would they even have been given the same freedoms that had been newly acquired by the Protestants? Needless to say, historians differ profoundly in their responses to these questions.

---

[2] For a detailed discussion of the Metz contest as well as the prize-winning essays, see F. Malino, *A Jew in the French Revolution: The life of Zalkind Hourwitz* (Oxford, 1996), pp. 14–37.

The private correspondence of those most involved in addressing the question of the Jews suggests a profound ambivalence towards proposing a change in their status. Malesherbes, who, after preparing the edict of 1787 had been instructed by the king to turn his attention to the Jews, personally both distrusted and feared them.[3] Although the Jews themselves were divided over the inclusivity of Jewish law and tradition, they were united over the need to retain their separate corporate existence – which, of course, directly contradicted the intentions of the reforming ministers. Ironically, if anything changed from the time the Metz Academy announced its question concerning the Jews (1785) to the awarding of the prizes in the summer of 1788, it was that the actual status of the Jews of France appeared less rather than more secure. For now, in contrast to Protestants and foreigners, only the Jews were explicitly prevented from entering more fully into the economic life of the kingdom. Understandably, then, the rabbis at the end of the nineteenth century reminded their co-religionists of the benefits to them of the French Revolution. But what they failed to convey was also important. Following the decree of 27 September 1791, emancipation was renegotiated, both during the Directory and again during the First Empire. When it was finally brought to a formal closure in 1831, the process not only transformed the intent of the early Revolutionaries concerning the Jews but also bequeathed to the *Israélites* of France a set of expectations and presumptions that would define their relationship with the state for more than a century.

II

The public had been privy to arguments for welcoming the Jews into the body politic as early as the spring of 1789, when the prize-winning essays from the Metz contest were published and reviewed in the important journals of the capital. Although all three laureates – Henri Grégoire, the *curé* of Embermènil, Claude-Antoine Thiéry, Protestant lawyer to the parliament of Nancy, and the Polish Jew, Zalkind Hourwitz – had demanded that the Jews dress like the French, that they dwell alongside them instead of in Jewish quarters and that they be relieved of collective guilt, their positions were profoundly if subtly different.[4] Both Grégoire and Thiéry

---

[3] F. Malino, 'Les communautés juives et l'Edit de 1787', *Bulletin de la Société de l'histoire du protestantisme français*, 134 (1988), 313–28.

[4] Hourwitz, *Apologie des juifs* (Paris, 1789), C.-A. Thiéry, *Dissertation sur cette question: est-il des moyens de rendre les juifs plus heureux et plus utiles en France?* (Paris, 1788). H. Grégoire, *Essai sur la régénération physique, morale et politique des juifs* (Metz, 1789).

considered Judaism inferior to Christianity and the Jews in need of 'correction'. Thiéry had more respect than Grégoire for the religious integrity of the Jews and more concern for their freedom to remain faithful to their traditions. But this came at a price. For when he was asked whether the Jews would be able to rule, his answer was simple: they would not.

Although Grégoire's reformed Judaism presented no such impediments, he believed the Jews themselves might present some of their own. One should never loose sight, he warned, of the character of the people one proposes to correct. Hourwitz, on the other hand, vehemently denied that the faith of the Jews stood in the way of full equality, that their 'character' required 'regeneration', or that they needed first to demonstrate their worth. Of the three, Hourwitz alone gave voice to the new ideal of citizenship – democratic, non-corporatist and inclusive – which reached fruition in the Declaration of the Rights of Man and the Citizen of August 1789. It was also this ideal of citizenship, in contrast to the arguments of Grégoire and Thiéry, which the Parisian Revolutionaries embraced when they welcomed the Jews as active participants in the Revolution: on the streets, in the cafes and clubs, and in the uniform of National Guardsmen, and also when they petitioned the Constituent Assembly in January–February 1790 on behalf of the Jews.

Revolutionary ideals notwithstanding, the Assembly found it necessary to decide formally whether 'non-Catholics' could in fact be active citizens. During these debates, distinctions between Protestants and Jews were once again made. And once again, as with the edict of 1787, a decision concerning Jews was postponed. 'It has just been established', the *Courrier de Gorsas* announced sarcastically on 26 December 1789, 'that on principle one cannot decide a question as important as that of the Jews'.[5] Although the Jews of France responded immediately to the adjournment by the National Assembly, they did not do so with one voice. The more privileged *portugais* prepared their own *Adresse à l'Assemblee nationale*, sent delegates to Paris, engaged in a sophisticated lobbying of the deputies and won from Talleyrand the promise to bring their cause, separated from that of the majority of the Ashkenazic Jews, before the Constituent Assembly. On 28 January 1790, its numbers reduced as much by fatigue and hunger as by politics, the Assembly decreed that the *portugais* and *avignonnais* Jews of France were to continue to enjoy the rights they had enjoyed previously, including that of active citizenship. This was not, however, to presume any decision concerning the Ashkenazim of the northeast. The vote, twenty times begun amid 'cries' and 'tumult' in an

---

[5] *Courrier de Gorsas*, 26 December 1789.

atmosphere Mirabeau's *Le Courrier de Provence* likened to a 'synagogue,' was finally tallied at 374 to 224.

The enfranchisement of the *portugais* was a vindication less of the principles of the Revolution than of the privileged position these few thousand Jews of southwestern France had consistently enjoyed in the France of the *ancien régime*. Yet the decree of 28 January 1790 was significant. It not only communicated to the rest of the Jews the necessary terms for their citizenship but also empowered them in their response to its postponement. The next year and a half saw the old regime confronting the new each time citizenship for the Jews was raised. Not surprisingly, the concerns and reservations abundant in the debates at the end of the *ancien régime* found a receptive audience among those who sought to postpone indefinitely the granting of equal rights to the Jews. When emancipation finally came, in contrast to the debates of December 1789 as well as those of January–February 1790, the vote had little to do with the Jews, their patriotism or their equality. On the contrary, their citizenship had been subtly transformed into a vote on the credibility of France's constitution, as Adrien Duport persuaded his fellow deputies that freedom of religion allowed no distinction in the political rights of citizens because of their faith.

When the deputies left the Assembly on 27 September 1791, they believed that the decree they had adopted made further discussion of the Jews unnecessary:

> The National Assembly, considering that the conditions requisite to be a French citizen and to become an active citizen, are fixed by the constitution ... annuls all adjournments, restrictions and exceptions contained in the preceding decrees affecting individual Jews who will take the civil oath.[6]

The next day, however, Victor de Broglie requested that citizenship for the Jews carry an explicit and formal renunciation of their 'civil and political laws'. While the deputies assented, Louis-Pierre-Joseph Prugnon called their attention to the implications of the request: 'The civil laws of the Jews are identified with their religious laws and it is not our intention to require that they renounce their religion'.[7] Suggesting that 'privileges' be substituted in place of 'civil and political laws', Prugnon carried the vote. The following phrase was then added to the decree: 'which shall be considered as a renunciation of all privileges and exceptions introduced previously in their favour'. Before the discussion ended and much to the

---

[6] *Archives parlementaires*, 27 September 1791.
[7] *Ibid.*, 28 September 1791.

increasing chagrin of the deputies, Jean-François Reubell demanded that citizenship for the Jews of Alsace be linked to economic regulations ensuring the liberation of Alsatians from 'usurious' debts. His proposal – that within one month the Jews of Alsace were to produce detailed lists of their credits – ended the debates. On 13 November 1791, the first decree to grant citizenship to the Jews became law.

III

By persuading the deputies to permit discrimination against the Alsatian Jews collectively at the very moment they denied them their corporate existence, Reubell had demonstrated just how easily the prejudices of the old regime could be fitted into the new. Insignificant though it appeared at the time (the lists of credits from the Jews of Alsace never materialised) his victory must be seen as prophetic. It anticipated decisions made by the Directory and, even more significantly, during the First Empire.

Jewish historians have paid far too little attention to the Directory. For it was then, amid rampant inflation and endemic speculation, that the spectre of the usurious Jew reappeared – in journal articles, in debates concerning citizenship for the Jews in the newly formed Helvetic Republic and, more subtly, in the debates concerning nationalisation of the debts of the former Jewish communities. The problem of Jewish debts was hardly new; on the contrary, the Metz Academy had required Grégoire and Hourwitz to address it in their prize-winning essays. Now three separate commissions reported to the Directory's Council of Five Hundred. Endorsing the request of the Jewish communities, these commissions reminded the legislators that the decree nationalising the debts was based on the union of all Frenchmen in one social order:

> Let it be known finally that there can no longer be *tolerated bodies* or *intolerant domination*. What importance is the difference of religious opinions, when it is a question of civil or political interests? The Jews are French citizens: treat them as such so their dissolved community will not lie under an odious exception.[8]

An 'odious exception,' however, prevailed. The Council of Five Hundred, ignoring the reports of the commissions, found that the Jewish communities had never been organised as corporations and thus could not have been and were not included in the October 1790 order of dissolution. The decision ensured that the majority of the Jews of France would be saddled

---

[8] *Rapport fait par Riou sur les pétitions des juifs de Metz & Avignon, au nom d'une commission spéciale.* Séance du 4 Frimaire, An 6. *Archives nationales,* ADXVII 49.

with burdensome debts. They would also be required to organise some semblance of communal organisation to ensure payment and prosecute delinquents. In this it was not emancipation and the Revolution but rather the *ancien régime* which triumphed.

During the First Empire the emancipation of the Jews was actually sent back to the negotiating table. Napoleon had returned from a visit to Strasbourg (23–24 January 1806) committed to addressing the question of the Jews. But it would not only be on the issue of their organisation and their desire to establish the parity of rabbis with priests and pastors; it would also be on their presumed usury and what measures might be necessary to satisfy the interests of the peasant population of northeastern France.

Within a month the stage was set for a second round of debate concerning citizenship for the Jews. 'The evil done by the Jews', Napoleon would tell his Council of State on 7 May 1806 'does not come from individuals but from the very temperament of this people'.[9] The only remedy for their time-honoured habit of usury, the Parisian lawyer Louis Poujol argued in his pamphlet of 1806, was to withdraw their citizenship and establish exceptional legal measures.[10] Napoleon's Minister of Justice soon proposed this course of action to the Council of State.[11] If it did not appear in the terms of the imperial decree of 30 May 1806, which placed a moratorium on all debts owed to the Jews by non-commercial farmers of the northeast and ordered the convening of an Assembly of Jewish Notables, it was only because some members of the Council of State, consistently challenging Napoleon's views during three heated meetings, finally convinced the emperor that the Jews were perfectible and that they could and should participate in their own regeneration. Napoleon presented the Assembly of Jewish Notables, which met in Paris in the summer of 1806, with twelve specific, carefully worded questions. In all twelve answers the deputies eloquently affirmed their commitment to France, their determination to abandon any religious practices which interfered with their military and civic duties and their identification as Frenchmen. Their answers were subsequently codified by the Grand Sanhedrin, convened by Napoleon from February to April 1807.

On 17 March 1808, Napoleon approved a series of three decrees. The first two secured the foundation of French Judaism by assuring the Jews

---

[9] Quoted in S. Schwarzfuchs, *Napoleon, the Jews and the Sanhedrin* (London, 1979), p. 50.

[10] L. Poujol, *Quelques observations concernant les juifs en général et plus particulièrement ceux d'Alsace* (Paris, 1806).

[11] R. Anchel, *Les juifs de France* (Paris, 1946), p. 240.

of France an official consistorial organisation comparable to that of the Protestants.[12] The third, the 'Infamous Decree', subjected the majority of the Jews of France, although not the *portugais* of the southwest, to particular economic, geographic and military restrictions.[13] There is no doubt that these decrees complemented the Concordat with the Church and the Organic Articles for the Protestants. Yet in raising anew the question of citizenship for the Jews and in requiring from them, in contrast to 1791, doctrinal as well as concrete economic guarantees, Napoleon had inextricably linked their emancipation to a regeneration demanded only of them. In so doing he had interwoven *ancien régime* ambivalence and suspicion of the Jews with revolutionary universalism, religious freedom and the application of the constitution to all residents of France. Put somewhat differently, Napoleon ensured the preservation in the new public sphere of discourse of the particular and 'alien' quality of the Jew.

This did not mean, however, that Jewish and non-Jewish advocates of emancipation were left with profoundly different expectations. Both presumed a diminution of Jewish identity, the ending of a distinct corporate existence, and the replacement of the *ancien régime* Jew with that of the newly enfranchised *Israélite*. Nor, ironically was there dissonance in the acknowledgement of a need to regenerate the Jews. On the contrary, the Jewish leadership made this their primary task. One need only turn to Berr Isaac Berr's impassioned *Lettre d'un citoyen* addressed to his co-religionists on the eve of their emancipation.[14] Lastly, both Jews and non Jews agreed to a profound change in their traditional dialogue. Instead of questioning whether the Jews as men were to be included in the body politic, the Jews were now to demonstrate that they themselves consi-

---

[12] A synagogue and consistory were to be established in every *département* which contained two thousand individuals professing the religion of Moses. The functions of the consistories were fourfold: to assure that the rabbis acted in accordance with the decisions of the Assembly and Sanhedrin, to maintain order within the synagogues, to encourage Jews to engage in useful occupations and report those without any means of existence and to inform the authorities of the number of Jewish conscripts each year. The consistories were to be responsible for paying, with sums levied on each district, the expenses of the rabbis as well as other expenses of worship.

[13] Every Jew, wishing to engage in any form of commerce was required to obtain a special licence, issued annually and revocable when warranted. No Jew could henceforth establish residence in the *départements* of the Haut- and Bas-Rhin (*ancien régime* Alsace) and no Jew would be allowed to reside in the other *départements* unless he acquired a rural property and devoted himself to agriculture. Every Jewish conscript was to be subject to personal service. The decree was to last ten years, with the hope that at its expiration there would be no difference between the Jews and other citizens of France.

[14] Berr Isaac Berr, *Lettre d'un citoyen membre de la ci-devant communauté des juifs de Lorraine à ses confrères, à l'occasion du droit de citoyen actif, rendu aux juifs par le décret du 28 Septembre 1791* (Nancy, 1791).

dered the French as their brethren and France as their country. There was one critical area, however, in which expectations might and indeed would diverge. While there were non-Jews for whom the regeneration of the Jews had merely replaced the need for their conversion, virtually no Jew assumed that regeneration necessitated an abandonment of their Jewish identity and fusion with the non-Jewish community.

IV

Successfully uniting the Jews of France, emancipation had simultaneously welcomed them individually as full and active citizens – although not until they took the *serment civique*.[15] Predictably, the immediate impact on the Jews was far less radical than the change in their status. To be sure, Jews in Bordeaux and Bayonne became active in political life and some even occupied prominent positions; those from the northeast and the former papal provinces joined political clubs, volunteered for service in the army and participated in elections. In the capital, the Jews saw their population triple – by 1809 there were 2,908 Jews in Paris.[16] But even more significant was the continuation of traditional economic practices on the part of the majority of Jews (in fact, there was a substantial increase in money-lending after the emancipation decree of 1791) as well as the continuation of discrimination towards them – for example, arguments of physical repugnance were used to justify preventing the Jews from joining the National Guard. Perhaps there was more justice than previously, the Prefect Laumond wrote a decade after emancipation: 'One no longer confuses all Jews in one category, and public respect accompanies those in small number who make themselves worthy'.[17]

Only with the July Monarchy was the formal process of Jewish emancipation finally brought to a close. To be sure, under the Restoration Napoleon's 'Infamous Decree' of 1808 was not renewed, as it could have been in 1818. Yet, along with the empowerment of the Church and the pervasive influence of Catholicism, the Restoration also saw increasing hostility to Jews and Judaism. Prejudicial barriers blocked the careers of talented intellectuals like Léon Halévy. Well publicised competitions, such as those of the *Académie royale des inscriptions et belles lettres* (1821)

---

[15] The civic oath was simple and brief: 'Je jure d'être fidèle à la Nation, à la Loi et au Roi, et de maintenir de tout mon pouvoir la constitution du Royaume, décrétée par L'Assemblée nationale constituante aux années 1789, 1790 et 1791'.

[16] Census carried out by the Consistory in 1809, Jewish Theological Seminary, Mic. 8138.

[17] R. Reuss, 'Quelques documents nouveaux sur l'antisémitisme dans le Bas-Rhin de 1794–1799', *Revue des études juives*, 59 (1910), 275–6.

and the *Société des sciences, agriculture et arts* of Strasbourg (1825), questioned whether the Jews were useful citizens.[18] Emancipation was precarious; indeed, in the minds of some, it may even have been rescindable.

Not until the reign of Louis-Philippe, with the law of 8 February 1831, was parity finally established between Jews and non-Jews. Rabbis, previously paid by the Jewish consistories, were now to be paid by the public treasury, as were Catholic priests and Protestant pastors. In 1846, thanks to the influence and efforts of Adolphe Crémieux, future Minister of Justice, the *more judaico*, a special oath Jews had been forced to swear in the courtroom, was abrogated. Little wonder, then, that after praising the revolutionaries and the Revolution, Rabbi Félix Meyer had concluded his sermon with the words of Louis-Philippe:

> Full of confidence in God and of hope in the future, we desire ... the fulfilment of these beautiful words addressed ... by a French sovereign to the *Consistoire israélite* of Paris: 'Just as water which falls drop by drop finishes by piercing the hardest rock, so will the unjust prejudice which besets you evaporate before the progress of reason and of philosophy'.[19]

V

By the Second Republic, although major demographic, economic and cultural transformations were yet to come, the parameters of French Judaism had been clearly delineated. The consistories, which were hierarchical, centralised and dominated by lay leaders, dedicated themselves to the moral and social regeneration of their co-religionists. They protected Jewish interests, created Jewish charitable institutions (for example, orphanages, a hospital, primary and vocational schools) and supervised the training of future religious leaders. At their head stood the *Grand Rabbin* of France. His position of public authority resembled that of the Catholic archbishop.[20] After the decree of 1831, Jewish religious and educational institutions became financially dependent upon the state. This involved the state in more than just matters of funding, for it saw itself as being directly concerned with the development of Jewish education. French, Greek and Latin, which were common to all French institutions

---

[18] A. Rodrigue, 'Léon Halévy and modern French Jewish historiography'. Lecture delivered at the Ecole normale supérieure, April, 1997.
[19] *Discours prononcé* (see note 1).
[20] E. Benbassa, *Histoire des juifs de France* (Paris, 1997), p. 146.

of higher learning although they were hardly central to the duties of the rabbis, were made essential parts of the curriculum of the rabbinical seminary. State financing also directly influenced the decision in 1859 to move the seminary from its traditional residence in Metz to the more cosmopolitan Paris.[21]

If its institutions were centralised, French Jewry itself remained diversified. The traditionalism of the Alsatians, for example, bore little resemblance to the radicalism of a minority of reformers in Paris or even to the moderate majority whose positions found expression in two important Jewish journals, the liberal *Archives israélites,* founded in 1840, and the more orthodox *Univers israélite,* which was founded by the secretary of the central consistory in 1844. When in 1856 a rabbinical conference was convened, it carefully avoided a confrontation with the more orthodox by concretising a number of minor reforms and leaving to local communities the freedom to introduce other reforms, such as the reduction of the number of traditional prayers, the use of an organ in the synagogue and the introduction of a ceremony for all newborns. Since no other conferences took place (it had been assumed that they would be held every five years) official French Judaism remained moderately traditional. The numerous and often stately synagogues that were constructed throughout the nineteenth century, however, provide a striking metaphor for the success of its modernisation and integration.

The transformation of French Judaism – its orderliness and decorum, the elegant dress of its rabbis and the diminution of their authority, the subservient role assigned to Judaism in Jewish primary and vocational schools and the 'catechism' prepared for Jewish students – all speak to the direct effects of Jewish emancipation and to the indirect influence of the Catholic Church. Much to the chagrin of the rabbis, moreover, for whom many of these changes were already problematic, emancipation also brought in its wake a rapid and visible acculturation.

In contrast to their co-religionists in central Europe, whose emancipation was delayed until the second half of the century, a new generation of French-speaking Jews enrolled in universities, practised law, joined political parties and, in the case of a few, embraced the messianic world view of the Saint Simonians. During the Second Republic, Michel Goudchaux successfully served as Minister of Finance, along with Adolphe Crémieux as Minister of Justice. During the Second Empire, Achille Fould was appointed Minister of Finance. Jews also entered the

---

[21] J. Haus, 'The practical dimensions of ideology: French Judaism, Jewish education and state in the nineteenth century' (unpublished Ph.D. thesis, Brandeis University, 1997).

worlds of music, art, literature and the press and a number occupied posts at the *Ecole pratique des hautes études*, the *Sorbonne* and the *École normale supérieure*.

Needless to say, integration was neither immediate (it spanned the Restoration, the July Monarchy, the Second Republic and the Second Empire) nor without expressions of prejudice. When, for example, the brilliant philosopher Solomon Munk was appointed in 1864 to the Chair of Hebrew Language and Literature at the *Collège de France*, there was conflict and controversy, fear of 'disorder' and 'tumult' as a number of faculty argued that the occupant must believe in the divinity of Jesus Christ.[22] Paradoxically, emancipation also had a direct influence on the rate of conversion. Some examples notwithstanding, only one hundred well-known families converted between 1808 and 1840, even fewer under the Second Empire and none by the end of the century.[23] This, however, differs sharply from the situation in Germany where, as Heinrich Heine noted sarcastically, conversion had become a necessary ticket to enter society. Significantly, and again unlike Germany as well as the other countries of Europe, the Jews of France found little reason to leave their country.

Although emancipation brought about profound and observable changes in the behaviour, dress, language, professions and religious practices of the Jews of France, the most significant demographic and economic changes were not so much the effect of emancipation as the increasing urbanisation and industrialisation of nineteenth-century France. Without emancipation, of course, the Jews could never have taken advantage of, or participated in, these developments. And they did so, in even greater numbers than the non-Jewish population. In spite of the dire warnings of those who fought against their emancipation, Jews never formed more than one quarter of one per cent of the population; their numbers did increase from nearly fifty thousand in 1808 to more than eighty thousand in 1861, but they returned to less than fifty thousand with the loss of Alsace and Lorraine in 1870.[24] These numbers do not, however, convey the extraordinary inner migration of the Jewish population – one third to one half of the Jews of Alsace emigrated between 1820 and 1870 – or that by 1872 a largely rural and traditional community had been transformed into an urban population that was

---

[22] Of course, that Munk was to succeed the recently dismissed Ernst Rénan only complicated matters. For the position at the *Collège de France*, see *Archives nationales* F17 13556, dossier 36.

[23] Benbassa, *Histoire des juifs*, p. 191.

[24] *Ibid.*, p. 156.

predominately engaged in commerce, trade and banking and was increasingly identified as bourgeois.[25] Emblematic of this transformation is the three-generation odyssey of the Dreyfus family, from Jacob, a peddler and money-lender in the Alsatian village of Rixheim, to his son Raphael, a textile manufacturer in the city of Mulhouse, and finally to his grandson Alfred, an officer on the French General Staff. Along the way, the family made its name more French, adopted an *haut-bourgeois* way of life and educated its two youngest sons in elite schools. They, in turn, identified fully with French republican culture.[26]

Should one, however, only describe French Jewry in terms of a linear process of assimilation? Was there throughout the nineteenth century an increasingly attenuated Jewish identity and commitment to Judaism? Or was the acculturation and integration of the Jews more nuanced, more diverse, perhaps even concomitant with a retention of religious and, in spite of the nature of the French integrationist nation state, what we might now call ethnic identity?

The early Revolutionaries who supported emancipation, for example Brissot, Gorsas and Mirabeau, concerned themselves very little either with a particular regeneration of the Jews or with a shedding of their Judaism in favour of French norms. But the discussions and debates concerning the Jews at the end of the eighteenth century, influenced by Enlightenment ideals of moral virtue and economic utility, had found their way into Napoleon's resolution of the Jewish question. By 1808, regeneration of the Jews of France had become the dominant theme not only in their own emancipationist ideology but also in the expectations of their non-Jewish compatriots. For the Jews, however, their regeneration did not mean fusion with the majority population. On the contrary, throughout the nineteenth century many struggled to give meaning to their Jewish identity and content to their Judaism, while simultaneously expressing their full commitment to French values and French culture. Debates concerning religious observance, education, even the role of Jewish women, filled the pages of their two largest periodicals. Teachers and directors of Jewish schools discussed privately among themselves how best to instil in their students knowledge of and pride in their religious heritage. Nothing, however, captures more dramatically this emerging Franco-Judaism than the creation of the *Alliance Israélite Universelle*. With its network of schools, its international diplomacy and

---

[25] Although the majority of the Jews (sixty per cent) resided in Paris, other important urban centres were Marseille, Lyon, Bordeaux and Nancy.

[26] M. Burns, 'Majority faith: Dreyfus before the affair', in F. Malino and D. Sorkin (eds), *From east and west: Jews in a changing Europe 1780–1870* (Oxford, 1989), pp. 57–82.

its determined emancipationist ideology, the *Alliance* wove together seamlessly the diverse, often paradoxical, threads of *ancien régime* ambivalence, Revolutionary universalism, French patriotism, and collective Jewish responsibility.

VI

Founded in Paris in 1860 by six young, acculturated French Jews, and by 1881 numbering 24,176 members in Europe and the United States of America, the *Alliance* had from its inception clearly defined goals: 'to work throughout the world for the emancipation and moral progress of the Jews; to help effectively all those who suffer because they are Jews; to encourage all publications designed to achieve these results'.[27] The heart-wrenching Damascus Blood Libel of 1840, in which Jews living in Damascus were accused by Christian Arabs of the ritual murder of a Capuchin monk, and the Mortara kidnapping case of 1858, in which the Catholic Church refused to return a young Jewish boy to his parents after he had been secretly baptised by his nursemaid, provided the immediate catalysts for the formation of the *Alliance*. Emancipated Jewry, under the inspiration and leadership of the Jews of France, resolved to come to the aid of their persecuted and vulnerable co-religionists.[28]

Motivated by a genuine sentiment of Jewish solidarity wedded to the conviction that French civilisation was both normative and universally applicable, the *Alliance* set itself the task of 'regenerating' the Jews of the world – vocationally, linguistically, morally and spiritually. The means? Modern, intellectually rigorous schools for young girls and boys. By 1900, the *Alliance* had established one hundred schools from Morocco to Iran. Some were co-educational, most were primary, a few were vocational. Although the teachers were originally chosen from graduates of Jewish schools in France as well as the rabbinical seminary in Paris, they were subsequently recruited from *Alliance* schools in the Ottoman Empire, North Africa and the Middle East. Brought to Paris at the age of fourteen or fifteen, the males were trained at the *Ecole normale israélite orientale*. Young girls attended the *Institut Bischoffsheim*, the private schools of Madame Isaac or Madame Weill-Kahn and, finally, after 1922, the *Alliance Ecole normale* for women in Versailles.

[27] 'Appel à tous les Israélites', *Alliance Israélite Universelle* (Paris, 1860), 39.
[28] Michael Graetz has argued persuasively that the founders of the *Alliance Israélite Universelle* were drawn from an intellectual elite alienated from the Jewish consistorial establishment and influenced by republicanism, Saint Simonism and positivism. M. Graetz, *The Jews in nineteenth-century France: From the French Revolution to the Alliance Israélite Universelle*, trans. J. M. Todd (Stanford, 1996).

After four years of study in Paris, these newly westernised teachers, armed with their *brevets supérieurs* and a ten-year mandatory commitment to the *Alliance*, returned to such communities as Tetuan, Tripoli, Bagdad or Bursa. There they introduced young children, who were often painfully poor and from very traditional families, to the French language, culture and value system, to modern hygiene and the means to earn a livelihood, to a knowledge of and pride in Judaism. If they were vectors of modernisation and missionaries of westernisation, the *Alliance* teachers also qualified as ethnographers and informants.[29] Most importantly, they testified to the superiority of France, the strength of French Jewry and, through the trajectory of their lives, the future emancipation of their fellow Jews.

Less successful or enduring than this educational network, although no less indicative of the *Alliance*'s self-defined mandate, was its sophisticated lobbying and tireless diplomacy on behalf of persecuted Jews in Switzerland, Russia, Romania, Greece, North Africa, the Ottoman Empire and the Middle East.[30] Benefiting from the prestige and leadership of such men as Crémieux, Sylvain Lévi, Jacques Bigart, Lucien Wolf (England) and Gerson von Bleichröder (Germany), the *Alliance* drew public attention to its political activities. Simultaneously, it negotiated in private with diplomats, ambassadors and ministers of state.

In an extraordinary process of internalisation and displacement, the Jews of France brought to their co-religionists of the 'Orient' many of the prejudices and assumptions their grandparents had encountered among French advocates of tolerance and reform. They also brought confidence in their own successful model of emancipation. Both of these – a disdain for the traditions, 'superstitions' and languages of their 'less civilised' fellow Jews and pride in their own accomplishments and status – spoke to the delicate situation of emancipated French Jewry. It was simultaneously powerful, yet vulnerable; French, yet somehow also distinctly Jewish; committed to the individualism of citizenship in a modern nation state, yet inextricably linked to the fate of Jews outside of France. Understandably, the increasing anti-Semitism in the Third Republic, as well as the subsequent arrival in France of Jewish immigrants, challenged the identity of French Jews and threatened to test the success of their emancipation.[31]

[29] A. Rodrigue, *Images of Sephardi and eastern Jewries in transition: The teachers of the Alliance Israélite Universelle, 1860–1939* (Seattle, 1993).
[30] This lobbying was made even more urgent by the potential threat to emancipated Jewry of an influx of Jews from traditional societies.
[31] Jewish immigration to France came later than to England or to the USA. Only after 1905, with the failure of the Revolution in Russia and the restrictive legislation in England, was there a substantial immigration from Eastern Europe to France. It is important to keep in mind that Jewish immigrants also came from North Africa and the Ottoman Empire. By the First World War, immigrants formed nearly half of the Jewish population of Paris.

VII

Historians often look to the failures of emancipation to explain or at least hint at the sources of French nineteenth-century anti-Semitism. Admittedly, if one were to juxtapose the expectations of those who supported Jewish emancipation – that the Jews would become peasants and craftsmen, that they would abandon not only their languages and their corporate autonomy but also their particularity, their tendency to dwell apart, their endogamy – with the socio-economic and cultural realities of an urbanised, bourgeois, self-assertive Jewish population, one can easily imagine the French of the Third Republic, both from the right and the left, suggesting that Jewish emancipation had indeed failed. But to attribute political anti-Semitism to emancipation's presumed failure is not only to make anti-Semitism rational but also to connect it to the behaviour of the Jews.

Arguments against the Jews calling attention to their prominence as bankers, financiers and large-scale retailers, their political influence as civil servants, army officers, magistrates and members of the legislature, their support for and benefit from the increasing secularisation of French society, and their presumed membership in an inferior race, were largely rationales for a phenomenon that, in essence, had less to do with Jews or Judaism than with the political conflicts, economic fears, psychological anxieties and pseudo-science of late nineteenth-century France. These arguments also spoke to the vitality and endurance of a hostility rooted in medieval Christianity and re-substantiated in an emancipatory process that had particularised the Jews by presenting them with separate criteria for their citizenship.

By the last third of the century, anti-Semitism could be found in a broad political spectrum ranging from the anti-Judaism of the right and the clergy, to the anti-modernism of the populists and the anti-capitalism of the socialists. Linked with Freemasons and Protestants (who were often portrayed as half-Jews), Jews were accused of having instigated the French Revolution, its anti-clericalism and its destruction of traditional, Christian French civilisation. They were also seen as the embodiment of the modern capitalist spirit. The Jews, in short, were identified as the cause of the malfunction of modern society.

No one gave more eloquent voice to this emerging anti-Semitism than the journalist Edouard Drumont. His passionate and vitriolic *La France juive* (1886) sold more than one hundred thousand copies in its first year of publication. Yet not even Drumont could transform this rhetoric into the platform of an anti-Semitic political party. Within a year the *Ligue antisémitique*, which he founded with Jacques Biez in 1888, was dissolved. Little wonder, then, that in their centennial commemorations of the Revolution, Jewish leaders and rabbis, including Félix Meyer, spoke of Revolutionary heroes, Jewish emancipation and the republican tradition. For them the diatribes of a Drumont stood in stark contrast to the prestigious positions occupied by their co-religionists, the state support, even protection, which the schools and personnel of the *Alliance Israélite* received, and the knowledge that nowhere else in Europe were Jews as successfully and fully integrated into political life than in France.[32] Only in 1894, when the Alsatian Jew, Captain Alfred Dreyfus, was charged with treason, was a relatively weak anti-Semitic movement empowered. *La Libre Parole*, the daily paper Drumont had begun to publish in 1892, and the Catholic newspaper, *La Croix*, successfully provided the fuel.

The contemporary debate over Dreyfus's guilt or innocence – which rent families asunder, called into question political alliances, ignited anti-Semitic waves of violence throughout France and, especially, Algeria and initially saw even the Jews themselves divided – has been replaced by divided opinion over the nature of the Affair. Some argue that it really had nothing at all to do with the Jews; others suggest that it identified nineteenth-century France as being more hospitable to anti-Semitism than its German neighbour. Although these interpretations leave room for a more nuanced appreciation both of the vulnerability and marginality of the Jews and, paradoxically, of the full extent of their equality, neither really challenges the legacy of the Affair – either for France or for the Jews.

In 1906, eleven years after his court martial and public degradation ceremony, Alfred Dreyfus was finally vindicated. That vindication, which was inextricably linked to the separation of the Church and the state in 1905 and to the reaffirmation of the civilian Third Republic, secured French Jewry's emancipationist ideology and re-enforced its identification with and indebtedness to republican France. Most importantly, it ensured that the Franco-Judaism of the nineteenth-century, in spite of subsequent challengers, would remain the dominant identity of French Jews until Vichy.

---

[32] For a discussion of the emergence and self-identity of this Jewish political and administrative elite, see P. Birnbaum, *The Jews of the republic: A political history of state Jews in France from Gambetta to Vichy*, trans. J. M. Todd (Stanford, 1992).

6

German Catholics

Wolfgang Altgeld

The consciousness of being a minority – a 'born minority' – was part of the innermost self-understanding of Catholics in the new German nation state of 1871; it lay at the very core of the classification by which the political and journalistic spokesmen of Catholicism defined themselves. The term was brought into play when a description of the political situation of the Catholics was required in relation to the different administrative levels of the German Empire and the respective political elites that determined them. It was used to contrast the particular Catholic social conditions or to pinpoint the place of Catholics within the wider national culture. Above all, the term was utilised in order to justify the call for absolute unity among Catholics and to inculcate the idea that 'Catholics in the German Empire [were] a born minority; only through their unity against their divided opponents [did] they exert a substantial influence'.[1]

Historians have adopted this common and all-encompassing Catholic usage of the term 'minority', but they have rarely reflected upon its problematic application or developed it into a starting-point to guide historical research on German Catholics in the nineteenth and twentieth centuries. Characteristically the term appears most commonly in studies evaluating the role of Catholic party politics within the general political spectrum of Imperial Germany and the Weimar Republic.[2] In this context 'minority' is entirely appropriate in view of the numbers of Catholic political representatives and potential voters and here its colloquial usage does not

---

[1] Letter from Franz Xaver von Balestrem to Georg von Hertling, 10 April 1991, in E. Heinen (ed.), *Staatliche Macht und Katholizismus in Deutschland*, vol. 2 (Dokumente des politischen Katholizismus von 1867–1914) (Paderborn, 1971), pp. 239–41. The topic of the letter was the question of who should succeed Ludwig Windthorst as leader of the Centre Party.

[2] See, for example, W. Becker (ed.), *Die Minderheit als Mitte: Die deutsche Zentrumspartei in der Innenpolitik des Reiches, 1871–1933* (Paderborn, 1986).

cause any problems. However, the more recent research into social history does not operate with the technical term 'minority' but, on the whole, with the term 'milieu',[3] which signals that the main research interest focuses on the internal condition of the denominational group. Historical research of milieus has to start at the local and regional levels in order to give substance to its ambitious programme. Naturally, the geographical areas of investigation are those in which the formation of a dense Catholic milieu was possible because Catholics were the majority population, such as in the Rhineland or Westphalia.[4] Accordingly, the importance of the issue of being a minority is in general frequently overlooked in the study of milieu formation.[5] This corresponds to a tendency in German historical scholarship since 1945 to consider separately the large denominational groups and their social, cultural, political and religious manifestations and to avoid overlapping explorations, as if there were a danger of reopening old wounds. It is at any rate evident how willing comparatively uninhibited non-German historians are to apply overarching perspectives and confront problems and, by so doing, contribute substantially to a more precise understanding of the development of Catholic Germany and therefore German history as a whole.[6] German Catholics did not develop in a vacuum but very much in opposition to other particular segments of German society in the course of the building of the German nation before and after 1871.

[3] See M. R. Lepsius, 'Parteiensysteme und Sozialstruktur: Zum Problem der Demokratisierung der deutschen Gesellschaft', G. A. Ritter (ed.), *Deutsche Parteien vor 1918* (Köln, 1973; first edn, 1966), pp. 56–80.

[4] For this growing field of studies, see for example, J. Sperber, *Popular Catholicism in nineteenth century Germany* (Princeton, 1984), which, despite the title, researches the constitution of the Catholic milieu in the Rhineland and Westphalia between 1850 and 1870; E. Föhles, *Kulturkampf und katholisches Milieu 1866–1890 in den niederrheinischen Kreisen Kempen und Geldern und der Stadt Viersen* (Viersen, 1995); C. Rauh-Kühne, *Katholisches Milieu und Kleinstadtgesellschaft: Ettlingen 1918–1939* (Sigmaringen, 1991).

[5] Similarly, this statement is valid for research on Catholic popular piety (*Volksfrömmigkeit*), not least because situated at the core of this approach is the revelation of opposition to Catholic elite culture and to the elitist authoritarian Church. Though this approach may be used in research into milieus, which itself needs to address the development of popular piety, it stands separately because of its ethnological roots and its orientation towards the history of mentalities and everyday life. See W. Schieder (ed.), *Volksreligiosität in der modernen Sozialgeschichte* (Göttingen, 1986), who identifies (pp. 11–12) the main areas of research, which since have been surpassed by a number of excellent studies such as D. Blackbourn, *Volksfrömmigkeit und Fortschrittsglaube im Kulturkampf* (Stuttgart, 1988) and D. Blackbourn, *Marpingen: Apparitions of the Virgin Mary in Bismarckian Germany* (Oxford, 1993).

[6] See, *inter alia*, M. L. Anderson, 'The Kulturkampf and the course of German history', *Central European History*, 19 (1986), 82–115; H. Walser Smith, *German nationalism and religious conflict: Culture, ideology, politics, 1870–1914* (Princeton, 1995); Blackbourn, *Marpingen*.

German Catholics became a minority in the process of this nation building, not because they entered the *kleindeutsch* nation state as a quantitative minority after the first division of Germany in 1866 and the decisions of 1870–71 but because they found themselves confronted with a politically dominating majority which rigorously attempted to force the homogenisation of their peculiarities. After the successful foundation of the nation state, Catholics experienced this situation as oppression and disadvantage. It reinforced their own narrow insularity and also frustrated their own efforts at integration. What follows will be an attempt to approach these particular problems of the Catholic minority in four stages: first, by some observations regarding the antecedents in the first two thirds of the nineteenth century, second, by evaluating the confrontation during the time of the *Kulturkampf* (struggle between the State and the Catholic Church during the 1870s), third, by a characterisation of the Catholic section of the population, and finally, by discussing the extent of their national integration in Wilhelmine Germany.

I

Around sixteen million Catholics, ten million Lutherans and two million members of the Reformed Church lived within the borders of the Holy Roman Empire of the German Nation on the eve of its dissolution. In the two decades between 1795 and 1815 they experienced fundamental changes to their daily life and to the order to which they had been accustomed. These changes took place in several phases, were of varying magnitudes and were by and large confirmed in the post-Revolutionary re-ordering of Central Europe in the Congress of Vienna.[7] From a denominational perspective, Catholics, especially outside Austria, were without doubt most severely affected by these changes. Napoleon's policy on Germany enforced or, depending on one's perspective, made possible the Enactment of the Delegates of the Empire (*Reichsdeputationshauptschluß*) of 1803, which destroyed the once magnificent Imperial Church (*Reichskirche*), with its prince bishoprics (*Fürstbistümer*) and Imperial abbeys (*reichsunmittelbare Abteien*), which had guaranteed Catholic predominance in the Empire. As a result, about 3.2 million people, almost exclusively Catholics, fell under the rule of Protestant rulers in pre-

---

[7] Among the many useful overviews of this period of radical change are K. O. Freiherr von Aretin, *Vom Deutschen Reich zum Deutschen Bund* (Göttingen, 1980); H. Möller, *Fürstenstaat oder Bürgernation: Deutschland, 1763–1815* (Berlin, 1994; first edn, 1989).

dominantly Protestant states. The decree of 1803 also provided the opportunity to dissolve the monasteries and convents that were freeholds (*landsässige Klöster und Stifte*). This was carried out everywhere with extreme rapidity and with a destructive ruthlessness reminiscent of the actions of the French Revolutionaries against the Church a decade earlier. The social and cultural consequences of this internal secularisation for Catholic Germany, especially for the lower middle class of artisans and small tradesmen and for elementary and secondary education, cannot be described in detail here. The catastrophic ruin of the Church's organisation at different levels as a result of this secularisation process took decades to redress.[8] It is therefore not surprising that many astute contemporaries saw the Catholic Church as being generally in decline or that, especially in the beginning of the nineteenth century, irenically-minded Christians earnestly debated the possibility of a reunification of the denominations.[9]

Article 16 of the Federal Constitution (*Deutsche Bundesakte*) of 8 June 1815 stated very clearly: 'The differences between the Christian religious parties cannot establish a difference in the enjoyment of civic and political rights in the states of the German Confederation.'[10] This one sentence fundamentally determined the emancipation (in the sense of formal equality or, in contemporary parlance, parity) of Catholics as well as Lutherans and members of the Reformed Church in all German states: to belong to a minority denomination in states ruled by houses of different denominations, or under the governments of the three free cities, or (apart from the Grand Duchy of Baden) where there were majority populations of different denominations, would no longer constitute grounds for restrictions in civil rights. This breakthrough, which only a few years earlier, in the Enactment of 1803, had not been achieved, implied a new notion of the state: the concept of the denominationally neutral state, which had only begun to emerge in the liberal legislation of a number of the more enlightened absolutist German states from the late eighteenth

---

[8] See F. Schnabel, *Deutsche Geschichte im neunzehnten Jahrhundert* (Munich, 1987; first edn, Freiburg, 1937), vol. 5; A. Langner (ed.), *Säkularisation und Säkularismus im 19. Jahrhundert* (Paderborn, 1987). Shorter useful overviews on these and following developments are H. Hürten, *Kurze Geschichte des deutschen Katholizismus, 1800–1960* (Mainz, 1986); K. Schatz, *Zwischen Säkularisation und Zweitem Vatikanum: Der Weg des deutschen Katholizismus im 19. und 20. Jahrhundert* (Frankfurt, 1986).

[9] See G. May, *Interkonfessionalismus in der 1. Hälfte des 19. Jahrhunderts* (Paderborn, 1969).

[10] Quoted in E. R. Huber (ed.), *Dokumente zur Verfassungsgeschichte* (Stuttgart, 1961), vol. 1, p. 80.

century to the downfall of the Empire in 1806.[11] This idea derived from the Enlightenment. Politics was pressured to follow it by the necessity to integrate large denominational minorities: Protestants in Bavaria and Catholics in Prussia, Hanover, Württemberg, Nassau, Hesse-Cassel, Hesse-Darmstadt and, indeed as a majority, in Baden. By elevating the former parity legislation of individual states to an all-German standard a basis for the German Confederation was secured under which only Bavaria, and of course Austria, remained Catholic in the traditional sense, but the other thirty-seven states were regarded as Protestant, which meant a complete reversal of the conditions before 1803.

The principle of full civic equality of the three Christian denominations, which enjoyed public acknowledgement since the Peace of Westphalia, was also enshrined in the constitutions subsequently created by individual representative states.[12] In other German states older regulations needed to comply with Article 16 of the Federal Constitution. In Prussia these were the stipulations of the civil code of 1794 (*Allgemeines Landrecht*), in Austria those of the Edict of Toleration of 1781, which was by now comparatively narrow, and in other states merely administrative practice. During the *Vormärz* the restrictions of civic equality to the members of the three Christian denominations were lifted only rarely and with great hesitation, the first occasion being the constitution of Hesse-Cassel.[13] This was a trend-setting step on the way to the modern constitutional state, religiously neutral with respect to civic rights, which asserted itself in Germany in 1871 with the adoption of the corresponding previous legislation in the North German Confederation (1869).

Constitutional paragraphs, laws of equality or administrative practice stemming from Article 16 of the Federal Constitution were by no means tantamount to the abandonment of traditional denominational ties or of

---

[11] Many of these toleration edicts – for example, Prussia (1794), Bavaria and Württemberg (1803) or Baden (1807) – are collected in E. R. Huber and W. Huber, *Staat und Kirche im 19. und 20. Jahrhundert: Dokumente zur Geschichte des deutschen Staatskirchenrechts* (Berlin, 1961), vol. 1, part A. See also H. Conrad, 'Religionsbann, Toleranz und Parität am Ende des alten Reiches', in H. Lutz (ed.), *Zur Geschichte der Toleranz und der Religionsfreiheit* (Darmstadt, 1977), pp. 155–92.

[12] Such as in the Bavarian constitution of 1818 (title IV, § 9), of Baden of the same year (§§ 9, 18, 19), of Württemberg of 1819 (§ 27) and of Saxony of 1831 (§ 33).

[13] The constitution mentioned full equality for all adherents to the Christian faith and also envisaged a future regulation of the status of the Jewish inhabitants. This was accomplished in the law of 29 October 1833. Texts in Huber and Huber (eds), *Staat und Kirche*, vol. 1, pp. 148–50. The historic relevance of this and further developments for Jews has been emphasised by H. Berding, *Moderner Antisemitismus in Deutschland* (Frankfurt, 1988), pp. 31–43. However, the stipulations were also of importance for adherents to Christians sects and secessionist movements.

the religious inclinations of the respective kings and the political and administrative elites; for many influential personalities of the time, personal faith was far too important for their lifestyle and their very self-understanding. Even for those who were alienated from the Church or for the quietly agnostic, the deep-seated conviction remained that religious, cultural and political matters were one. Furthermore, Protestant rulers were the head of the Church in their individual territories and therefore felt committed to promote the interests of their *Landeskirche* (Church of an individual state or territory) and of Protestant matters in general. Personal roots and the denominational traditions, based on dynasty and state, were not easily abandoned.[14] The often quoted declaration of the Prussian Minister of Culture, Karl von Altenstein, in a memorandum of 1819, could also have come (with the necessary variations) from officials of other states with significant new minority denominations:

> The Prussian state is a Protestant state and has over one third of Catholic subjects. The relationship is difficult. It is right for the government to care for the Protestant Church with love and for the Catholic Church with duty. The Protestant Church needs to be favoured. The Catholic Church should not be treated unfairly – its best interests will be dutifully cared for.[15]

With the ruling elites professing such positions, it was inevitable that there would be conflicts with the minority Church, all the more because, as Altenstein's statement suggests, every state claimed wide-ranging supervisory and controlling powers over all Churches, which in most contemporary constitutions or quasi-constitutions were defined as virtual state institutions. Conflicts became unavoidable as soon as the interests of the Prussian state and the Catholic Church contradicted each other and as soon as there emerged forces within the Churches that abandoned the initially dominant attitudes of the state Church and did not shy away from confrontation with the state. Some Churches – in particular, because of German conditions, the Catholic Church – came into conflict with authorities of different denominations and distanced themselves earlier

---

[14] Accordingly, several of the smaller north German states continued to grant exclusive rights to their respective Protestant *Landeskirche* and massively restricted Catholic religious practice. On the other side, Austria acted similarly against its Protestant minority. E. R. Huber, *Deutsche Verfassungsgeschichte seit 1789* (second edn, Stuttgart, 1967), vol. 1, pp. 412–15.

[15] Quoted in R. Lill, 'Preußen und der Katholizismus', in M. Richter, *Kirche in Preußen* (Stuttgart, 1983), pp. 141–2. See also D. Höroldt, 'Preußische Konfessionspolitik am Rhein im 19. Jahrhundert', *Monatshefte für Evangelische Kirchengeschichte des Rheinlandes*, 31 (1982), 147.

and more completely than the Churches that considered themselves tied in an unbroken tradition to the respective dynasty or ruling elite. Confrontations between state and Church inevitably turned into general minority conflicts, when denominational minorities, or at least larger parts of public opinion, began to see such state politics as an attack against their own cultural and social identity and civic status. They understood this confrontation in the wider context of conflict and organised public opposition. This last development showed itself during the *Vormärz* only in some isolated conflicts between individual states and Churches, the most pronounced area in Catholic Germany being in Prussia's western provinces. This was a significant harbinger of future constellations in the national context.[16]

When Prussia took possession of the Rhineland and Westphalia in 1815, there was scepticism against the new rulers within the predominantly Catholic population but no rejection on grounds of faith. In the dispute which soon evolved between the Prussian government and part of the Catholic clergy about marriages between partners of different denominations, some Catholic priests fought with great journalistic fervour but without any noticeable effect on local opinion.[17] Broadsheets appeared in 1830–31, especially in the border area of Aachen, calling on the people of the Rhineland to follow the example set by the Belgians, but this attempt to translate the denominational situation into anti-Prussian political sentiments at that time remained marginal in its effect. The arrest of the Archbishop of Cologne at the beginning of the *Kölner Wirren* (Cologne disturbances) of 1837 provoked hardly any unrest in the city itself and elsewhere: the man was quite unpopular. However, when Pope Gregory XVI instantly made a public protest, a whole host of pamphlets were let loose all over Germany, protesting against this neo-absolutist Prussian Church policy. Joseph Görres' *Athanasius* was published, resistance at the local level manifested itself against further police measures and against priests co-operating with the government, and the Catholic nobility and bourgeoisie made known their dissent from this element of Berlin Church politics. After this, broad segments of the Catholic population of the Rhineland and Westphalia showed that they were conscious of their minority status. The actions of the Prussian state were now judged to result from its Protestant character and not to be merely a

---

[16] Confines of space prevent a fuller exploration of the different developments in other states, in particular Baden, Silesia and Prussia proper. The same is true for Protestant problems with the state Church in Austria and also in Bavaria, from where Catholic circles contributed vehemently to the defence of co-religionists in Prussia.

[17] For legal aspects of the problem of mixed marriages in Prussia in 1815–42 see, *inter alia*, Schatz, *Zwischen Säkularisation und Zweitem Vatikanum*, pp. 85–92.

consequence of its generally neo-absolutist Church policy. Lamentations about the persecution of the Church were combined with protests against the systematic violation of Catholic equality, first of all in the oppression of their Church and religious practice and then, closely following this, in the restrictions to their career opportunities in the state and, with respect to their civil rights in their own provinces, in their treatment at the hands of civil servants who were, insofar as they occupied key positions, almost exclusively Protestant.[18] If these were indications of the existence of politicised middle and upper classes, then the enormous turnout at the pilgrimage to the Holy Coat in Trier in 1844 demonstrated the increasing relevance of such identifications for the masses.[19] It is particularly telling, however, that this development continued to strengthen, even though the cause of the conflict of the opposing views of Church and state concerning mixed marriages had been removed in a way that particularly favoured the former, through a compromise reached by the pope and the new Prussian king, Frederick-William IV. The reign of the 'romantic on the throne' (1840–1858/61) was regarded by the Catholics in the Empire as a golden age. The king stood against the neo-absolutist *Staatskirchentum* and for a rapprochement of the denominations. The Prussian constitution of 1850 granted more freedom to the Catholic Church than they had in many Catholic states.[20] Yet, the process of self-identification of Catholics as a denominational and at the same time a social and political minority had already moved on from being merely a matter of the formal relationship between Church and State.

II

The developments outlined above demonstrate the manifestation of a new factor in German history: the reawakening of Catholicism as a new and modern phenomenon which connected religion, the Church and the ideo-

---

[18] The goal of Catholic citizens of the Rhineland and Westphalia now had to be: 'the complete realisation of the solemnly declared freedom of religion and the promised political and civic equality of the denominations to the fullest extent without danger or attack. See Joseph Görres, *Athanasius* (Regensburg, 1838), p. 156. Others interpreted the conflict as the consequence of an almost national antagonism between *Rheinländer* and Prussians.

[19] See W. Schieder, 'Kirche und Revolution: Zur Sozialgeschichte der Trierer Wallfahrt von 1844', *Archiv für Sozialgeschichte*, 14 (1974), 419–54; corrected by R. Lill, 'Kirche und Revolution: Zu den Anfängen der katholischen Bewegung im Jahrzehnt vor 1848', *Archiv für Sozialgeschichte*, 18 (1978), 565–75.

[20] Of great significance was Frederick-William's personal involvement in the completion of Cologne Cathedral as a symbol of Christian national unity, culminating in the festivities of 1842. See R. Lill, 'Der Kölner Dom und der deutsche Katholizismus im 19. Jahrhundert', in O. Dann (ed.), *Religion – Kunst – Vaterland: Der Kölner Dom im 19. Jahrhundert* (Köln, 1983), pp. 96–108.

logical, cultural, social and, last but not least, political make-up of the Catholics.[21] The development had its origins in the ruins of the old Church and the devastation of Catholic life at the beginning of the century. Its basis had initially been provided by small, scattered circles of mostly younger clerics and committed laymen. It had its roots in Romantic ideas of a Christian renewal of Europe after the Revolution, but also beyond that in the Reformation,[22] in the Enlightenment and also in rationalistic absolutism. The Church gradually began to reorganise itself and became in many ways a new Church: in its social structure, in the education of its priests and in its willingness to integrate into its dogma and calendar elements of popular belief that had previously been fought against by the Catholic Enlightenment. The Catholic Church was new also in its increasing ultramontane orientation. There were several reasons for this. First, secularisation had destroyed a previously strong episcopalism; second, it was the pope who conducted the negotiations with the now chiefly Protestant governments about the reconstruction of the Catholic Church in Germany; and third, there was a new type of priest who resolutely favoured it.[23] Since its former means of wielding political influence had been lost for good, the Church took up modern methods of political mass mobilisation in order to renew its secular power. This happened hesitantly and with modest success until the middle of the 1830s but received a sudden push during the *Kölner Wirren*.

The initiative and participation of the clergy in the founding and leadership of Catholic literary, philanthropic and socio-political associations as well as in the general organisation of German Catholics, especially during the revolutionary period of 1848–49, could hardly be overlooked. The same was true for Catholic journals, newspapers and publishing houses.[24] However, it does not necessarily follow that the

---

[21] For Catholicism as a phenomenon of modernity, see: Hürten, *Kurze Geschichte des deutschen Katholizismus*, pp. 7–10; also A. Rauscher (ed.), *Entwicklungslinien des deutschen Katholizismus* (Munich, 1983).

[22] See Novalis (Friedrich von Hardenberg), 'Die Christenheit oder Europa', an essay of great importance for the development of early Romanticism, written in 1799 but first published widely in 1826.

[23] See O. Weis, 'Der Ultramontanismus: Grundlagen – Vorgeschichte – Struktur', *Zeitschrift für Bayerische Landesgeschichte*, 41 (1978), 821–77; H. Raab, 'Zur Geschichte des Schlagworts "ultramontan" im 18. und frühen 19. Jahrhundert', *Historisches Jahrbuch der Görres-Gesellschaft*, 81 (1962), 159–73; E. Weinzierl (ed.), *Die päpstliche Autorität im katholischen Selbstverständnis des 19. und 20. Jahrhundert* (Salzburg, 1970).

[24] Information on this long and complex process of internal Catholic organisation is provided in K. Bucheim, *Ultramontanismus und Demokratie: Der Weg der deutschen Katholiken im 19. Jahrhundert* (München, 1963); A. Rauscher (ed.), *Der soziale und politische Katholizismus: Entwicklungslinien in Deutschland, 1803–1863*, 2 vols (Munich, 1981);

Catholicism that spread in modern forms over decades, the *Kulturkampf* of the 1870s and beyond, was either steered exclusively by the Church or merely a grandiose manipulation of the Catholic masses by the clergy for the furtherance of its own power. Certainly, the mobilisation of the Catholics was undertaken from a perspective of Church objectives, but security and freedom of the Church in society and state were likewise prime concerns of Catholics, whose identity was so absolutely intertwined with the old Church (which in many respects had become a new Church) and expressed itself so significantly in the activities of the numerous emerging institutions close to the Church. The clergy, especially priests, were an integral part of the Catholic world and, owing to the special educational and elite structures of Catholic Germany, their involvement in the development of Catholicism was as inevitable as it was natural to the Catholics. On the other hand, a natural disparity of interests was bound to exist, since the purposes of the Catholic Church as a universal community of believers went beyond the purposes of each Catholic population, and vice versa, because the Catholics as a social group and as citizens were also interested in goals other than the existence of the Church.

This disparity may be illustrated by looking at the differences between political Catholicism and Catholic politics. The former aimed essentially at the reconstruction of the Church and at the strengthening of its influence in the society and state of the nineteenth century, after *the* Revolution. Catholic politics, on the other hand, endeavoured to shape a new outlook and to influence changes in the state and society on the basis of Christian values, whereby the goals of political Catholicism were sometimes sidelined or lost their relevance altogether. Political Catholicism manifested itself in different political trends, sometimes several at the same time. This was demonstrated in the Frankfurt National Assembly of 1848, where Catholic deputies of numerous factions co-operated with the Liberals in order to bring about the end of the *Staatskirchentum* and to fight some narrow-minded restrictions on the full freedom of the Church – this time against the Liberals – but otherwise pulled in different directions. Catholic politics, on the other hand, because of its comprehensive political claims, needed its own permanent organisation and needed to become a party in competition with other parties in the development of democracy in the nineteenth century.[25]

H. Heitzer, *Der Volksverein für das katholische Deutschland im Kaiserreich, 1890–1918* (Mainz, 1986).

[25] For a discussion of the terms, see H. Maier, *Revolution und Kirche: Zur Frühgeschichte der christlichen Demokratie* (München, 1975; first edn, 1959), pp. 22–8.

Their ideological presumptions originated from the beginning of the nineteenth century, their internal organisation from the 1840s. They had attempted in Prussia in the 1850s to progress from the mere defence of Church rights to a more wide-ranging construction of Catholic political interests, but this had not been a lasting success among Catholic deputies of the *Landtag* (Prussian Diet) and among Catholic voters.[26] It is doubtful whether further attempts would have brought about substantial success, if there had not been a new minority situation for Catholics and Catholicism in the 1860s that was finally confirmed through the successful foundation of the nation state. This process was characterised, as the development in Baden since 1860 had already shown,[27] by a power-sharing compromise between conservative elites, who were prepared for partial modernisation, and liberal bourgeois forces. These two endeavoured to assert their own interests and values in the national context and to suppress dissenting voices. In fighting the Church, Catholics and Catholicism they themselves both resorted to, and even exacerbated, absolutist methods of traditional etatistic Church policies.

In the Empire, the open attack on the Church, which was especially severe in Prussia from late 1871, was directed against its influence on important social areas: education, the training of priests and any political statements that went beyond preaching the Gospel and providing spiritual guidance.[28] Apart from that, however, it was an attack against Catholicism and the opportunities for Catholic politics, as shown by the experiences in Baden.[29] It was hoped to destroy both the ideological and

[26] See K.-E. Lönne, *Politischer Katholizismus im 19. und 20. Jahrhundert* (Frankfurt, 1986), pp. 123–39; K. Rohe, *Wahlen und Wählertraditionen in Deutschland: Kulturelle Grundlagen deutscher Parteien und Parteiensysteme im 19. und 20. Jahrhundert* (Frankfurt, 1992), pp. 73–83.

[27] See L. Gall, 'Die partei- und sozialgeschichte Problematik des badischen Kulturkampfes', *Zeitschrift für die Geschichte des Oberrheins*, 113 (1965), 151–96; J. Becker, *Liberaler Staat und Kirche in der Ära von Reichsgründung und Kulturkampf* (Mainz, 1973); G. Zang (ed.), *Provinzialisierung einer Region. Regionale Unterentwicklung und liberale Politik in der Stadt und im Kreis Konstanz im 19. Jahrhundert* (Frankfurt, 1985).

[28] Details of anti-Catholic laws in Baden since the 1860s and on the national level, especially in Prussia, can conveniently be found in R. Lill, *Der Kulturkampf* (Paderborn, 1997). A comprehensive modern survey is lacking. Aspects of the *Kulturkampf* can be found in G. Besier, *Kulturkampf* (Theologische Realenzyklopädie, Bd. 20) (Berlin, 1990), pp. 209–30 and T. Nipperdey, *Deutsche Geschichte, 1866–1918* (Munich, 1992), vol. 1, pp. 364–81.

[29] For the translation of the liberal experience in Baden into a national programme, see J. C. Bluntschli, *Charakter und Geist der politischen Parteien* (Nördlingen, 1869). It may be added in defence against studies which claim that the foundation of the Centre Party was a general attack by ultramontanism and that the *Kulturkampf* was a liberal self-defence, that the chronology in Baden was absolutely clear: first there was the liberal anti-Church legislation, then the organisation of Catholic politics. See J. Dorneich, 'Der Kulturkampf in

the organisational foundations of the Church by rigorously curtailing its impact. In the long run, even the particularities of the Catholic existence in the nation in the making would be dissolved. The result of this aggressive attempt at integration by way of all available state power was an accelerated internal integration of Catholic Germany. The other results were the general politicisation of Catholicism and the permanent establishment of Catholic politics in the Centre Party, an organisation that emerged during the first national elections in 1871 with a sufficiently large and secure electorate to be able, at the height of the so-called *Kulturkampf*, to win more than four in five Catholic votes.[30]

The vast majority of Catholics not only saw their Church in danger and thus closed ranks in its defence but also felt that, along with the Church, their identity was threatened. This encompassed more wideranging political interests than those which were directly connected with their faith and affiliation to their Church. The Centre Party won the votes of those who felt that they had been forced on to the defensive by everything the Liberals praised as 'progress' and by everything they attempted to push through politically and legislatively in concert with neoconservative 'white revolutionaries'. It won the votes of rural and *petit bourgeois* voters, who were increasingly marginalised by the rapid development of industrial capitalism, and of uprooted workers of the first generation, who settled in the slums of the booming industrial cities.[31] The Centre likewise profited from the votes of citizens resident in the territories that had been annexed by Prussia in 1866 and degraded to peripheral provinces, and the party was favoured by many who generally opposed Prussian hegemony in the new nation state. It gained such electorates not on an anti-liberal platform but as a force against the elitist

---

Baden (1860–1876) und die katholische Gegenbewegung', *Freiburger Diözesan-Archiv*, 94 (1974), 547–88.

[30] Still indispensable because of its rich collection of materials is J. Bachem, *Vorgeschichte, Geschichte und Politik der Deutschen Zentrumspartei, 1815–1914*, 9 vols (Cologne, 1927–1932). For a more recent overview, see E. L. Evans, *The German Centre Party, 1870–1933. A study in political Catholicism* (Carbondale, 1981); for the party's foundation period, see Chr. Weber, *'Eine starke, enggeschlossene Phalanx': Der politische Katholizismus und die erste deutsche Reichstagswahl 1871* (Essen, 1992); for Bavaria, see F. Hartmannsgruber, *Die Bayerische Patriotenpartei, 1868–1887* (Munich, 1986). For data on Catholic voting that are still relevant, see J. Schauff, *Das Wahlverhalten der deutschen Katholiken im Kaiserreich und in der Weimarer Republik* (Mainz, 1975; first edn, 1928).

[31] This factor in the constituency of the Centre Party was important until the turn of the century and has been studied at the local level in N. Schloßmacher, *Düsseldorf im Bismarckreich: Politik und Wahlen, Parteien und Vereine* (Düsseldorf, 1985). See also K. M. Mallmann, 'Ultramontanismus und Arbeiterbewegung im Kaiserreich: Überlegungen am Beispiel des Saarreviers' in W. Loth (ed.), *Deutscher Katholizismus im Umbruch zur Moderne* (Stuttgart, 1991), pp. 76–94.

bourgeois (and hardly democratic) Borussian liberalism, as well as against an etatistic neo-conservatism.[32] But it was for the same reason as that which had enabled the party to establish itself permanently that it could win electorates with such motivations only among Catholics: the nationalist denominational refashioning of the state's fight against the Church into a *Kulturkampf* by the forces 'sympathetic towards the *Reich*', which entailed a sharp exacerbation of denominational differences. Catholics were not only a quantitative minority but also a qualitative one,[33] ostracised and self-isolated by comparison with the multifarious majority of Protestant Germany, which could be considered to be united only in its opposition to Catholicism. The impossibility for non-Catholics to vote for the Centre Party was not the least significant characteristic of the Catholic minority situation.[34] Under such conditions it was impossible for the Centre Party to develop into an inter-denominational Christian party, although some of its prominent leaders earnestly wanted this. The party's claim to be not denominational but Christian-political was nevertheless justified, because the programme of the Centre was by no means limited to serve the goals of political Catholicism. It called for freedom for the Church in the framework of more general demands for securing the natural rights of individuals and their pre-state communities against the modern tendency, which favoured an omnipotent state.[35]

Conflicts between the modern national 'cultural state' and the Catholic Church, especially over the assertion of a state monopoly on education and more generally over the implementation of a secular state and a religiously egalitarian bourgeois society, were part and parcel of Euro-

[32] In the Prussian Parliament and the *Reichstag* the Centre Party under the leadership of Ludwig Windthorst often defended liberal principles far more vigorously than the Liberals, particularly the National Liberals. See M. L. Anderson, 'Liberalismus, Demokratie und die Entstehung des Kulturkampfes', in R. Lill and F. Traniello (eds), *Der Kulturkampf in Italien und in den deutschsprachigen Ländern* (Berlin, 1993), pp. 109–25.

[33] In 1871 the Catholic proportion of the population in the Empire, including Catholics from ethnic minorities, was a little over 34 per cent. It rose to almost 36 per cent in 1890 and to 36.5 per cent in 1912.

[34] See G. A. Ritter, *Die deutschen Parteien, 1830–1914* (Göttingen, 1985), p. 55. There were significant individual exceptions and one major exception, namely Protestant voters in former Hanover, due above all to electoral agreements. See H.-G. Aschoff, *Welfische Bewegung und politischer Katholizismus, 1866–1918: Die Deutschhannoversche Partei und das Zentrum in der Provinz Hannover während des Kaiserreichs* (Düsseldorf, 1987).

[35] See D. Blackbourn, 'Catholics and politics in Imperial Germany: The Centre Party and its constituency', in his *Populists and patricians: Essays in modern German history* (London, 1987), pp. 188–214. A compilation of the most important sources for its ideological foundation and programme is R. Morsey (ed.), *Katholizismus, Verfassungsstaat und Demokratie: Vom Vormärz bis 1933* (Paderborn, 1988). For the place of the Centre in Christian party politics, see W. Becker and R. Morsey (eds), *Christliche Demokratie in Europa: Grundlagen und Entwicklungen seit dem 19. Jahrhundert* (Cologne, 1988).

pean history in the second half of the nineteenth century. Although the *Kulturkampf* in its general function can be classified in this context, it nevertheless remains a unique event.[36] It was determined by the attempt of the elites who had founded the nation state to remedy the reality of a denominational rift, which was perceived as the central problem facing national unity, to sponsor Protestant (or what they declared to be Protestant) cultural patterns and modes of behaviour and, if need be, force them upon Catholics as a minority. Moreover, the elites that had established themselves during the successful foundation of the nation state not only saw themselves as completing the German awakening to civic and national freedom, which Luther had begun, but also identified the national and the nation with Protestantism, or rather its secular manifestations. At the same time, they denounced the Catholic Church because of its universalism and its subordination to the 'Roman papacy' – which they nationalistically misconstrued as foreign rule – as *volksfremde* (alien to the people) and, worse, *nationalfeindliche* (hostile to the nation) forces throughout German history. From that vantage point, recent Roman undertakings, such as the dogma of the Immaculate Conception of Mary (1854), the *Syllabus Errorum* (1864) and the dogma of papal infallibility (1870), and also the establishment of Catholic politics at home were regarded as an all-out attack on modern civilisation in general and on German efforts to create a nation state in particular.[37] The accusation of being 'enemies of the Empire' (*Reichsfeinde*) had been made against the Catholic clergy and politicians, and against Catholics in general, even before the Empire existed.[38] It remained current in different spheres thereafter: when (after 1871) the Centre became something of a refuge for 'particularists' and Catholic ethnic minorities, when it defended the Prussian Poles against Bismarck's Germanisation policies in the mid-1880s,[39]

---

[36] See W. Becker, 'Der Kulturkampf als europäisches und als deutsches Phänomen', *Historisches Jahrbuch der Görres-Gesellschaft*, 101 (1981), 422–46. A different opinion is presented in G. Besier, 'Der Kulturkampf als europäisches Phänomen? Zur Relativierung einer Kulturkampfhistoriographie aus katholischer Sicht', *Monatshefte für evangelische Kirchengeschichte des Rheinlandes*, 37/38 (1988/1989), 515–27.

[37] See W. Becker, 'Luthers Wirkungsgeschichte im konfessionellen Dissens des 19. Jahrhunderts', *Rheinische Vierteljahrsblätter*, 49 (1985), 219–48; W. Becker, 'Liberale Kulturkampf-Positionen und politischer Katholizismus', in O. Pflanze (ed.), *Innenpolitische Probleme des Bismarck-Reiches* (Munich, 1983), pp. 47–71.

[38] For a collection of quotes and cases see 'Die Katholikenhetze in Preußen während des deutsches Krieges', *Historisch-Politische Blätter für das katholische Deutschland*, 58 (1866), 654–60.

[39] See H. Neuback, *Die Ausweisungen von Polen und Juden aus Preußen, 1885/86* (Wiesbaden, 1967). For the preceding period, see Z. Zielinski, 'Der Kulturkampf in der Provinz Posen', *Historisches Jahrbuch der Görres-Gesellschaft*, 101 (1981), 447–61.

when it argued under Ludwig Windthorst's leadership against anti-Semitic attacks on the civic emancipation of the Jews or against special laws against the Socialists,[40] or when it voted for the curtailment of the budget for German South-West Africa in 1906–07 because of grave violations of human rights in the German colonial administration.[41] The Centre Party was constantly accused of providing a dangerous platform for Catholic 'particularistic' interests. In reality the party contributed, wherever possible, to the integration of the Catholics into the nation state, a state that had been accepted by the Catholics from the very beginning. The party's representatives wanted to collaborate in the building of the Empire, but at the same time they wanted to contribute Catholic national traditions and ideas to that effort. These, however, had developed in confrontations with the traditions and ideas of the liberals, especially with *kleindeutsch* Prussian-oriented liberals, who wanted to elevate Protestant culture to a principle of national politics[42] and who were determined to achieve a truly German religious ethos, morality, culture and politics, precisely by excluding anything Catholic. The *Kulturkampf* was about the relationship between Church and state, but at the same time it was about the questions of which inheritance from pre-national cultures should be woven into the new national culture, which leitmotif should be stamped on it and which groups would therefore be privileged. This was responsible for the singular fierceness of the *Kulturkampf* in attack and in defence.

III

The *Kulturkampf* was carried out in the following manner. At the level of the individual states, or the Empire, the forces that 'supported the *Reich*' promulgated laws which were designed to abolish the public influ-

---

[40] See W. Altgeld, 'Windthorst und die konfessionellen Probleme Deutschlands', in *Ludwig Windthorst, 1812–1891: Christlicher Parlamentarier und Gegenspieler Bismarcks: Begleitbuch zur Gedenkausstellung aus Anlaß des 100. Todestages* (second edn, Meppen, 1992), pp. 44–56; W. Altgeld, *Katholizismus, Protestantismus, Judentum: über religiös begründete Gegensätze und nationalreligiöse Ideen in der Geschichte des deutschen Nationalismus* (Mainz, 1992), pp. 35–45. The rejection of the law against the Socialists was not supported by a growing minority during the successive votes on its extension.

[41] See W. Becker, 'Kulturkampf als Vorwand: Die Kolonialwahlen von 1907 und das Problem der Parlamentarisierung des Reiches', *Historisches Jahrbuch der Görres-Gesellschaft*, 106 (1986), 59–84; W. Loth, *Katholiken im Kaiserreich: Der politische Katholizismus in der Krise des wilhelminischen Deutschlands* (Düsseldorf, 1984), pp. 113–30.

[42] For the development of this antagonism, see Altgeld, *Katholizismus, Protestantismus, Judentum*, pp. 158–65.

ence of the Church and which therefore interfered deeply with internal Church affairs and the Church's formative social influence. The expected resistance to these laws from the Catholic clergy of all strata gave justification for a second wave of legislation aimed at breaking such resistance. The defence of the Catholic clergy by laymen led to a third stage of legislative and persecutory measures. In 1878 the situation in Prussia, the main theatre of action, comprising two thirds of the Empire, was that only three out of twelve bishops were still in office, 1,125 out of 4,600 parishes were vacant and 601 had long been completely abandoned, since the majority of the clergy was not prepared to be sworn in under the new Church laws and the communities did not accept the few 'state priests'. State commissaries administered Church funds in most dioceses; the usual state subsidies were blocked almost completely after the so-called *Brotkorbgesetz* (bread-basket law) of 1875,[43] which within a few years amounted to a sum of 16 million Reichsmarks. Since the banning of religious orders, beginning with the Jesuits in July 1872, close to three hundred monasteries and religious orders had been shut down and nearly four thousand members had been forced into exile along with about 260 priests and six bishops. In the first four months of 1875 alone – before a further massive clampdown – 241 members of the Prussian clergy were fined or sent to prison, mostly because they had performed baptisms, confessions or burials illegally. In the same period, Prussian courts convicted 210 laymen for supporting such clergy and 136 journalists who wrote for Catholic papers for reporting critically about such events. Additionally, numerous newspapers were confiscated, Catholic associations and assemblies dissolved, houses searched and individuals expelled or interned. The police traced the whereabouts of newborn babies and the recently deceased in order to follow the trail of obstinate priests, some of whom were consequently arrested in the middle of services. Subsidies and assignments of premises that were statutorily due to Catholics were often allocated to minuscule communities of 'Old Catholics'.[44] Large Catholic gatherings, such as the annual adoration of the Virgin Mary in Marpingen, were guarded by the military. Almost no Catholics were employed by the civil service, and even an unproven

---

[43] The law stipulated that all state subsidies for bishops and priests should be cut, unless the individual cleric committed himself in writing to adhering to all Prussian and German Church laws.

[44] The Old Catholics, who had developed in opposition to the dogma of Papal infallibility, were promoted by liberals and the state as the alternative to ultramontanism and had about seventy thousand members in 1890. See O. R. Blaschke, 'Der Altkatholizismus 1870–1945: Nationalismus, Antisemitismus und Nationalsozialismus', *Historische Zeitschrift*, 261 (1995), 51–99.

suspicion that a civil servant harboured ultramontane convictions was sufficient grounds for forcible retirement. The chances of Catholic academics entering university careers, modest as they had previously been, were now nil, and many universities now (as before) excluded the appointment of Catholics in their statutes. Catholic veterans of the war of 1870–71 were excluded from ex-servicemen's associations or their membership rights were curtailed.

All in all, the Church organisation was effectively destroyed.[45] Open community life was largely impeded and its underground continuation inevitably meant resistance. Being a Catholic was tantamount to belonging to a second-class minority, which was in some way under special jurisdiction and living in a special situation *vis-à-vis* the rest of the nation. Catholics lived as it were under the 'ministerial dictatorship' that the left-Liberal Rudolf Virchow had demanded as a measure against them in Prussia. The 'pariah community'[46] of Catholics even had to regard itself as a minority whose status of citizenship was doubtful, since the 'Law concerning the prevention of unauthorised practice of Church offices' of 4 May 1874 decreed that 'the clergy or other religious servants' contravening it could lose their citizenship and be expelled from Germany.[47] Heinrich von Sybel, the famous historian and National Liberal Member of Parliament, stated cynically: 'Whoever feels uncomfortable when a nation frames its legislation at its own discretion and demands obedience to that legislation from every inhabitant of the land, can only be advised to leave a place which pleases him so little'.[48]

Resistance had been expected but not to such an extent – presumably because the central importance of the clergy and clericalism in the everyday life of Catholics was lost on the Liberals who were either remote from the Church or Protestants. It remained almost exclusively a passive resistance, whose activities ranged from spontaneous local mass gatherings of protest against the arrests of priests, or against the auctioning of property belonging to convicted clerics, to collections for the replacement of Church funds blocked by the state, social ostracism of state bodies (and particularly of state priests), aiding the escape of priests faithful to the Church and the organisation of an underground Church. Cohesion

---

[45] R. Morsey, 'Der Kulturkampf', in Rauscher (ed.), *Der soziale und politische Katholizismus*, vol. 1, p. 91. The extent and impact of the repression is heavily underestimated by R. Ross, 'Enforcing the Kulturkampf in the Bismarckian state and the limit of coercion in Imperial Germany', *Journal of Modern History*, 56 (1984), 456–82.

[46] Blackbourn, 'Catholics and politics', p. 206

[47] Quoted in Huber and Huber, *Staat und Kirche*, vol. 2, pp. 632–3. This was popularly named the 'law of expatriation'.

[48] H. von Sybel, *Klerikale Politik im neunzehnten Jahrhundert* (Bonn, 1874), p. 115.

was demonstrated through participation in pilgrimages and processions, which were often banned, as were any Catholic celebrations for the thirtieth year of reign of Pope Pius IX. For their part, Catholics in many places refused to take part in any national celebrations, such as the birthday of the emperor and, especially in entirely Catholic regions, the anniversary of Sedan. In his call to Catholics in his diocese to abstain from attending, Bishop Ketteler of Mainz explained that the celebrations did not spring from the people at large but only from the Liberal *Kulturkämpfer*.

Under the surface, a massive reaction took place against what was perceived, on the other side, as German culture with, concomitantly, the creation of a separate, Catholic German culture. It possessed its own forms and themes of folk literature, favoured neo-gothic church architecture, a somewhat late Nazarene art, had its own history and was at pains to create a comprehensive Catholic scholarship with special publishers and associations for the dissemination of Catholic culture among Catholics. Naturally, this also included a Catholic press which, despite oppression by the police and judiciary, grew strong during the *Kulturkampf*.[49] The process was carried out by committed clerics and Catholic intellectuals, who stood no chance of being employed in universities or as journalists, or who were discriminated against by publishers. It could not (and presumably also was not intended to) have an influence outside the Catholic sphere. In the wider bourgeois social world the conviction was widely held that Catholic material was unreadable anyway.

All these confrontations and exclusions kindled latent prejudices against adherents of other denominations[50] and, in many areas with a mixed population, disrupted the formerly peaceful co-existence. We hear about brawls in public houses after Johannes Janssens' disrespectful interpretation of Luther, of broken windows and boycotted shops of Protestants who had acquired at auction goods that had been confiscated from Catholic priests, of complaints about the slander of the pope and mutual disregard of religious holidays and more of the same. Quite a few Catholic high school students (*Gymnasiasten*) may have suffered discrimination from *kulturkämpferisch* teachers and persecution from

---

[49] See Smith, *German nationalism and religious conflict*, pp. 42–9; A. Rauscher (ed.), *Religiös-kulturelle Bewegungen im deutschen Katholizismus seit 1800* (Paderborn, 1987); J. Osinsky, *Katholizismus und deutsche Literatur im 19. Jahrhundert* (Paderborn, 1993).

[50] See C. Köhle-Hezinger, *Evangelisch – Katholisch: Untersuchungen zu konfessionellem Vorurteil und Konflikt im 19. und 20. Jahrhundert vornehmlich am Beispiel Württembergs* (Tübingen, 1976). Since historians have not researched this aspect extensively, the following is compiled from local and regional studies.

Protestant classmates, as Rupert Mayer did around 1890.[51] For these reasons he was forced to leave his school in Stuttgart and attend another one in the predominantly Catholic area of Ravensburg. Similar conflicts raged at many universities, especially when anti-Catholic orators, like the former Jesuit Paul von Hoensbroech, were giving lectures. The opinion of the German academic community about Catholic scientists and teachers, and also implicitly about Catholic students, was made public by the Prussian Minister of Culture during the open debate about the appointment of the historian Martin Spahn to the University of Freiburg in 1901.[52] It is hardly surprising that Catholic students preferred specific universities, such as Freiburg, and shied away from attending others.

At the time of the Freiburg controversy the 'official' *Kulturkampf* had ended almost two decades earlier and the conflict between state and Church had been settled with a compromise. Below this official level, however, the conflict continued, since it had always been more than a quarrel about the position of the Church in the state. Around the turn of the century new crises erupted, fanned especially by associations such as the large Protestant League (*Evangelischer Bund*), the anti-ultramontane Reichsverband or the radical nationalistic Pan-German League.[53] They were motivated by the concern that at times the decisive significance of the Centre Party in the ability of the government to assert its power in Parliament could have brought to the fore ultramontanism and thus ushered in the end of the German character (*deutsches Wesen*). In such an ingrained perspective of the Catholic Church Catholicism and Catholics remained the problem minority that threatened the nation, irrespective of whether the Centre Party supported or opposed the government. Radical *völkisch* circles began therefore to look for a way out, beyond the denominational split, in the construction of a native Christianity (*arteigenes Christentum*), or even in the reconstruction of a pre-Christian Germanic national religion.

IV

The political and cultural representatives of German Catholics did not need to be 'converted' to the idea of the nation after the hiatus of the

---

[51] Father Rupert Mayer (1876–1946) was repeatedly arrested as an opponent of National Socialism, and finally sent to Sachsenhausen concentration camp, where he remained for the rest of the war; he was beatified in 1987.

[52] See Chr. Weber, '*Der Fall Spahn' (1901): Ein Beitrag zur Wissenschafts- und Kulturdiskussion im ausgehenden 19. Jahrhundert* (Rome, 1980).

[53] Smith, *German nationalism and religious conflict*, pp. 206–32.

Kulturkampf,[54] nor to its concrete manifestation in the foundation of the nation state between 1866 and 1871, though Pan-German ideas and nationalistic reminiscences of the 'old Empire' were part of the undercurrents of Catholic thinking. Catholics accepted the new reality pragmatically. Even those who had vowed after Königgrätz not to engage in politics any more naturally collaborated with the development of Catholic politics in the new Empire. They did not oppose the national state but only its anti-Catholic disposition.[55] It may be argued that after the *Kulturkampf* the Catholic masses were incorporated into the process of nation-making at a slower pace. This was possibly indicated by the fact that Catholic participation in general elections was always two to three per cent below average. That, however, was more likely to be a consequence of the more rural and small-town Catholic social structure which slowed Catholic politicisation than a rejection of the German nation. The nationalisation of Catholics, in the sense of normal integration, was proved in the years after the end of direct state oppression, when Catholic voters slowly began to support other parties and the formerly total identification with the Centre Party crumbled more and more with each successive election.

The observation that Catholic unity was waning in this respect provided an impetus for the younger, post-*Kulturkampf* Catholic elites to seek the further rapprochement of Catholicism and the wider German society and culture. Unlike the Catholic leadership during the *Kulturkampf*, which was largely composed of aristocrats and notables, these circles were recruited predominantly from the bourgeoisie. They were much more open-minded to the successes, requirements and opportunities arising from the German ascent to a modern industrial nation and to the transition to world politics during the Wilhelmine era, and they also approved in principle of the imperialist and colonial politics. Not very different from modern liberals such as Friedrich Naumann or Max Weber, they hoped to achieve a widening of political participation and

---

[54] E. Deuerlein, 'Die Bekehrung des Zentrums zur nationalen Idee', *Hochland* 64 (1970), 432–49. This was especially true for those marginalised Catholics who, as liberals, attempted to escape from the polarisation of the *Kulturkampf*. For an account of part of these see W. Grohs, *Die liberale Reichspartei, 1871–1874: Liberale Katholiken und föderalistische Protestanten im ersten Deutschen Reichstag* (Frankfurt, 1990).

[55] See. R. Lill, 'Katholizismus und Nation bis zur Reichsgründung', in A. Langner (ed.), *Katholizismus, nationaler Gedanke und Europa seit 1800* (Paderborn, 1985), pp. 51–63; R. Lill, 'Großdeutsch und kleindeutsch im Spannungsfeld der Konfessionen', in A. Rauscher (ed.), *Probleme des Konfessionalismus in Deutschland seit 1800* (Paderborn, 1984), 29–48; R. Lill, 'Die deutschen Katholiken und Bismarcks Reichsgründung', in Th. Schieder and E. Deuerlein (eds), *Reichsgründung 1870/71* (Stuttgart, 1970), 344–64.

national-democratic integration of Catholic and German workers in general.[56] This 'return from exile' was to take place on all levels:[57] Karl Muth called for it in literature and art and promoted it from 1903 in his journal *Hochland*. Georg von Hertling called for it in the relationship between Catholicism and modern science; Ernst Lieber and Matthias Erzberger practised it in the leadership of the Centre Party in Parliament; and Julius Bachem called for the opening of the Centre Party for Protestant Christians in 1906, in order to provide a firm basis for Christian politics in modern Germany. All these approaches provoked friction and conflicts within Catholicism, for example, disputes with the rank and file of the party about approval of the very costly armament expenditures for the navy, or with integralists within the Catholic Church about the Church's attitude to German classical and modern literature, the relationship between religion and science, and the foundation of interdenominational trade unions. The prejudices and antipathies of non-Catholic Germans, however, were hardly affected by such endeavours.

Efforts to be more open towards wider national culture and politics, however, also provoked new confrontations, precisely because they implied a deeper and more intensive integration of Catholic Germany into the national community as a whole. Catholic social peculiarities had already been noticeable at the time of the foundation of the Empire, though they had not then created a marked gulf between the social conditions of Protestant Germans. Since then, however, within a mere generation, a predominantly agrarian economy had been transformed into a modern industrialised society.[58] The mainly Catholic regions were comparatively less involved in this stormy process of economic modernisation and social change and the Catholics were under-represented in occupations and enterprises in industry or in the service sector. Many of their political, cultural and, especially, spiritual leaders did not perceive this as a problem and even welcomed it as long as their thinking was rooted in a strong dichotomy between Christianity and modernity, or in other words, in the fundamentalist rejection of any modernisation that could be seen to be a path towards secularisation. The innovators in German Catholicism, however, viewed the discrepancy between the social structures of Catholic Germans and those of other Germans, which

---

[56] See H. Gründer, 'Nation und Katholizismus im Kaiserreich', in Langner (ed.), *Katholizismus, nationaler Gedanke und Europa seit 1800*, pp. 65–87.

[57] Hürten, *Kurze Geschichte des deutschen Katholizismus*, pp. 183–208.

[58] See M. Stürmer, *Das ruhelose Reich: Deutschland, 1866–1918* (Berlin, 1994; first edn, 1984), who presents the pace of this radical change between 1870 and 1890 as the central problem in the history of the Empire.

around 1900 had also been documented scientifically, as backwardness and above all as a motive for and obstacle to their efforts at integration.[59] The enormous under-representation of Catholics in all higher public offices, whether in the Empire or in an individual state, especially in Prussia,[60] could no longer be explained as the consequence of persistent discrimination during the *Kulturkampf*, if only half as many Catholics as non-Catholics earned high-school qualifications or university degrees. Beneath that, different social conditions became evident, expressed in the Catholic adherence to occupations and economic sectors that were in decline or in different reproductive patterns.

Pioneers of Catholic openness and renewal, such as Hertling, Bachem or Hans Rost, were prepared to understand the demand for 'parity' as part of their endeavours to integrate, and as a call on Catholics to adapt to the modern world and to cast off, for example, traditional reservations about modern education and science. But they were not prepared to concede the assertion of anti-ultramontanists of all sorts: namely that Catholic socio-economic 'inferiority' was caused by their religion and denomination and that it was the result of their being kept in continual ignorance – even brutalised by the Church 'hierarchy' – which explained their inferior position in the public life of the nation. These pioneers rightfully pointed to the history of the nineteenth century, which had begun with the destruction of Catholic culture and especially of the Catholic educational system. As a result, Catholics had become inward-looking on account of the rejection that they experienced from their environment.

---

[59] See M. Offenbacher, *Konfession und soziale Schichtung: eine Studie über die wirtschaftliche Lage der Katholiken und Protestanten in Baden* (Tübingen, 1900); H. Rost, *Die wirtschaftliche und kulturelle Lage der detuschen Katholiken* (Köln, 1911). M. Baumeister, *Parität und katholische Inferiorität: Untersuchungen zur Stellung des Katholizismus im Deutschen Kaiserreich* (Paderborn, 1987), contains a variety of statistical data.

[60] In the predominantly Catholic Rhine Provinces, Catholics still occupied 48 per cent of all higher public offices in 1850. In 1875 this had diminished to 39 per cent and to 34 per cent in 1905.

7

German Jews

Christopher Clark

In the middle decades of the nineteenth century many German liberals came to see 'emancipation' as a historical process no less inexorable than the emergence of modern society itself. Specific 'issues of emancipation', one author noted, were 'individual components or phases' in an irreversible 'universal emancipatory process'.[1] Emancipation, in other words, was identical with historical progress in general and with the political ferment of the contemporary era in particular. With their faith in the notion of history as a unitary, forwards-driving process whose ultimate telos was the liberty of mankind, these remarks carry the imprint of mid-nineteenth-century liberalism. They also reflect a semantic inflation of the term 'emancipation', which took place in the 1830s and 1840s and resumed in the wake of the civil rights movements of the 1960s and 1970s. This investment of the term with a progressive ideological freight has left its mark on the modern historiography of nineteenth-century German Jewry, which has repeatedly stressed the links between the removal of Jewish legal disabilities and broader processes of social and political emancipation.[2]

---

[1] K. H. Scheidler, 'Emancipation', in J. S. Ersch and J. G. Gruber (eds), *Allgemeine Encyclopädie der Wissenschaften und Künste* (Leipzig, 1840), Section 1, vol. 34, pp. 2–12.

[2] See, for example, W. Grab, *Der deutsche Weg der Judenemanzipation 1789–1938* (Munich, 1991), p. 7: 'the struggle for the emancipation of the Jews was from the very beginning part of the general struggle of the enlightened and the revolutionaries for human rights and social justice'; J. Katz, *Emancipation and assimilation: Studies in modern Jewish history* (Farnborough, 1972). For comments on this aspect of the literature, see M. Zimmermann, *Hamburgischer Patriotismus und deutscher Nationalismus: Die Emanzipation der Juden in Hamburg 1830–1865* (Hamburg, 1979), p. 11. For related 'revisionist' observations on Jewish societal emancipation, see J. Frankel, 'Assimilation and the Jews in nineteenth-century Europe: Towards a new historiography?' in J. Frankel and S. J. Zipperstein, *Assimilation and community: The Jews in nineteenth-century Europe* (Cambridge, 1992), pp. 1–37; P. Birnbaum and I. Katznelson, 'Emancipation and the Liberal offer', in P. Birnbaum and I. Katznelson (eds), *Paths of emancipation: Jews, states and citizenship* (Princeton N.J., 1995), pp. 3–36.

It is certainly true that the transformation of the Jews in the German territories from rightless aliens to fully entitled citizens was implicated in broader political, social and economic transitions: the ascendancy of the category 'citizen', the growth of liberal and radical movements committed to concepts of 'rights' and 'equality', the emergence of a Jewish middle class and transformations in Jewish religious and cultural practice, to name just a few. Nevertheless, the notion of emancipation as a forward-driven, unitary transformation defined teleologically by a striving for the liberation of society does only very partial justice to the historical experience of nineteenth-century German Jewry. The removal of Jewish legal disabilities was a drawn-out, haphazard affair that proceeded with halting steps at varying speeds in different times and places. It was not for the most part about rights, as we shall see, but about one-off concessions that could be delayed, reversed or reinterpreted. Nor was it always driven by a unified or consistent political intention; it was more often the outcome of momentary calculations, local conditions and shifting balances of social and political power. The emancipatory process was far from linear; it was, in the formulation of Reinhard Rürup, one of the foremost historians of the field, 'tortuous and thorny'. Indeed, one of the most recent treatments of the subject chose to metaphorise emancipation as a multitude of meandering 'paths' rather than a road plotted out in advance to reach a specific goal.[3] The following outline will therefore focus less on the gradual accumulation of a pro-emancipatory consensus than on the interaction of social and political forces that shaped the course of government policy regarding the Jews and obstructed emancipation for some six decades. It is important to look closely at the counter-currents in the history of Jewish emancipation, because they help us to understand, as I argue below, what was distinctive about the Jewish minority experience and why the 'Jewish Question' failed to go away, even after the emancipation question had ostensibly been resolved.

I

Jewish emancipation in the German states was tortuous and fragmented because it reflected the complex political and social geography of German Europe. A bewildering variety of 'Jew regulations' existed within the 300-odd territorial and ecclesiastical principalities represented at the Imperial

---

[3] R. Rürup, 'The tortuous and thorny path to legal equality: "Jew laws" and emancipatory legislation in Germany from the late eighteenth century', *Leo Baeck Institute Yearbook*, 31 (1986), 3–33; Birnbaum and Katznelson (eds), *Paths of emancipation*. See esp. the editors' introduction, p. 11.

Diet of the eighteenth-century *Reich*. Jewish settlement was encouraged in some territories for fiscal reasons, but was entirely prohibited in others, such as Bavaria and Saxony. The Jews in some principalities were divided into different categories of privilege according to their personal wealth and capacity to purchase specific concessions. Diverse as they were, these legal dispensations had several things in common: they imposed taxes and occasional levies that applied solely to Jews; they withheld from Jews the status of subjects, granting them instead the purely provisional title of 'tolerated' or 'protected' aliens; and they excluded Jews from the established branches of commercial and manufacturing activity (craft guilds, the keeping of shops, agriculture), while permitting them to engage in financial transactions, most commonly the provision of credit, and itinerant trade in non-restricted or second-hand goods.[4]

By the end of the eighteenth century, under the influence of the Enlightenment, the legal condition of the Jewish minority had been improved in piecemeal fashion in a number of territories. The famous 'edicts of emancipation' issued by Joseph II for the Habsburg lands in the early 1780s did not place Jews on an equal footing with other, non-Jewish subjects, but they did abolish the humiliating *Leibzoll* – a poll-tax levied on Jews at customs boundaries – and they authorised Jews to enter professions formerly closed to them by law. Jewish poll-taxes were abolished in several other German states around the turn of the century. A change in Prussian government attitudes after the accession of Frederick-William II was signalled by the official 'naturalisation' of several prominent Jewish figures who had rendered outstanding financial services to the Crown. Among them was the Berlin banker Daniel Itzig, whose 'Patent of Naturalisation' accorded him all rights possessed by Christian citizens in the entire territory of the monarchy.[5] Important as these changes were for the individuals involved and as tokens of an enlightened governmental sensibility, they hardly amounted to a concerted programme of reform. The chief stimulus for a more thoroughgoing and programmatic approach to the issue came not from the enlightened bureaucracies of the German states, but from Revolutionary and Napoleonic France.

The impact of the Revolution and its Napoleonic aftermath made itself felt in a number of ways. First, French law was introduced to those German territories occupied and subsequently annexed to metropolitan France in the 1790s and 1800s. Since the Jews of France had enjoyed full

---

[4] Rürup, 'Tortuous and thorny path', 5.

[5] S. M. Lowenstein, 'Jewish upper crust and Berlin Jewish enlightenment: the family of Daniel Itzig', in F. Malino and D. Sorkin, *From East and West: Jews in a changing Europe, 1750–1870* (Oxford, 1990), pp. 182–201, esp. p. 185.

citizenship rights since 1791, this meant that the Jews in those territories were relieved at one stroke of all their traditional disabilities. This happened, for example, in the German territories on the left bank of the Rhine that were annexed in 1797 and in the northwestern territories annexed under Napoleon in 1810. Second, various emancipatory legislations were introduced in the satellite entities created by Napoleon in western Germany following the dissolution of the old *Reich*. Thus, for example, the Jews of the Kingdom of Westphalia, founded in 1807 and ruled by Napoleon's brother Jérôme, acquired citizenship rights in January 1808.[6] A further factor accelerating reform was the redistribution of secularised territories under French auspices, a policy designed to provide Napoleon with a network of German client states. The Duchy of Baden, elevated by Napoleon to a Grand Duchy in 1806, was territorially enlarged to nearly seven and a half times its former size at the expense of various defunct minor principalities. As a consequence, it faced the task of administering a greatly enlarged Jewish population living under a bewildering array of 'Jew laws'. The example of French law, administrative efficiency and the self-interest of a government faced with the task of winning the hearts and minds of its new citizens all spoke in favour of the rationalisation and amelioration of Jewish entitlements. The result was the 'constitutional law' of January 1809 that abolished many, though not all, legal restrictions and confirmed that Jews enjoyed civic equality with other subjects of the Badenese state.

Lastly, the upheavals unleashed by Napoleon in German Europe assisted the cause of Jewish emancipation by helping, indirectly, to bring about the ascendancy of enlightened, reformist elements in a number of the German bureaucracies. The best example is Prussia, where the growing threat from France and the catastrophic defeats at Jena and Auerstedt brought a new cohort of administrators to the fore, most notably the minister and later State Chancellor Karl August von Hardenberg, whose 'Edict concerning the civic condition of the Jews in the Prussian state' of 11 March 1812 transformed the legal status of the Prussian Jews. Reinhard Rürup has rightly described this edict as 'a remarkable law, which to this day must be valued as one of the greatest documents of the history of emancipation in Europe'.[7] However, the emancipation made available by the edict was limited in several important respects: most significantly, it postponed judgement on the question of whether positions in government

---

[6] G. Hentsch, *Gewerbeordnung und Emanzipation der Juden im Kurfürstentum Hessen* (*Studien der Kommission für die Geschichte der Juden in Hessen*) (Wiesbaden, 1979), vol. 4, p. 24.

[7] Rürup, 'Tortuous and thorny path', 15.

service would be made available to Jewish applicants. It thus fell crucially short of the French emancipation of 1791, which had embedded Jewish entitlements in a universal endorsement of citizenship and political rights. By contrast, the language of the Prussian edict, which warned that the 'continuation of their allotted title of inhabitants and citizens of the state' would depend on the fulfilment of certain prior obligations, made it clear that the edict was about the concession of status rather than the recognition of rights.[8]

For all its transformative impact on the societies of the European states, the legacy of the Napoleonic era was double-edged, at least for the Jews of the German states. While it is true that the expansion of the French Republic/Empire brought to many of the Jews of the annexed and satellite German territories the benefits of the law of 1791, the momentum of these developments was partly reversed in 1806, when Napoleon was confronted with the problem of Jewish 'usurers' and money-lenders during a brief stay in Strasbourg. His initial response was to issue a decree on 30 May 1806 imposing a one-year moratorium on all outstanding debts owing to Jewish lenders by Christian agricultural workers in the eight German-speaking *départments* on the eastern fringes of the French Republic. This was followed by the far stricter *décret infâme*, the 'infamous decree' of 17 March 1808, which imposed constraints on the economic activities of Rhenish Jews that were to remain in force for nearly half a century. All Jews engaged in trade and manufacture were obliged to acquire a 'business patent' or a manufacturing licence; the supply of such documents by the provincial authorities was dependent upon good references both from Jewish and from the local Christian authorities (*Gemeinderat*), who were responsible for establishing that the applicant was not guilty of 'usurious' trading practices. At the slightest suspicion of improper practice patents could be withdrawn, leaving the individual concerned with virtually no honest alternative to beggary. Resettlement from one department to the next was permitted only on the condition that the Jew seeking resettlement became a farmer. The result was a somewhat anomalous situation in which Jews enjoyed 'citizenship rights' but were also subject to discriminatory and demeaning legal restraints.[9] The law of 1808 was important in that it identified Jewish

---

[8] The text of the edict may be found in A. Doll, H.-J. Schmidt, M. Wilmanns, *Der Weg zur Gleichberechtigung der Juden (Dokumente zur Geschichte der jüdischen Bevölkerung in Rheinland-Pfalz und im Saarland von 1800 bis 1945)* (Koblenz, 1979), vol. 2, pp. 45–8.

[9] On these developments, see the excellent analysis by D. Kastner, *Der Rheinische Provinziallandtag und die Juden im Rheinland 1825–1845: Eine Dokumentation* (Cologne, 1989), part 1, pp. 18–27.

economic activity in the credit sector as an obstacle to legal emancipation; for decades after it had lapsed in metropolitan France, the law of 1808 was retained on the statute books by the Prussian and Bavarian governments which inherited formerly French Rhenish territories after 1815, precisely on the grounds that it was deemed to contribute to the protection of the rural population from Jewish 'usury'.[10] French expansion into German Europe cannot, therefore, be said to have imparted an unequivocally positive momentum to the process of Jewish emancipation in the German states.

II

The decades between the end of the Napoleonic Wars and the revolutions of 1848 were characterised by the lack of a co-ordinated approach to Jewish legal reform, both between and within the German states. The plan, strongly endorsed by Hardenberg, to introduce a single emancipatory law for all the states of the new German Confederation was torpedoed by the resistance of several lesser territories, including particularly the Hanseatic cities. Instead, the Charter produced by the Vienna Congress in 1815 announced that the *Bundestag* (and Confederal Assembly) would at some future date provide a uniform regulation that would secure the 'enjoyment of civic rights' for the Jews in the member states. But this regulation, like the promised harmonisation of the German constitutions and the confederal regulation of customs duties, never materialised. The interests and circumstances of the respective member states were too diverse, and the centripetal forces within the Confederation too weak, to sustain a co-ordinated response to the issue of Jewish rights. In the meantime, responsibility for Jewish policy remained in the hands of the respective German governments. In some states the clock was actually wound back, as in the Duchy of Mecklenburg-Schwerin, where a law modelled on the Prussian edict and introduced in March 1813 was rescinded six months later. Even a state such as Prussia, which had installed prestigious emancipatory laws and was loath to rescind them, found it easy to minimise their effect through restrictive bureaucratic practice, the exploitation of legal loopholes and one-off restrictive decrees by the monarch, such as Frederick-William III's Cabinet Orders of 18 June and 4 December 1822

---

[10] By contrast, the Grand Duchy of Hesse-Darmstadt, like France and the Netherlands, allowed the decree to lapse after 1818.

prohibiting the promotion of Jewish soldiers into the officer corps, and the entry of Jews into academic and teaching posts.[11]

By far the most effective means of maintaining discrimination against the Jewish minority was simply governmental inaction. The Duchy of Nassau provides an excellent example of this principle in operation. After a few half-hearted gestures in the direction of educational and occupational reform in the years 1815 to 1819, the issue ceased to be pursued with any urgency at all. After two decades of virtual stagnation the government, under the new and more energetic sovereign Duke Adolf, began to address specific anomalies in such areas as taxation and poor relief, but a more ambitious initiative to redefine Jewish status stalled, and by the eve of the revolutions of 1848 the Jews of Nassau were in law and in fact what they had been under the old regime: *Schutzjuden*, protected Jews.[12] The decentralised character of the German Confederation created a welcome pretext for inaction; it was not uncommon for government officials and even parliamentary chambers to forestall initiatives in the sphere of Jewish entitlements on the grounds that it would be better to wait for the 'forthcoming' general revision by the Confederal Assembly.

The same governmental lassitude could be observed in Prussia. Here, the edict of 1812 was not extended beyond the four provinces (Brandenburg, Pomerania, Silesia and East Prussia) for which it had originally been issued. Hardenberg's hope that his edict would serve as a model for legislation throughout Germany thus remained unfulfilled, even within the borders of the post-Napoleonic Prussian state. The failure of the authorities to take responsibility for the rationalisation of Jewish status meant that Prussian Jews lived under some two dozen different regional jurisdictions during the *Vormärz* era. The Rhineland Province ceded to Prussia in 1815 provides a particularly crass example of the consequences of government immobility. In those parts of the province that had been *départements* of France the Jews were formally state citizens who lived under the stipulations of the 'infamous decree' of 1808. In those districts that had belonged to the Duchy of Nassau, including the Prussian enclave around Wetzlar, the Jews lived under a range of local 'Jew laws' inherited from previous administrations, none of which conceded civic rights of

---

[11] H. Fischer, *Judentum, Staat und Heer in Preußen im frühen 19. Jahrhundert: Zur Geschichte der staatlichen Judenpolitik (Wissenschaftliche Abhandlungen des Leo Baeck Instituts)* (Tübingen, 1968), vol. 20, pp. 122–3, 125.

[12] V. Eichler (ed.) *Nassauische Parlamentsdebatten*, vol. 1: *Restauration und Vormärz 1818–1847* (Wiesbaden, 1985), pp. 333–7.

any kind. Finally, the Jews residing in former territories of the Grand Duchy of Berg lived under a different dispensation altogether. The *Code Napoléon,* which assumed the political equality of all citizens and made no legal distinction between Christians and Jews, had been introduced into the Duchy in November 1809, and remained in effect thereafter, but the 'infamous decree' was never formally gazetted in the territory and consequently never became law there. After 1815 this placed the Jews in formerly *Bergisch* districts, at least in theory, on an almost equal footing with their Christian neighbours.[13] Unlike most of their co-religionists throughout the monarchy, these Jews actually benefited from the administrative lethargy of the Prussian state. Moreover, the fact that the Berlin government generally took its cue from district and provincial administrations, rather than conceiving and enforcing a unified policy from the centre, meant that the legislative landscape gradually became more complex, as new concessions were made to local interests. In the Prussian province of Westphalia, for example, where the 'infamous decree' had never been applied, a special law, harsher in some respects than the Napoleonic original, was introduced to suppress Jewish trade in four rural districts.[14]

Governments, local administrations and other opponents of emancipation justified the withholding of Jewish entitlements with a range of substantive arguments. They warned that the preferment of Jews to public offices or to positions of authority over Christians would compromise the Christian character of the state. In Prussia, this view generated a growing emphasis upon conversion as the only means of incorporating the Jewish minority into the mainstream community. In 1824, when the mathematician David Unger applied for a teaching position at the Berlin Academy of Engineering, he was advised personally by King Frederick-William III that his application would be reconsidered after his conversion to the Evangelical Church.[15] Prussian provincial administrators also favoured state measures to speed the pace of Jewish conversion, either through compulsory adult education schemes or through the retention of demoralising legal restrictions on those who refused to convert.[16] The government even provided a royal 'christening present' of thirty marks for those converts who entered the monarch as their 'godfather' in the

---

[13] Kastner, *Der Rheinische Provinziallandtag,* p. 21.
[14] *Ibid.,* p. 44.
[15] Frederick-William III, Order of 14 June 1824, reproduced in Bildarchiv – Preußischer Kulturbesitz (ed.), *Juden in Preußen: Ein Kapitel deutscher Geschichte* (Dortmund, 1981), p. 195.
[16] Fischer, *Judentum, Staat und Heer,* p. 95.

church registry books.[17] In the 1840s the 'Christian state' became one of the *idées reçues* of the emancipation debate; a book entitled *The Christian State principle* by the Privy Councillor Anton Edler von Krauß appeared in Vienna in 1842, arguing that Christianity was the highest form of wisdom and knowledge known to mankind and ought therefore to inform the public life and governance of every Christian polity. In the same year the term was invoked by opponents of emancipation in the Baden Chamber of Deputies; the Jewish journal *Der Orient* described it in 1843 as 'the very latest pretext for refusing us our rights'.[18] Interestingly enough, it was the constitutional lawyer Friedrich Julius Stahl, a convert from Judaism with close ties to Protestant missionary circles, who produced the most influential and theoretically coherent formulation of Christian statism. Stahl's book, *The Christian State* (1847) warned that the admission of Jews (and deists!) to positions of public authority would lead to the 'complete de-Christianisation of the state'.[19]

It was also common for governments to reject emancipation on the grounds that it would provoke protest from various vested interests, or would stir up opposition and unrest in the Christian population. As Gerhard Hentsch demonstrated in a study of Jewish emancipation in Hesse-Cassel, the reluctance of the government to dismantle guild privileges, despite considerable pressure from liberal circles, was a serious obstacle to the integration of Jews into the 'Christian' economy.[20] In this context, it is worth recalling that the work of legal homogenisation and rationalisation, undertaken with such energy by the French and by indigenous reforming bureaucracies around the turn of the century, was at best half-finished after 1815. Most German societies remained cellular in character; guilds continued to dominate the manufacturing sector in many areas, on occasion despite government edicts proclaiming 'freedom of occupation'. 'Citizenship' in the full sense depended as much upon the concession of rights within a specific municipality (*Gemeinde*) as it did on recognition from the state; indeed it was often at the local level that

---

[17] C. M. Clark, *The politics of conversion. Missionary Protestantism and the Jews in Prussia 1728–1941* (Oxford, 1995), pp. 99–100.

[18] For Jewish comments on the Christian state, see esp. 'Ulm, 12 September', *Der Orient*, 3 (1942), 342–3; 'Vorwärts oder Rückwärts in der Judenemancipation: Ein offenes Sendschreiben', *Der Orient*, 4 (1843), 106; 'Tübingen, im Februar', *Der Orient*, 5 (1844), 68.

[19] F. J. Stahl, *Der Christliche Staat und sein Verhältniß zum Deismus und Judenthum: Eine durch die Verhandlungen des vereinigten Landtages hervorgerufene Abhandlung* (Berlin, 1847), pp. 31–3.

[20] Hentsch, *Gewerbeordnung und Emanzipation*, pp. 68–9; on the exclusion of Jews from guild-controlled crafts in Hamburg, see Zimmermann, *Hamburgischer Patriotismus*, pp. 25–6, 59.

emancipation took longest to be realised. In Baden, for example, the problem of communal (*gemeindebürgerlich*) emancipation remained unresolved until the early 1860s.[21] The Jews of Baden had formally enjoyed the status of 'state citizens' since the legislation of 1809 but were excluded from residence in over eighty per cent of Badenese municipalities, and therefore also from the constitutional 'freedom of movement' enjoyed by the Grand Duchy's Christian inhabitants.[22] This dimension of complexity in Jewish 'citizenship' requires that we move beyond the bipolar fixation on Jews and states that has been a characteristic of some recent work.[23] The state may have been the Jews' chief interlocutor in negotiations over emancipation and the ultimate guarantor of legal entitlements once granted, but it was not, in Germany at least, the only agency to determine the course of emancipation or the meanings of 'citizenship'.

Underlying the reluctance of many Restoration governments to take the initiative in Jewish emancipation was a fear of threats to public order. The potential of the Jewish issue to spark conflict in this period should not be underestimated. As early as 1803, the Prussian government forbade the publication of pamphlets for or against Jewish emancipation, on the grounds that they would 'merely prompt excesses on the part of one side or the other'.[24] The so-called Hep!-Hep! riots, a wave of anti-Jewish demonstrations and attacks on Jewish property that swept through the south and west of Germany in 1819, were interpreted in many states as a warning of what would follow upon precipitous attempts to liberate the Jews from their traditional disabilities.[25] In Hamburg, where there were repeated anti-Jewish tumults after 1830, the City Senate was successful in using arguments for safeguarding public

---

[21] P. Nolte, *Gemeindebürgertum und Liberalismus in Baden 1800–1850: Tradition – Radikalismus – Republik* (Göttingen, 1994), pp. 340–1.

[22] R. Rürup, 'Die Emanzipation der Juden in Baden', in R. Rürup, *Emanzipation und Antisemitismus* (Frankfurt am Main, 1987), pp. 58–9.

[23] Cf. Birnbaum and Katznelson (eds), *Paths of emancipation*, esp. p. 22, where the editors note that 'Our ... focus on the form and content of citizenship made available to Jews impels us to adopt ... a national framework for our cases. In each instance, we have tried to highlight the distinctive character of transactions between the state and civil society, the domain of citizenship.'

[24] Privy Financial Councillor Borgstede to Hardenberg, 8 September, 1803, transcribed in L. Geiger, *Geschichte der Juden in Berlin: Als Festschrift zur zweiten Säkular-Feier. Im Auftrag des Vorstandes der Berliner Gemeinde* (Berlin, 1871), p. 313.

[25] See, for example, Rürup, 'Emanzipation der Juden in Baden', p. 53; W. Wippermann, *Jüdisches Leben im Raum Bremerhaven: Eine Fallstudie zur Alltagsgeschichte der Juden vom 18. Jahrhundert bis zur NS-Zeit* (Bremerhaven, 1985), p. 44.

order to justify delaying emancipatory measures.[26] This logic was even more compelling in the volatile 1840s when food riots and episodes of local unrest grew increasingly common and not infrequently incorporated an anti-Jewish element.[27]

However, the argument most consistently advanced by legislators and their informants and advisers throughout the era of emancipation related to a deeply-held conviction that Jewish legal equality ought to be conditional upon the 'self-improvement' of the Jewish minority. From the very outset, bureaucratic legislators linked the granting of emancipation with the idea of transforming the social and economic character of the Jewish communities. An example is the work of Christian Wilhelm Dohm, an enlightened Prussian civil servant and friend of Moses Mendelssohn, whose essay, *Concerning the civic betterment of the Jews,* appeared in 1781.[28] Historians have often commented on the ambiguity of the term 'betterment' (*Verbesserung*), which was used by Dohm in a transitive sense to denote the relief of Jewish disabilities by the state, but also in a reflexive sense to describe the process of social self-improvement that could be expected to follow the legal admission of Jews into Christian society. Dohm did not dissent from the contemporary consensus that the Jewish character was 'more morally corrupt than [that of] other nations', but he took the view that this character was the result, rather than the cause, of Christian discrimination. Once the pressure of legal discrimination were removed, it would become possible to woo the Jews away from the 'sophistic sayings of [their] rabbis' and divest them of their 'clannish religious opinions', inspiring them instead with patriotism and love for the state. And since it was primarily the 'limitation of the Jews to commerce which has had a detrimental influence on their moral and political character', Dohm proposed that the state might take action to 'dissuade the Jews from commercial occupations' and direct them towards professions that would foster 'a diametrically opposed spirit and character', by which he meant 'artisan occupations'.[29]

---

[26] Zimmermann, *Hamburgischer Patriotismus*, pp. 49–50. On the 'psychological shock' unleashed by Hep!-Hep!, see Rürup, 'Emanzipation der Juden in Baden', p. 51.

[27] On the volatility of the 1840s, see esp. M. Gailus, 'Food riots in Germany in the late 1840s', *Past & Present*, 145 (1994), 157–93.

[28] C. W. Dohm, *Über die bürgerliche Verbesserung der Juden* (Berlin and Stettin, 1781). For commentaries on the book and its context, see esp. R. Liberles, 'The historical context of Dohm's treatise on the Jews', in Friedrich-Naumann-Stiftung (ed.), *Das deutsche Judentum und der Liberalismus – German Jewry and liberalism* (Königswinter, 1986), pp. 44–69.

[29] The translations given here are based on the excerpts in P. Mendes-Flohr and J. Reinharz (eds), *The Jew in the modern world: A documentary history* (New York, 1980), pp. 27–34.

The link asserted here between occupational migration and the 'betterment' of Jews is one of the abiding themes in the modern history of German Jewry. An antagonism to trade and 'middle men' that had deep roots in the moral economy of traditional Christianity joined forces with secular, eighteenth-century assumptions about what was 'productive' in the economy and what was not. The Prussian pietists of the mid-eighteenth century, for example, saw the exclusion of Jews from 'productive' sectors of the economy as the chief obstacle to their ultimate conversion and absorption into the Christian majority, while the Hesse-Darmstadt Privy Councillor Georg Konrad Stockhausen, an enlightened physiocrat, took the view that the barriers of traditional prejudice could only be surmounted if the Jews were comprehensively weaned from petty trade.[30] Legislators and publicists continued to link emancipation with occupational reform after 1815, but with a somewhat changed emphasis. Whereas Dohm had seen the social transformation of Jewry as a consequence of emancipation, the trend after 1815 was to insist on social restructuring as the *precondition* for legal emancipation. In the words of a Bonn jurist whose advice on the rationalisation of Jewish status in the Rhineland was sought by the Prussian government: 'It is a precondition that they [the Jews] may only partake of civil rights to the extent that they prove capable of civic improvement (by which we also mean moral improvement)'.[31] Most legislators of the Restoration era took the view that it was the responsibility of the secular authorities to facilitate the social restructuring of Jewry through the provision of laws; the faith in the ameliorative, pedagogical mission of the state, which had been such a mainstay of the Enlightenment, remained undiminished in the Restoration era.[32]

Throughout the Restoration and *Vormärz* period this commitment to state-sponsored Jewish self-reform was reflected in the proliferation of decrees that aimed to lever the Jews out of their traditional economic niches into allegedly less harmful and more 'productive' areas of the economy. A resolution issued by the Privy Council of Hesse-Cassel in October 1815, for example, proposed that civic rights should be withheld

---

[30] Clark, *Politics of conversion*, esp. pp. 33–82, 108–18, 144–7; A. M. Keim, *Die Judenfrage im Landtag des Großherzogtums Hessen 1820–1849: Ein Beitrag zur Geschichte der Juden im Vormärz* (Darmstadt and Marburg, 1983), p. 15.

[31] Report by the Royal Justice Commission to the Minister of State for Legal Revisions and Judicial Organisation in the New Rhine Provinces, Cologne, 30 January 1819, in Doll et al. (eds), *Der Weg zur Gleichberechtigung*, p. 54.

[32] M. Richarz (ed.), *Jüdisches Leben in Deutschland: Selbstzeugnisse zur Sozialgeschichte 1780–1871* (Stuttgart, 1976), vol. 1, p. 22; R. Rürup, 'Judenemanzipation und bürgerliche Gesellschaft in Deutschland', in Rürup, *Emanzipation und Antisemitismus*, p. 14.

from individuals who, 'failed to sever themselves from activities dishonourable to the citizen ... [such as] brokering, peddling, personal loans and the sale of second-hand goods.' An ordinance published in February 1819 – just one of many similar initiatives from the years 1815–20 – declared: 'no Jew will in future be permitted to establish more than one son in the retail trade'; the stated aim was to 'direct the Jews towards other more useful activities'. An ordinance of 30 December 1832 'concerning the general conditions of the Israelites' was even clearer about the government's intentions, stipulating that it was the responsibility of rabbis and communal elders to see to it that young boys dedicated themselves to 'agriculture and other orderly vocations'.[33] The extremely oppressive Bavarian law of 1813, which remained in force until 1861, made permission to reside in the kingdom dependent upon possession of a 'matricular number', which could only be bequeathed to the eldest son; younger sons were only permitted to settle if they earned their livelihood from a craft trade, agriculture or manufacturing.[34] This fetishisation of the 'productive professions' was even internalised by prominent figures in many Jewish communities, who founded some fifty societies for the promotion of craft trades during the *Vormärz* era.[35]

The success of governments and independent Jewish initiatives in bringing about a transformation in the occupational structure of the Jewish population was very modest. There was a marked increase in the percentage of Bavarian Jews who embarked on artisan training, though many of these did so purely in order to obtain their 'matricular number' and never actually practised their trade. Even after the law of 1813 had been in place for thirty-five years Jews were still three times more likely than Christians to be working in trade and eight times less likely to be working in the agricultural sector.[36] In Bavaria, as in the other German states, the ideal of a Jewish minority that replicated *in parvo* the occupational proportions of the non-Jewish majority remained hopelessly remote.

The most important consequence of restructuring policies was therefore the potentially endless deferral of legal emancipation.[37] Jewish populations were subject to constant government scrutiny in the form of

---

[33] Hentsch, *Gewerbeordnung und Emanzipation*, pp. 43–4.

[34] Richarz, *Jüdisches Leben*, p. 24.

[35] A. Herzig, 'Das Problem der jüdischen Identität in der deutschen bürgerlichen Gesellschaft', in Grab (ed.), *Deutsche Aufklärung und Judenemanzipation*, pp. 243–64, here pp. 251–2; J. Katz, *Emancipation and assimilation*, pp. 91–110; Richarz, *Jüdisches Leben*, p. 32.

[36] J. F. Harris, *The people speak! Antisemitism and emancipation in nineteenth-century Bavaria* (Ann Arbor, 1994), pp. 32–3.

[37] On the impact of policies aimed at occupational restructuring, see also Rürup,

head counts or of highly tendentious local enquiries into Jewish commercial activity.[38] Throughout the *Vormärz* local and provincial authorities, as well as Conservative and even some Liberal parliamentary deputies, repeatedly voiced their 'disappointment' at the failure of the Jews to assimilate their occupational structure to that of the non-Jewish majority. There was a self-defeating logic in the notion of emancipation through occupational 'improvement'. In the first place, the economic environment of the 1830s and 1840s offered few incentives for a move into the artisan sector, large parts of which were suffering visibly from overcrowding and insufficient demand. Second, as we saw, in many areas of the German states, the skilled crafts remained under the control of Christian guilds with exclusive membership criteria; it was easy for the state to formulate intentions but difficult to realise them in practice – further reminder of the plurality of social agencies, some of them beyond direct state control, that helped to set the parameters of emancipation.[39] Moreover, the ultimate objective of the entire process of 'improvement' remained diffuse and ill-defined: at what precise point would the Jews have 'improved' themselves sufficiently to be deemed deserving of emancipation? Finally, as Rainer Erb and Werner Bergmann have pointed out, assessments of the 'civic-moral condition' of the minority were based not on the disinterested interpretation of 'direct, daily experiences and contacts' but on a 'collective, negative image'. It followed that 'improvements were *per se* undetectable by the opponents of emancipation, whose perceptions, mediated by schemata and stereotypes, were highly selective'.[40]

By contrast with occupational restructuring, where state policy ran against the current both of Christian interests and of economic rationality, the German states were relatively successful in improving the

---

'Emanzipation der Juden in Baden' p. 55; Richarz, *Jüdisches Leben,* p. 33; Eichler (ed.), *Nassauische Parlamentsdebatten,* vol. 1, p. 336; B. Brilling, *Die jüdischen Gemeinden Mittelschlesiens: Entstehung und Geschichte* (Stuttgart, 1972), p. 53; A. Prinz, *Juden im deutschen Wirtschaftsleben: Soziale und wirtschaftliche Struktur im Wandel 1850–1914,* ed. A. Barkai (Tübingen, 1984), p. 22; on the Prussian figures, which show a rise from 5 to 10.7 per cent in the numbers of Jewish artisans despite the absence of occupational laws, see J. Toury, *Soziale und politische Geschichte der Juden in Deutschland 1847–1871: Zwischen Revolution, Reaktion und Emanzipation* (Düsseldorf, 1977), p. 72.

[38] On biased reporting of Jewish economic activity by local officials, see M. Naarmann, *Die Paderborner Juden 1802–1945 (Paderborner Historische Forschungen 1),* (Paderborn, 1988), pp. 78–80.

[39] See., for example, V. Berbüsse, *Geschichte der Juden in Waldeck: Emanzipation und Antisemitismus vor 1900* (Wiesbaden, 1990), esp. pp. 70–1.

[40] R. Erb and W. Bergmann, *Die Nachtseite der Judenemanzipation: Der Widerstand gegen die Integration der Juden in Deutschland 1780–1860* (Berlin, 1989), pp. 38–9.

standard of Jewish schooling. A school founded by the enlightened Jewish elite in Berlin in 1781 met with state approval, and early Prussian proposals to standardise Jewish education foreshadowed the creation of state-supervised schools catering specifically for the Jewish population. In 1793, Karl von Hoym, minister of Silesia and South Prussia and a supporter of the emancipationist Christian Wilhelm Dohm, called for schools with 'rational' educators who could teach the Jews 'proper religious ideas and make them useful to the state as soldiers'.[41] The second and third partitions of Poland in 1793 and 1795 brought many more Jews under Prussian authority and prompted ministerial discussion on the ways in which schools might be used to render Jewish natives 'useful citizens'. Government enquiries in the newly acquired provinces of South and New East Prussia revealed that Jewish schools there were poor in quality, confined to the larger towns and hopelessly inadequate to the task of 'improvement' envisaged by the Prussian authorities. The subsequent General Jewish regulation of 1797 made provision for the appointment of state-paid instructors who would teach German, Polish and elementary mathematics to Jewish children of school age. The standardisation of Jewish schooling had scarcely begun, however, when the Peace of Tilsit (1807) removed these provinces from Prussian control.[42]

A number of states subsequently launched initiatives to improve the standard of Jewish elementary education, but the emphasis was generally on integration rather than segregation. The most important innovation, from the vantage point of the great majority of Jews, was the introduction and enforcement of universal compulsory education. Between 1809 and 1825 Baden, Bavaria, the Hessian principalities, Prussia and Württemberg all passed laws along these lines.[43] Jewish-run schools were tolerated, though their funding in many areas remained insecure, as long as they and their teachers conformed to the guidelines set out by departments of education. At the same time, the makeshift 'corner-schools' that had served many rural communities were abolished on the grounds, as one Prussian official put it, that children who were taught part-time by kosher butchers and cantors would be incapable of developing into 'fully-

---

[41] Quoted in W. W. Hagen, *Germans, Poles and Jews: The nationality conflict in the Prussian east 1772–1914* (Chicago, 1980), p. 60.

[42] A. Warschauer, 'Die Erziehung der Juden in der Provinz Posen durch das Elementarschulwesen', *Zeitschrift für die Geschichte der Juden in Deutschland* (1889; repr. Nendeln-Liechtenstein, 1975), vol. 3, p. 31.

[43] W. E. Mosse, 'From "Schutzjuden" to "Deutsche Staatsbürger jüdischen Glaubens": The long and bumpy road of Jewish emancipation in Germany', in Birnbaum and Katznelson (eds), *Paths of emancipation*, pp. 59–93; here p. 78.

fledged members of the state'.[44] In areas where there were no Jewish schools, or none of adequate standard to receive state recognition – as was the case in most rural areas – Jews were obliged to attend Christian schools. In the formerly Polish province of Posen, where Jews were numerous and schools were in short supply, the Prussian authorities even encouraged missionary organisations such as the 'London Society for the Promotion of Christianity among the Jews' to establish 'Jewish free schools'; the parents of children who failed to attend faced daily fines from the local police.[45] The result of these policies was a total transformation in the educational experience of the German Jews. The one-room *cheder* that had been the corner-stone of Jewish elementary schooling virtually disappeared, and the first half of the nineteenth century saw the substantial absorption of the Jewish minority into the state education systems of the German territories. By 1839 fifty-five per cent of German Jewish children attended Jewish schools; by 1867 the figure was twenty-five per cent.[46] The reason for this lay not merely in the geographical dispersion of the Jewish minority, which made confessional schools impractical, or in the scarcity of communal resources, but also in the readiness of most Jewish parents to embrace state education as a means to the cultural and social emancipation of their children. Nowhere is this more clearly demonstrated than in that flagship of German educational culture, the *Gymnasium*, where Jewish attendance came to outstrip that of Christians by a factor of around six to one. It is here above all that the state and its institutions contributed to the sociocultural integration of the Jewish minority, even as it withheld legal recognition of Jewish equality.

III

The 1840s saw a dramatic shift in the tone of public discussion on Jewish emancipation in many German states. A pioneering role was played by the provincial parliament of the Prussian Rhineland Province, which became, in 1843, the first German *Landtag* to pass a motion calling for full Jewish equality.[47] The motion was not put into practice by the government of the new monarch, Frederick-William IV, which embarked

---

[44] Düsseldorf Government to Oberpräsident Rhine Province, 1 August 1823, in T. Zimmer (ed.), *Inventar der Quellen zur Geschichte der jüdischen Bevölkerung in Rheinland-Pfalz und im Saarland von 1800/1815 bis 1945* (Koblenz, 1982), p. 67.
[45] Clark, *Politics of conversion*, pp. 202–4, 207.
[46] Richarz, *Jüdisches Leben*, pp. 51–2.
[47] Kastner, *Der Rheinische Provinziallandtag*, pp. 55–6.

during the same decade on a retrograde and ultimately unsuccessful campaign to corral the Jews into neo-medieval corporate entities known as *Judenschaften*, but it signalled the growing pro-emancipationist consensus within the liberal-minded propertied bourgeoisie whose voice in parliamentary debate was amplified by the elitist Prussian franchise. In 1846, after a period of declining support among the Liberals for emancipation, the Badenese Chamber suddenly followed suit, voting with a two-thirds majority for full Jewish equality. There were heated debates on the question in virtually all the German diets. Backed by an increasingly vociferous Liberal press and by unprecedented waves of petitions from Christians and Jews alike, Liberals and Democrats throughout the German states became increasingly confident that history was on their side and that restrictive 'Jew laws' were an anachronism that would soon succumb to the movement and ferment of the times. As the *Rheinische Zeitung* put it in 1842: '[the emancipation issue is] one of those questions that are no longer questions'.[48]

Developments in the late 1840s failed to bear out this optimism. In 1847 the Prussian United Diet that had been so forthright in its call for a constitution failed to pass a motion for emancipation of the Jews. The revolutions of the following year brought spectacular breakthroughs: the *Reich* Constitution drawn up by the Frankfurt Parliament proclaimed civic and state citizenship rights to be independent of religious affiliation, and was subsequently endorsed by twenty-nine of the lesser German states, excluding Austria, Bavaria, Prussia, Saxony and Hanover. In the last three, constitutions issued in 1849 abolished all legal disabilities. And in a remarkable turnabout the Bavarian government took the initiative in pressing for all-out emancipation. However, many of these successes were to prove as short-lived as the revolutionary situation that had given rise to them. The 'Basic Rights' set out in the Frankfurt Constitution were repealed by the re-formed Confederal Assembly, and the official endorsements of 1849 were thereby rendered meaningless. A number of states, including Saxony, Württemberg and some lesser territories, did move to retain equality of rights, but in many other states the emancipatory process was halted or even reversed. In the electorate of Hesse-Cassel political rights were withdrawn and the government even took measures to introduce segregated schooling. In Bavaria the government's proposal for emancipation collapsed in the Upper House in the face of a concerted opposition whose objections centred on the allegedly Christian character of the state. In Prussia the revised constitution of 1850 reaffirmed (Article

---

[48] *Rheinische Zeitung*, January 1842, no. 22, quoted in *Ibid.*, p. 337.

12) that civic and citizenship rights were independent of confession, but also asserted (Article 14): 'the Christian religion shall form the basis of all institutions of the state concerned with religious practice'. Throughout the 1850s and early 1860s Article 14 was invoked to maintain the exclusion of Jews from virtually all state employment. Only in the 1860s, with the growing dominance of Liberal factions in the various representative assemblies of the German states, was there a uniform trend towards emancipation throughout Germany, with the exception of the notoriously reactionary Duchies of Mecklenburg, which reluctantly conceded emancipation at the last hour. The comprehensive abolition of all legal disabilities was finally enshrined in the constitution of the North German Confederation, which was drawn up and signed in 1866–67. It became binding for all member states of the German Empire in 1871.[49]

With this law, the long road of Jewish emancipation appeared at last to have reached its destination. In the course of over sixty years of balking, delay and prevarication by the state authorities the German Jews, for their part, had undergone a profound socio-cultural self-transformation. Its most conspicuous consequence was the conscious shedding, within a generation or two, of many outward signs of difference. In the 1810s and 1820s the Jewish journal *Sulamith*, the foremost German-language organ of the early emancipation era, propagated a cult of middle-class respectability (*Sittlichkeit*) and personal formation (*Bildung*).[50] Yiddish and 'Jewish-German' soon made way for High German at home and in public. In 1833 one Jewish author invited his readers to 'consider the immense changes that have taken place in language, apparel, way of life, in requirements and amusements, in manners and customs'. 'Even their external appearance, how it has changed since those times.'[51] This transformation in styles represented, as many scholars have noted, an assimilation to the habitus of the emergent German *Bürgertum*, and it was in the venues and institutions of the bourgeoisie – *Gymnasien*, universities, coffee houses, concert halls and clubs – that integration was most pronounced.

Analogous developments could be detected in the sphere of synagogue worship, where the efforts of religious reformers in Berlin produced a new style of observance that was modelled in some respects on Protestant

---

[49] An excellent concise outline of these developments, on which the preceding paragraph is based, may be found in Rürup, 'Tortuous and thorny path', 26–33.

[50] G. L. Mosse, 'Jewish emancipation: Between *Bildung* and respectability', in J. Reinharz and W. Schatzberg (eds), *The Jewish response to German culture: From the enlightenment to the Second World War* (Hanover, N.H., London, 1985), pp. 1–16; here pp. 3–4.

[51] M. B. Lessing, *Die Juden und die öffentliche Meinung im preussischen Staate* (Altona, 1833), cited in Mosse, 'The long and bumpy road', p. 79.

worship. In 1820 a pious Christian journal observed with approval that there was now a 'fine synagogue' in Berlin, where 'solemn singing by the whole congregation' had replaced 'the horrible tinkling of the bell-ringers' and where a German liturgy had been installed in place of 'the senseless blabbering of prayers in a language most of them [did] not understand'.[52] The reform movement was initially quashed in Berlin by a government allergic to all manifestations of sectarian separatism, but it soon took off in other states, often with the approval and support of state authorities bent on purging Jewish worship of its more conspicuous peculiarities.[53] Since the propensity to reform differed from community to community and most states lacked a rabbinical body capable of imposing uniformity, the result of these innovations was an increasingly nuanced spectrum of religious practices ranging from neo-orthodoxy – a modernised and historically informed revival of traditional practice – to those extremist reformers of the Berlin *Genossenschaft für die Reform im Judentum* (Society for Reform in Judaism) who campaigned to have synagogue services moved to Sunday.[54]

What is striking about these developments is the complex interplay they reveal between Jewish aspirations and Christian expectations. While it is important to recognise the role played by endogenous cultural factors in the refashioning of nineteenth-century German Judaism, it is also necessary to acknowledge that the very protractedness of the emancipatory process, the tantalising juxtaposition of obstacle and opportunity over more than half a century, gave the German Jews, as David Sorkin has observed, ample time to 'internalise its terms'.[55] Christian legislators expected the Jews to pay for emancipation in the coin of a 'political and moral self-improvement' (*sittliche und moralische Bildung*) that would embrace religious practice, education and economic behaviour. The Jews, for their part, accepted the bargain on the terms set by the tutelary state. They had little choice, of course, for there were virtually no influential figures in government, politics or society who spoke out in favour of a genuinely pluralistic or multicultural 'solution' to the problem of the Jewish minority. Liberals and Democrats insisted as adamantly as their Conservative opponents that the Jewish 'personality must disappear with equalisation'. 'It is my conviction', the pro-emancipationist Josef Merk

---

[52] Anon., 'Juden in Deutschland', *Neueste Nachrichten*, 4 (1820), 286.

[53] See, for example, Mosse, 'Jewish emancipation', pp. 6–7; Rürup, 'Emanzipation der Juden in Baden', p. 54; Wippermann, *Jüdisches Leben*, pp. 64–5.

[54] Richarz, *Jüdisches Leben*, p. 47.

[55] D. Sorkin, 'The impact of emancipation on German Jewry: A reconsideration' in Frankel and Zipperstein (eds), *Assimilation and community*, pp. 177–98; here p. 184.

told the Lower House of the Badenese Chamber of Deputies in 1833, 'that nothing remains but to throw the Israelites, with equal rights, into the mass of the Christian population, so that, ripped along by the torrent, like the pebbles rolling along in a riverbed, they round themselves off and fit themselves in'.[56]

IV

What general conclusions can be drawn from the above outline of emancipation in the nineteenth-century German states? One could begin by re-emphasising the largely reactive role played by state administrations. More often than not, the German governments of the *Vormärz* were content to leave old laws in place, or to adjust them piecemeal. They were extremely reluctant to tamper with vested interests, most notably those of guilds and communes, partly because they feared the consequences for public order. They rarely grasped the initiative in legislation pertaining to the Jews, preferring to take advice from district and regional officials on what measures local conditions would tolerate. They deferred, and not always out of sheer expediency, to popular sentiment. They saw themselves as the 'protectors' of Christian rural populations against the depredations of Jewish 'usury', but failed to address the problem directly by providing cheap government credit for hard-pressed farmers or encouraging private banks or co-operatives to give credit. Their approach to reform, in this as in so many other areas, was pragmatic and timorous. The record we have surveyed is a reminder of how feeble the state remained in the face of the many groups among whose interests it had to mediate. This, perhaps, is part of what was specifically 'German' about the 'thorny' path to emancipation: German societies remained cellular and highly regionalised, and this diversity found political expression in a way that was not true, or possible, for France or Great Britain. The path to emancipation was 'tortuous' in part precisely because, in the absence of a consistent impetus from the state, it wove among so many disjointed interests – impecunious peasants, rebellious artisans in the cities and towns, cameral liberals, and the burghers of the local communes (*Gemeinden*) that in many regions remained the fundamental building-blocks of German public life.

A second point that arises from our overview concerns the ambivalent relationship between emancipation and 'modernisation'. Did the ultimate

---

[56] Quoted in D. Herzog, *Intimacy and exclusion. Religious politics in pre-revolutionary Baden* (Princeton N.J., 1996), pp. 57–8.

success of Jewish emancipation depend on the modernisation, and thus emancipation, of German society as a whole? There is much that speaks for this view. After all, emancipation became the catch-cry of a political movement, liberalism, that saw itself as the organisational incarnation of modernity. The very idea of legal emancipation and the concept of citizenship as undifferentiated and universal presupposed the transition from a law that was religious and personal to the kind of abstract, formal and impersonal legal system we associate with modern polities. Secularisation, generally deemed a standard feature of modernising societies, was also implicated in Jewish emancipation, which required that the state distinguish between religious and political entitlements and thereby surrender, in theory at least, the claim to be essentially 'Christian'. Moreover, as we have seen, the full realisation of Jewish citizenship rights required that some of the hardiest survivals of the traditional social order – guilds and communal authorities – were either demolished or substantially undermined by unilateral action on the part of the state. Lastly, Jewish *societal* emancipation was closely intertwined with other processes implicated in the transition from traditional to modern societies: urbanisation, professionalisation and the emergence of a highly acculturated bourgeoisie.[57]

If, however, we take the broadening of political participation to be a defining characteristic of modernisation, then the link with emancipation becomes ambiguous. For even at the height of liberal agitation for emancipation, there were signs that enthusiasm for the cause of the Jews was confined to that wealthy and largely urban social stratum that dominated cameral politics and the free-thinking press, and that a more equitable representation of public opinion might place the entire project in jeopardy. At the Rhenish provincial parliament of 1842, which famously passed a motion in support of full emancipation, there was an ominous

---

[57] On the urbanisation of German Jewry, which began earlier and proceeded at a faster pace than among non-Jewish Germans, see U. O. Schmelz, 'Die demographische Entwicklung der Juden in Deutschland von der Mitte des 19. Jahrhunderts bis 1933', *Bulletin des Leo Baeck Instituts*, 83 (1989), 15–62, here pp. 16, 20, 22–4. On professionalisation, see M. Richarz, *Der Eintritt der Juden in die akademischen Berufe: Jüdische Studenten und Akademiker in Deutschland, 1678–1848* (Tübingen, 1974) and I. Schorsch, 'Emancipation and the crisis of religious authority: The emergence of the modern rabbinate', in I. Schorsch, *From text to context: The turn to history in modern Judaism* (Hanover, N.H., 1994), pp. 9–50. On the emergence of a Jewish middle class, see especially J. Toury, 'Der Eintritt der Juden ins deutsche Bürgertum', in H. Liebeschütz and A. Paucker (eds), *Das Judentum in der deutschen Umwelt, 1800–1850* (Tübingen, 1977), pp. 139–242; M. A. Kaplan, *The making of the Jewish middle class: Women, family and identity in Imperial Germany* (New York, Oxford, 1995). Concise general discussion: S. M. Lowenstein, 'The pace of modernisation of German Jewry in the nineteenth century', *Leo Baeck Institute Yearbook*, 21 (1976), 41–56.

divide between the votes of urban and rural deputies, which suggests that the countryside, where most Germans still earned their keep, remained as yet unconvinced of the benefits of emancipation. That this was indeed so is demonstrated by recent studies that have shown that violence against Jews and Jewish property was far more widespread throughout the Restoration and *Vormärz* era than previously thought.[58] The hungry 1840s brought increasingly frequent attacks on Jewish property in small towns and villages across Germany, and during the revolutionary unrest of 1848–49 alone Helmut Berding counted no fewer than 180 instances in which angry mobs attacked and plundered Jewish homes, businesses and warehouses.[59] Those local and regional officials who held out against emancipation were thus in some respects better representatives of 'public opinion' than the Liberals of the parliamentary chambers. That this anti-Jewish mood could be captured for political purposes was demonstrated beyond doubt by the extraordinary petition campaign mobilised against emancipation in Bavaria during debate over the government's proposal to grant legal equality in 1849. It was partly as a result of this mobilisation of an extensive rural and small-town constituency which lay beyond the margins of the parliamentary electorate that the ministry's emancipation bill failed in the Bavarian Upper House. As James F. Harris has shown, this was 'an episode in the expansion of political participation' but emphatically not a chapter in the onward march towards emancipation.[60] A similar claim could be made for the innovative techniques of rural political mobilisation adopted by anti-Semitic agitators in the early 1890s.[61]

Were the German Jews a 'religious minority' comparable with other confessional groups? Certainly it was the ostensible aim of emancipation, legal and societal, to transform the Jews into a confessional group like any other. Hence the mid-century preference for the term 'German citizen of Mosaic faith' and the tendency to shed the ethno-cultural components of observance while foregrounding the subjective and 'positive' dimensions of faith. The same reasoning lay behind the drive to dislodge the Jews from their traditional niches in the economy and to promote their cultural integration through schooling.

[58] D. Preissel, *Frühantisemitismus in der Freien Stadt Frankfurt und im Großherzogtum Hessen, 1810 bis 1860* (Heidelberg, 1989); Erb and Bergmann, *Die Nachtseite*, pp. 217–68.
[59] H. Berding, *Moderner Antisemitismus in Deutschland* (Frankfurt, 1988), p. 74.
[60] Harris, *The people speak!*, p. 40.
[61] See G. Eley, 'Antisemitism, agrarian mobilisation and the Conservative Party: Radicalism and containment in the founding of the Agrarian League, 1890-93', in L. E. Jones and J. N. Retallack (eds), *Between reform, reaction and resistance: Studies in the history of German Conservatism from 1789 to 1945* (Providence, 1993), pp. 187–227, esp. pp. 204–6, 224–5.

Moreover, as David Sorkin has demonstrated, the comparison between the German Jews and the English Catholics, who also passed through a protracted phase of legal and social emancipation, reveals informative parallels.[62] Indeed, when the term 'emancipation' passed into general currency in the German states around 1830, it was initially associated not with the Jews, but with the legal relief of the English Catholics.[63] There were analogies too in Protestant perceptions of the two minorities; the charges laid by Protestant polemic against Catholic observance – namely, that it was purely formal, ritualistic and lacked the true subjectivity associated with 'positive religion' – also featured prominently in contemporary critiques of Judaism. And like the Jews, the Catholics, especially in the 1870s, were accused of forming more than merely a confession, of constituting an alien polity. Just as the Christian reactionary Ludwig von Thile could argue in 1847 that the true 'fatherland' of the Jews was not Germany but 'Zion', so the political loyalty of the Catholics of the German Empire could be questioned on the grounds of their alleged fealty to Rome; though it must be said that nothing in the Jewish experience corresponded with the assault on Catholic religious personnel launched by the Bismarck government under the auspices of the *Kulturkampf*.[64] The term 'state within a state' was used by Protestants of Catholics (and of Jesuits in particular) long before it passed into the lexicon of the anti-Semites.[65] German Jews and German Catholics alike suffered the effects of state discrimination after 1871, despite the absence of a legal sanction for such a policy. Both minorities were under-represented in the upper echelons of the imperial and Prussian governments; historically, the Prussian state had long discriminated against both Catholics and Jews in academic appointments;[66] both groups had difficulty gaining access to certain sections of the bureaucracy, especially the diplomatic corps. Catholics and Jews alike faced discrimination within the Prussian – and hence much of the German – military.[67] The shared experience of dis-

[62] D. Sorkin, 'Juden und Katholiken: Deutsch-jüdische Kultur im Vergleich 1750–1850', in S. Volkov and E. Müller-Lückner (eds), *Die Juden und die Moderne* (Munich, 1994), pp. 9–30.

[63] J. Katz, 'The term 'Jewish Emancipation': Its origin and historical impact' in J. Katz, *Zur Assimilation und Emanzipation der Juden: Ausgewählte Schriften* (Darmstadt, 1982), pp. 99–123.

[64] On Ludwig von Thile, who made these remarks at the 31st session of the United Prussian Diet of 1847, see Clark, *Politics of conversion*, pp. 130, 165–6.

[65] J. Katz, '"A state within a state". The history of an anti-semitic slogan', in Katz, *Zur Assimilation*, pp. 124–53.

[66] I. Schorsch, 'The religious parameters of *Wissenschaft*: Jewish academics at Prussian universities', in Schorsch, *From text to context*, pp. 51–70, here p. 59.

[67] On discrimination against Catholics and Jews within the judiciary, see esp. P. Pulzer,

crimination does seem to have produced a transient sense of solidarity between Jews and Catholics in Protestant-dominated Prussia, particularly during the 1850s,[68] but mutual suspicion prevailed and there was never any prospect of a fully-fledged alliance. After 1871 the organs of Jewish opinion took a variety of positions on the *Kulturkampf*: the *Allgemeine Zeitung des Judentums* was generally supportive of the Bismarckian policy on the grounds that the existence of the German Jews was 'tied to the liberal state' and that the revival of ultramontanism would have 'the saddest consequences' for the Jewish population. On the other hand, Jewish Reichstag deputies and left–liberal journals, such as the Jewish-owned *Frankfurter Zeitung,* opposed on principle such discriminatory legislation as the Anti-Jesuit Law.[69]

Notwithstanding important parallels and connections with the experience of the Catholic minority, the Jewish case was in some respects obviously quite unique. The 'Jewish question', which produced such an unabating flood of pamphlets, books, newspaper articles and political speeches from the middle of the century onwards, had no direct parallel in the historical experience of the other minorities. No other minority faced a concerted campaign of vilification to compare with the assault mounted by the political anti-Semites against the German Jews. If we survey the history of the 'Jewish question' in the German states, two factors emerge above all as distinctive throughout: the persistent sense that 'Jewishness' retained an indissoluble core of 'ethnicity'; and a concern verging on obsession with the location of the Jews within the economy. These preoccupations were mutually reinforcing: the concentration of Jews in the credit and commercial sector was only perceptible and significant because Jews were deemed to constitute a group 'foreign' to the Christian population. Conversely, the distinctive 'ethnicity' of the Jews was almost always defined in terms that were related, directly or indirectly, to perceptions of their economic activity.

It is remarkable how ubiquitous this circular interweaving of 'religious', socio-ethical, economic and ethnic themes was in the various discourses of German anti-Semitism. The Talmud was impugned in the nineteenth century above all – if we leave aside the lunatic fringe that claimed to find in it sanctions for the practice of ritual murder – for its

---

Jews and the German state: The political history of a minority, 1848–1933 (Oxford, 1992), pp. 44–68. On the army, see W. T. Angress, 'Prussia's army and the Jewish reserve officer controversy before World War I', *Leo Baeck Institute Yearbook*, 17 (1972), 19–42; esp. 27.

[68] A. Herzig, 'Die Juden in Preußen', in P. Freimark (ed.), *Juden in Preußen – Juden in Hamburg* (Hamburg, 1983), p. 40.

[69] Pulzer, *Jews and the German State*, p. 327.

endorsement of usury against Christians and for an ethical exclusivity that allegedly excluded Jews from the community of trust essential to benign economic traffic between human beings. Nor were such arguments confined to the anti-Semitic movement; Werner Sombart's famous and influential sociological study, *The Jews and modern capitalism*, asserted, for example, that the roots of the Jews' special eminence within the capitalist economy lay in the doctrines of their religion.[70] Moreover, many of the characteristics associated by Germans with 'the Jew' as a distinctive type were little more than metaphors for their commercialism: the 'nervousness'[71] of the Jews was the nervousness of the haggler or speculator, their cultural sterility an index of the middle man's alienation from genuinely productive labour, their disquieting 'mobility' (*Beweglichkeit*)[72] a personification of the self-generated velocity of speculative capital. 'Who nowadays', as one Christian Conservative asked in 1871, 'is as passionately engaged in the mobilisation of capital, in goading it through a thousand hands, in chopping up the landed estates and trading in them ... as a great number of the Jews?'[73]

V

These reflections take us back to the starting-point of our survey. In 1750, according to one estimate, some fifty per cent of German Jews were unemployed or destitute; perhaps two per cent were wealthy. By 1870, eighty per cent were bourgeois and sixty per cent within the upper-income groups.[74] But whereas emancipation and assimilation had radically transformed the earning power of German Jewry, the occupational structure of the Jewish population remained remarkably stable. Even in areas like Rhineland-Westphalia where industrialisation was transforming the economy and the physical environment, Jews 'held fast to their traditional vocations, above all in retail and a number of preferred "Jewish" economic sectors', strong evidence that 'group-specific

---

[70] W. Sombart, *Die Juden und das Wirtschaftsleben* (Leipzig, 1911), esp. pp. 24–5, trans. M. Epstein as *The Jews and modern capitalism* (New York, 1951). On Sombart's position, see P. Mendes-Flohr, 'Werner Sombart's "The Jews and modern capitalism". An analysis of its ideological premises', *Leo Baeck Institute Yearbook*, 21 (1976), 87–107.

[71] On 'Jewish nervousness', see esp. S. Gilman, *The Jew's body* (New York, 1991).

[72] 'diesem beweglichen und doch so unfruchtbaren Semitenthum', H. von Treitschke, 'Das konstitutionalle Königtum in Deutschland' (1869), cited in W. Boehlich, *Der Berliner Antisemitismusstreit* (Frankfurt, 1965), p. 244.

[73] J. F. A. de le Roi, *Stephan Schulz. Ein Beitrag zum Verständnis der Juden und ihrer Bedeutung für das Leben der Völker* (Gotha, 1871), p. 197.

[74] Sorkin, 'The impact of emancipation', p. 179. The figures are from Toury, *Soziale und politische Geschichte*, pp. 114, 277.

factors', rather than local economic forces, were at work.[75] By the last decades of the nineteenth century the listing of occupational statistics had become a commonplace in the discourse of the 'Jewish question'; some anti-Semitic works, such as Theodor Fritsch's infamous *Handbuch der Judenfrage* (Handbook of the Jewish question), were little more than paranoid compendia of statistical tables demonstrating alleged anomalies in the collective profile of German Jewry.[76] That this economic 'obduracy' should have seemed so problematic to non-Jewish contemporaries reflects one of the most fateful continuities that dogged the Jews on the long road to emancipation – namely, the persistence, in many spheres of German society, of a pre-modern moral economy that distinguished between morally upright and productive forms of economic activity (manufacture, agriculture, manual labour) and the sterility, parasitism and immorality associated with credit provision, brokerage, currency dealing and small trade. The prevalence of this moral economy should not be underestimated – it can be seen at work in the attempts of the Prussian finance ministry to obstruct the formation of joint stock companies in the 1840s, in the rapid institutionalisation of Marxism as the political philosophy of the German left, in the novels of Freytag and Fontane and in the ideologically freighted concept of a 'Cartel of the Productive Estates' (*Kartell der schaffenden Stände*) launched by the Prussian Finance Minister Johannes Miquel in the 1890s. Germans, to put it crudely, lacked language or arguments with which to articulate the virtues or embrace the necessity of the more rarefied forms of financial and economic mediation. The impact of this state of affairs on German perceptions of Jews can hardly be overemphasised; the reasons for it – the persistence of fiscal absolutism and the lack of a language of public credit? the survival of corporate structures and mentalities? the absence of a 'gentlemanly capitalism' sustained by colonial commerce? – must lie beyond the scope of this chapter.

---

[75] A. Barkai, 'Die sozio-ökonomische Entwicklung der Juden in Rheinland-Westphalen in der Industrialisierung (1850–1910)', *Bulletin des Leo Baeck Instituts*, 66 (1983), 53–81, here 66–7; A. Barkai, *Jüdische Minderheit und Industrialisierung: Demographie, Berufe und Einkommen bei den Juden in Westdeutschland 1850–1914* (Tübingen, 1988).

[76] T. Fritsch, *Handbuch der Judenfrage. Eine Zusammenstellung des wichtigsten Materials zur Beurteilung des jüdischen Volkes* (26th edn, Hamburg, 1907); the book was initially published under the title *Antisemiten-Katechismus* (Leipzig, 1888).

8

Italian Protestants

Gian Paolo Romagnani

One cannot refer to the emancipation of religious minorities in Italy before 17 February 1848, at which date new edicts were promulgated in Piedmont and Tuscany that granted civil and political rights to non-Catholics. The year 1848 will, therefore, be taken as the cornerstone of the periodisation of the topic under discussion. First we deal with what was essentially the only Protestant minority in Italy, the Waldensians in Piedmont. Later we turn to the emancipatory process and the gradual diffusion of Protestantism in Italy brought about by the work of preachers and missionaries.

I

With the exception of western Piedmont, where the presence of the Waldensians in three valleys (Val del Pellice, Val del Chisone and Val Germanasca) went back to the Middle Ages, there were no other substantial Protestant minorities in any other Italian state at that time. The history of Italian Protestants is therefore, above all, the history of a minority that fluctuated between 15,000 and 20,000 inhabitants and were concentrated in a tiny Alpine region on the French border. They constituted the only 'Protestant island', known as the 'Alpine ghetto', in Italian territory, and had joined the Reformation movement in 1532. Their internal organisation resembled that of the Calvinists and consisted of parishes, the consistory and the synod, which was the representative assembly that elected the 'Table' presided over by the Moderator. The term 'Alpine ghetto' appeared for the first time in 1798 following the collapse of the Savoy monarchy and the installation of the provisional Republican government in Turin, which decreed the end of all religious discrimination and proclaimed the legal equality of all citizens. It was thanks to the French armies that the process of the Waldensians' emancipation began, and it was consolidated later, during the fifteen-year period

(1800–14) during which Piedmont was part of France. Although the history of Italian Protestants was therefore, at this point, part of the history of the French Protestants, the specificity of the Waldensians should not be forgotten. The population in the valleys was made up for the most part of peasants, with isolated scatterings of lower middle-class people who were predominantly engaged in commerce or textile manufacturing. An equally small minority consisted of pastors and schoolteachers, who were fairly well educated but of a very modest social standing none the less. It is among these educated villagers of the lower middle class that Revolutionary ideas became most popular, as the result of frequent contact with the Swiss and through reading the works of Jean-Jacques Rousseau. Between 1792 and 1798 a political awareness developed rapidly among the Waldensians, as a consequence of which the arrival of the French was greeted as a liberation, with manifestations of joy and the planting of trees of liberty as a mark of freedom. In contrast to other agricultural areas in Piedmont, where the French were viewed as invaders, the communities in the Waldensian valleys took an active part in the provisional administrations and collaborated with the French.[1]

The election of the Moderator of the Waldensian Church, Pietro Geymet, to the provisional government (where he even served as president for a short time before the brief restoration in 1799), can be seen as a foreshadowing of the Protestants' future emancipation. Two years later, in 1801, following the French victory in Marengo and the annexation of Piedmont to France, Geymet was elected subprefect of Pinerolo, the district which included the Waldensian valleys, and was a highly competent public administrator for the next fourteen years. Although he abandoned his ecclesiastical offices he maintained his informal role of interceding with the Parisian government on behalf of the Protestant minority.[2] Geymet was not unique: the Turin Academy of Science accepted Waldensians among its associated members. Waldensian students, on Geymet's recommendation, were accepted for the first time at Turin's National College, even if very few pursued university studies. The presence of Waldensians in public offices, as in the intermediate army ranks, was virtually nil on a quantitative level. What was more important to the Waldensians was the option now open to them of leaving the

---

[1] D. Jahier, 'Le Valli valdesi durante la Rivoluzione, la Repubblica e l'Impero francese', *Bollettino della società di studi valdesi*, 52 (1928), 5–58; 54 (1929), 39–78; 60 (1933), 68–97; 61 (1934), 5–34; 62 (1934), 41–81; 64 (1935), 48–71, 65 (1936), 11–37; 66 (1936), 5–20.
[2] G. Jalla, 'Pierre Geymet, modérateur de l'Eglise Vaudoise et sous-préfet de Pignerol', *Bollettino della società di studi valdesi*, 61 (1934), 54–72.

ghetto and acquiring property outside the valleys' boundaries, in particular in the plains between Pinerolo and Turin. In the fifteen-year Napoleonic period, the economic role played by the valleys grew considerably – even during a time of economic stagnation – and a lower middle business class that had begun to develop at the end of the seventeenth century grew ever stronger. Moreover, there consolidated itself an intellectual lower middle class which, no longer excluded from studying and pursuing professional careers, ceased to be made up solely of pastors and school teachers. The possibility of taking part in elections was a complete novelty for the Waldensians. In April 1804, for example, 1141 voters participated in the election of the delegates of the Torre Pellice canton. Although numerous Waldensians were elected as delegates, only one was elected a member of Pinerolo's electoral college, a clear sign that the Protestant minority had not yet reached full social emancipation.

A clear indication of the degree of religious emancipation was the erection of a new temple in Luserna San Giovanni, which began in 1807. In Pinerolo, on the other hand, where many Waldensians had moved under Geymet's protection, only one chapel was opened, while in Turin no place of worship was built at all. After Napoleon's coronation at Nôtre Dame in Paris and the Concordat between the pope and the emperor, the Catholic Church rapidly regained the positions that it had previously lost, not only in the Italian *départements* but throughout France too. The Protestant churches had to struggle to preserve their own identity within the rigid framework of imperial society, subject as they were to numerous ministerial controls. According to the law of 7 April 1802, the churches in Piedmont, as in the whole of France, were organised into consistories. The pastors, paid by the state, were obliged to swear an oath of loyalty and became administrators of the national property assigned to them – property that had been taken from the abolished Catholic parishes. The annual Church assembly, which took the place of the Waldensian synod, thus became a kind of administration advisory board for the 'national Protestant Church'. On a formal level emancipation was complete, but on a more substantial level it can safely be said that no great changes had taken place. As far as the attitude of the Catholic population was concerned, the Waldensians were still a 'tolerated' minority, of which only a notable elite succeeded in integrating itself with reasonable prospects of stability. During the fifteen-year Napoleonic period a new Protestant presence – of foreign origin for the most part – began to take shape outside Piedmont. In Bergamo, for example, the Swiss Protestant community had an official pastor for the first time in 1807. In Leghorn the Dutch-German community was reorganised and in Florence the Genevese banker Jean-Gabriel Eynard was entrusted with assignments of some responsibility in the Kingdom of Etruria. Above all, it was during this period that the 'British and Foreign Bible Society' started diffusing copies of the Holy Scriptures and religious propaganda that was frequently linked with the undercover activities of the British agents.[3]

II

After 1815 Piedmont returned to its pre-1798 state. Jews and Protestants were again deprived of all civil and political rights. The Waldensian 'Table' had to return all property acquired under French rule to the Catholic parishes, lost its government subsidies and even had to contribute to the maintenance of the Catholic clergy. It was only thanks to deeds of indemnity granted in 1816 that the Waldensians were allowed to keep any property they had bought outside the valleys. They were made to relinquish any public offices they held. Geymet reverted to being a pastor and teacher in Torre Pellice, while businessmen withdrew behind the valley boundaries and attempted to renew their interrupted contacts with England and Germany. According to the edict of 1 March 1816, which redefined, with only a few amendments, the legislative structure of the *ancien régime*, the Protestant religion was only tolerated in the three valleys and even then only as long as it did not offend Catholic sensibilities. The building of new churches was forbidden, as was attendance at any public or private school outside the valleys and the rental or purchase of real estate outside the area. Residence in cities without authorisation was also prohibited, as were practising the liberal professions, attaining any academic or military qualifications and obtaining any civil post. Above all, the Waldensians could only be elected to the position of mayor or town councillor in a municipality where they represented the total population; in all other areas, where they had only a simple majority, they had to concede more than half the seats in council and the position of mayor to Catholics.[4]

In spite of the Holy Alliance's directives, post-Napoleonic Europe was not entirely unfavourable to the Waldensians. Diplomatic pressure from Prussia and England, allies of the Savoy State, prevented any serious outrages against the Waldensians. The presence of travellers as well as of Swiss, British and German missionaries in Piedmont favoured renewed

---

[3] G. Spini, *Risorgimento e protestanti* (Milan, 1989), pp. 56–66.
[4] D. Jahier, 'La Restaurazione nelle Valli valdesi', *Bollettino della società di studi valdesi*, 30 (1912), 21–60; 33 (1914), 5–64; 34 (1915), 5–41; 35 (1915), 5–76; 37 (1916), 9–55.

contacts with the European Protestant world. The same was true in the other Italian states, where the British and Prussian diplomatic missions led to a systematic policy of support of (for the most part foreign) Protestant minorities, and in Turin, Bergamo, Leghorn, Florence and Pisa Protestant chapels with Swiss or German pastors were opened. In Turin, from 1825, the English ambassador opened the doors of his private chapel, guaranteeing regular worship every Sunday. Two years later, on the initiative of the Prussian ambassador Friedrich Ludwig von Waldburg-Truchsess (1776–1844), the Prussian, English and Dutch embassies joined forces to fund a regular chaplain who was recruited from among the Waldensian pastors. In 1835 Waldburg-Truchsess was elected president of the Protestant Assembly Board in Turin, which consisted of the embassies' pastor, two Waldensians and two members of foreign Churches.[5] The most famous of the Waldensians' 'foreign friends' was Colonel Charles Beckwith (1789–1862), a British agent who established himself in Torre Pellice in 1827, and through whom there passed a consistent flow of money destined to sustain Protestant activities and above all to form an educated elite capable of leading the local communities towards emancipation. Beckwith struggled, albeit unsuccessfully, to have the Waldensian Church adopt a kind of episcopal structure, which, by strengthening the Moderator's position, would have had more in common with the Anglican than the Calvinist Church.[6]

Although what they did lacked public recognition, the Waldensians expanded the organisational basis of their community in the Restoration years by founding hospital and scholastic institutions in the main centres of the valleys, with the aid of subsidies from England, Switzerland, Germany and Russia. Hospitals were founded at Torre Pellice in 1824 and Pomaretto in 1828. Pomaretto's grammar school was established in 1830 and Torre Pellice's college in 1831.

At the same time more than 120 village schools opened their doors. The authorities, however, closed down the two institutions of higher education. The diffusion of popular education at village level on the Waldensians' initiative – already underway in the second half of the seventeenth century and further reinforced during the Napoleonic period – reached very significant levels in the first half of the nineteenth century, transforming the Waldensian valleys into a tiny island of literate peasants in a sea of illiterates. In the years between 1838 and 1865 the proportion

---

[5] D. Jahier, 'Il conte Waldburg-Truchsess', *Bollettino della società di studi valdesi*, 59, (1936), 55–69.

[6] J.-P. Meille, *Il generale Beckwith. Sua vita e sue opere in mezzo ai Valdesi del Piemonte* (Rome and Florence, 1879).

of literates in the Waldensian population fluctuated in the three valleys between sixty-two and seventy per cent, whereas among the Catholic population it did not exceed fifty per cent. In those years the level of literacy in the Waldensian valleys was comparable to that of the most advanced areas of Europe, and considerably higher than the Italian average of thirty to thirty-five per cent literate in 1861.[7] Outside Piedmont the Protestant presence was most evident in Tuscany, where the conversions of Duke Lucca Carlo Ludovico of Bourbon (1835) of the Florentine Count Pietro Guicciardini (1836) took place.[8]

III

After the accession of Carlo Alberto of Savoy-Carignano to the Piedmontese throne in 1831, modifications of the law in the direction of a less restrictive treatment of religious minorities were demanded by the more enlightened jurists. Between 1832 and 1837, during the preparations for the new civil code, Giuseppe Barbaroux, the Minister of Justice, in the course of raising the problem of civil and political emancipation of the non-Catholic subjects, came up against the opposition of the Conservatives. The Civil Code of 1837 only confirmed the already existing 'tolerance of customs and special regulations' for the Waldensians. But the authorities demonstrated that they were in fact less and less insistent on the strict enforcement of the law. The problem re-emerged in the mid 1840s, in the new climate of hope generated by the first reforms promised by the Savoy monarchy.[9]

Between 1843 and 1847 numerous intellectuals, Catholic politicians and others publicly supported the Waldensians' emancipation.[10] One of the most resolute advocates of the Waldensians' rights was the Prussian ambassador Waldburg-Truchsess, whom Carlo Alberto frequently consulted for advice. He died in Turin in 1844 and his remains were buried in the Waldensian cemetery in Torre Pellice. The funeral, which took place in August, in the presence of the ambassadors of the Protestant countries, reminded public opinion of the discrimination against Protestants. One month later Carlo Alberto visited Torre Pellice, accompanied

---

[7] M. G. Caffaro, 'Alfabetismo e analfabetismo nella prima metà dell'ottocento', *Bollettino della società di studi valdesi*, 167 (1990), 3–26.

[8] S. Jacini, *Un riformatore toscano dell'epoca del Risorgimento: Il conte Pietro Guicciardini (1806–1886)* (Florence, 1940).

[9] D. Jahier, 'Charles Albert et les Vaudois avant 1848', *Bollettino della società di studi valdesi*, 15 (1898), 1–32.

[10] R. Romeo, *Cavour e il suo tempo*, 3 vols (Rome and Bari, 1969–84).

among others by the Marquis Roberto d'Azeglio, to inaugurate the church of the Mauriziano order, which was built at the entrance to the village precisely to symbolise the intention of reconquering the valleys for Catholicism. The visit was turned into a first partial success for the Waldensians, as the king was sympathetic towards them, went without an armed escort, granted an audience to members of the 'Table' and decorated the Waldensian mayor of Torre Pellice with the Knight's Cross of Saint Maurice and Saint Lazarus.

In the years that followed d'Azeglio made more private visits to the valleys, meeting with Waldensian pastors and notables in order to learn about their lives. A fervent, yet enlightened Catholic, d'Azeglio believed that it was his duty as a Christian to do his utmost to have full civil and political rights and freedom of religion conceded to both Protestants and Jews. D'Azeglio's work, in which he was assisted by other intellectuals and liberal politicians, was the decisive factor in bringing about the edict of 17 February 1848, in which the king would grant civil and political emancipation to the Waldensians.[11] On 15 November 1847, at a time when Carlo Alberto was announcing important administrative reforms, the pastor Amedeo Bert, the chaplain of the foreign legations and the focal point for the Protestant community of Turin, received a visit from Roberto d'Azeglio. The result of their deliberations was that the Waldensian Church agreed to put their faith in d'Azeglio rather than deal officially with the sovereign. From that moment on, the pressure on the sovereign grew from day to day, whether through weekly meetings with d'Azeglio or through the mobilisation of liberal public opinion. A petition demanding the emancipation of non-Catholics was supported by Roberto d'Azeglio, Cesare Balbo, Camillo Cavour and more than six hundred Piedmontese individuals, among them sixty-five Catholic clergy. The petition was presented to the king on Christmas Eve 1847. A few days later, on 27 December, the Chamber of Commerce in Turin held a public banquet to celebrate the administrative reforms and to demand further political reforms. Among the 620 guests was pastor Bert who, to general applause, was asked to speak for the Waldensians. On 5 January 1848 Carlo Alberto assured the Waldensian 'Table' that he would do 'all that was possible' and entrusted the Conference Cabinet[12] with the task of drafting an emancipation edict for non-Catholic subjects.

---

[11] N. Nada, *Roberto d'Azeglio I. 1780–1846* (Roma, 1965); D. Bosio, 'Dove, quando e come fu formulato l'Atto di Emancipazione', *Bollettino della società di studi valdesi*, 15 (1898), 68–73.

[12] The Conference Cabinet consisted of the Cabinet and of the king's principal advisers.

IV

On 8 February 1848 Carlo Alberto publicly announced the imminent concession of a constitution, the *Statuto*. A few days later, the Conference Cabinet secretly discussed the project of emancipation prepared by d'Azeglio. Some ministers suggested that Article 1 of the *Statuto* be followed by a second article enshrining the equality of all civil and political rights of all non-Catholics. Carlo Alberto, however, insisted that the emancipation of the Waldensians be dealt with not in the constitution, which accorded the Catholic faith the status of the only 'state religion', but in a separate edict. The edict sanctioning the emancipation of the Waldensians was signed by the king on 17 February:

> Taking into consideration the loyalty and good character of the Waldensian population ... we have conceded ever greater relief to our subjects, granting frequent and long dispensation from observation of the laws. Now that the reasons for those restrictions have become obsolete, the system in their favour which has already been progressively adopted can reach its completion. We are happily determined to have them share in all the advantages which are reconcilable with the principles of our legislation ... The Waldensians are free to enjoy all the civil and political rights of our subjects; to attend schools as well as the university, and to obtain academic grades. Nothing has changed, however, concerning the practising of their religion and the schools directed by them.[13]

The content of the emancipation edict was made public on 24 February in the *Gazetta Piemontese*, while care was taken to postpone the publication of the actual text. The Turin Waldensians gathered at the pastor's house in order to celebrate and to find out all the details. Within a short time a large crowd had gathered and begun to chant patriotic songs hailing freedom. The theology student Jacques Parandier spread the good news in the valleys, while pastor Bert wrote a letter to the Moderator summoning all Waldensians to Turin on Sunday 27 February. On that day, at eight o'clock in the morning, the Waldensians gathered outside the Legations' Chapel to attend the first free Protestant worship in public. At ten o'clock they rejoined the crowd in the procession arranged to celebrate liberty. Roberto d'Azeglio greeted the Waldensians, arranging for them to be at the head of the procession which had reached Castello square, where the king was awaiting them. The official procession was opened by a blue silk flag with the Savoy coat of arms and the following

---

[13] Regie Patenti, 17 febbraio 1848.

words embroidered in gold: 'The Waldensians are grateful to Carlo Alberto'.[14] A new era was beginning for Italian Protestants. On 28 February a brief article appeared in *Il Risorgimento* in which pastor Bert regretted not having been able to celebrate the Waldensians' reconquered liberty with the Catholic clergy in a brotherly way, but hoping that the Catholics would understand the reasons for their happiness. On 4 March 1848 the *Statuto*, the new constitution of the kingdom was promulgated, which solemnly sanctioned the principle of civil equality of all subjects. Article 24 stated: 'all citizens of the kingdom, whatever their title and status, are equal in the eyes of the law. All shall enjoy civil and political rights equally and can be admitted to civil and military positions, except in the cases determined by law.'

This last clause, however, was dangerous, and did not escape the notice of more attentive readers; since freedom of religion had not been established in the *Statuto* and the Catholic religion had been defined as the 'state religion', there was nothing to prevent the 'exceptions' from affecting the rights of the non-Catholics.[15] The following March the new electoral law was published, which allowed electors to vote regardless of their professed religion. It was not yet entirely clear, however, if the extension of rights applied only to the Waldensians and the Jews or if it applied to anyone who professed a religion other than Catholicism. A special law was necessary to resolve the dilemma, which was proposed by a group of Liberal Members of Parliament and approved by a large majority in June 1848. The law stated: 'A difference in religion does not prevent the enjoyment of civil and political rights, nor the eligibility for civil and military office'.[16] It is only fair to note that at the beginning of 1848 the Piedmontese sovereign was not the only one to concede civil and political rights to non-Catholics. A similar initiative was also taken by the grand duke of Tuscany, Leopoldo II, who – as part of a wider plan of political and administrative reforms, and responding to demands by liberal public opinion, supported with particular force by the Catholic priest Raffaello Lambruschini – promulgated an edict in which he abolished legal discrimination towards religious minorities. In 1849, however, after a brief Republican interlude and the subsequent return of the grand duke backed by the Austrian military, all concessions were withdrawn.

[14] J.-J. Parandier, 'La fête du 17 février', *Bollettino della società di studi valdesi*, 15 (1898), 58–67; A. Jalla, 'Le manifestazioni valdesi del febbraio 1848', *Bollettino della società di studi valdesi*, 49 (1927), 56–62.

[15] E. Comba, 'L'interprétation progressive de l'Edict d'Emancipation en corrélation avec la Constitution et telle qu'elle a été provoquée par la Maison Évangélique Vaudoise', *Bollettino della società di studi valdesi*, 15 (1898), 75–94.

[16] *Atti del Parlamento Subalpino, Documenti, 1° legislatura, Sessione 1848*, pp. 64–5.

V

For a better understanding of the concept of 'emancipation' for Italian Protestants one has to start with an examination of the text of the edict of 17 February 1848 and of the *Statuto* of 4 March 1848 that succeeded it, which put an end, at least on a formal level, to any legal discrimination against non-Catholic subjects. The very definition of 'non-Catholics' reveals how far away the state still was from considering all religious faiths as equal.[17] According to the first article of the *Statuto*, the 'Roman Catholic faith' was the 'state' religion, while the two 'permitted' religions – Waldensianism and Judaism – enjoyed no more than public recognition. The *Statuto* of the kingdom of Sardinia – which served as the constitution of the new kingdom of Italy and remained officially in force until the declaration of the Republic in 1946 – confirmed, although with some ambiguity of expression, the edict of 17 February. The edict of 1848 did not amount to complete religious freedom: the Waldensians could be viewed as full citizens, or rather subjects, but, as the edict stated, 'nothing [had] changed, however, concerning the practising of their religion'. Theirs was a 'permitted religion', nothing more and nothing less.[18] The emancipation of the Waldensians and the Jews marked the end of a regime of religious intolerance that had already been progressively eroded in recent years and had appeared by then to be useless and counterproductive. But the concession of civil rights to the Waldensians represented above all a secure way of guaranteeing the support of Great Britain and Prussia for the king of Sardinia and his anti-Habsburg politics. The change of attitude of the Savoy authorities towards the Waldensian coincided with the political change in attitude of the leading liberal group, which still had strong links to the 'neo-Guelph' Catholic tradition in the early 1850s, became more laical in the 1860s and turned potentially anticlerical towards the end of the century. Although Catholicism remained officially the religion of the state, religious faith came more and more to be regarded as the private concern of the individual, who was expected to give public testimony of loyalty to the state and the monarchy rather than declare his or her religious convictions. The civil and political emancipation of the most significant Protestant minority in Italy coincided with the attainment of civil and political rights by all subjects of Savoy, who were the first among the Italians to become 'citizens'

---

[17] U. Marcelli, 'Dibattito al Parlamento subalpino sulla questione degli acattolici', *Bollettino della società di studi valdesi*, 102 (1954), 57–62.
[18] G. Peyrot, *Rapporti fra Stato e Chiesa Valdese in Piemonte nel triennio 1849–51* (Milan, 1955).

– albeit with many restrictions – of their country in March 1848. The two issues cannot be separated.

The right to take part in parliamentary elections was conceded in the *Statuto* as being independent of religious affiliation.[19] Also allowed to vote in local elections, the Waldensians in the period 1848–49 had already won nearly all the council seats and mayoral posts in those places where they formed a majority. Given their geographical concentration, it is possible to follow quite precisely the Waldensians' electoral behaviour from 1848 onwards. In spite of the fact that very few Waldensians were allowed to vote on account of the restricted franchise (only 450 out of the 22,000 valley inhabitants had the right to vote between 1848 and 1861), and even though they were always in the minority by comparison with the Catholic voters, their vote was initially concentrated on candidates from the liberal left. In the four parliamentary terms from 1849 to 1853 the Waldensians finally managed to have one of their own candidates elected: the entrepreneur and banker Giuseppe Malan, who was a political ally of Cavour and held his seat until 1859.[20] The entry of a Waldensian deputy into the Subalpine Parliament was undoubtedly a significant turning-point and a symbol of the political emancipation of the religious minorities. However, it was not until 1886 that the Waldensians managed to have one of their representatives returned to Parliament again. Both before and after the unification of Italy the Waldensians confirmed their loyalty to the government and to the monarchy, identifying themselves with the liberal and moderate politics of the 'Historical Right'. After having elected Giuseppe Malan for three legislative periods, the electorate of the valleys began to prefer the government's candidates. Between 1876 and 1886 they elected Colonel Geymet, a Catholic of Waldensian origin, who protected their interests. While this can be taken as an indication that a visible Protestant presence on a political-institutional level remained a problem, it can also be seen as a consequence of emancipation, or even as a symptom of successful integration. Within Italy's new liberal political class religious faith was no longer a defining element. National and, above all, political identification were more important. In 1889, thanks to the extension of the franchise, votes from the Waldensian valleys were divided between two candidates for the first time, both of whom were Waldensian, but each of whom belonged to different political parties. Between 1886 and 1897 the Conservative

---

[19] P. Notario and N. Nada, '*Il Piemonte sabaudo. Dal periodo napoleonico al Risorgimento* (Turin, 1993).

[20] W. Meille, *Souvenirs de Joseph Malan* (Turin, 1889); U. Marcelli, 'Alcuni rapporti fra Cavour e i Valdesi', *Bollettino della società di studi valdesi*, 104 (1958), 77–84.

candidate Giulio Peyrot had the upper hand, but between 1897 and 1911 his rival Enrico Soulier, supported by the Left, was elected. Figures of public standing excepted, it is difficult to make hypotheses about the political sympathies of Italian Protestants outside Piedmont. As far as the Waldensian urban population was concerned, it can be assumed that, notwithstanding a more marked inclination towards the Liberal party and a strong anti-Catholic bias, their political leanings did not differ substantially from those of the majority society. By contrast, the voting habits of the other Protestant denominations outside Piedmont, which were deprived of any territorial roots comparable to those of the Waldensians, leaned heavily towards the Left. Mainly originating from the ranks of Garibaldi, republicans and (later on) socialists, these Protestants were organised into the 'Free Christian Churches', the 'Church of Brethren', the 'Methodist Church' and many other groups. They never stood a chance of electing one of their own candidates and nearly always voted for the democratic opposition, in particular for the exponents of the radical and anticlerical Left.

VI

An important source for documenting the attitude of the Waldensians towards the vicissitudes of Italian politics is their principal newspaper, which directed public opinion from 1849 onwards. It was alternately called *L'Echo des Vallées* (Echo of the Valleys) and *Le Témoin* (The Witness) and was strictly Francophone until 1939. Although it seldom contained political articles as such, it did not show any liking for Mazzini and the republicans and was solidly pro-government. Between 1848 and the turn of the century the Waldensians' involvement in national politics was limited. Even the news of the *Risorgimento* seemed remote to the inhabitants of the valleys. When the Waldensians did take part in the unification process they nearly always did so within the official institutional boundaries. After the victory of the Piedmontese army at Goito on 30 May 1848, for example, the Moderator urged all the pastors to hold a solemn service.[21] In September the *Echo* advised Waldensians against evading military service. The Waldensian Church took on the task of making sure that the valley population fulfilled their 'patriotic' duties, thus contributing to the building of a 'national' identity. The day after the defeat at Novara in 1849 a 'Table' delegation met with the new king,

---

[21] Archivio della Tavola Valdese, Carteggio Tavola, vol II (1848–49), doc. 92: circular, 2 June 1848.

Victor Emmanuel II, to pay him homage and ask him to confirm their recently acquired liberty. The day after Cavour's death, on the 6 June 1861, the Waldensian newspaper, *La Buona Novella* (The Good News), featured a commemorative article. The Waldensians made countless protestations of loyalty to the sovereign, often accompanied by thanks for the freedom that they obtained in 1848. Some thousand Waldensian soldiers – nearly all of them peasants from the Valleys – participated in the 1866 war.[22] Among them was a non-commissioned cavalry officer, Enrico Gay, (1842–86), who participated in Garibaldi's attempt to liberate Rome the following year. In 1870 an unusual amount of space in the *L'Echo della Verità* (Echo of the Truth) was dedicated to the inauguration of the Ossuary of Saint Martin at the site of a battle in 1859, at which the pastor Giorgio Appia was present as a representative of the newly formed Red Cross. When Victor Emmanuel II died, the valleys held mourning processions. In the village of Perrero, in Val del Chisone, black ribbons were adjusted to attached to flags, while the members of the consistory wore black badges on their arms.

The process of integrating the Waldensians into the national Italian community was completed, at least on a symbolic level, with King Umberto I's two visits to the Valleys in September 1893, ten years after the writer Edmondo de Amicis had exalted the virtues of the small and freedom-loving mountain people as worthy of the admiration of all Italians. The two successive celebrations of the *glorioso rimpatrio* (glorious homecoming) in 1889 and the emancipation in 1898 were organised in concert by the Waldensian deputy, Giulio Peyrot, and the civil and military authorities of the liberal Italy. At the end of the century, these two festivities symbolised the beginning of a process that would take the Waldensian community, by now fully integrated into the national community, to the rediscovery of the historical key to its own identity. A clear indication of the 'nationalisation' of the Waldensians at the end of the century is their use of the term *rimpatrio* (homecoming) instead of *rentrée* (re-entry) to refer to the long march through the Alps which some thousand exiled Waldensians made from the banks of Lake Geneva to their valleys of origin. It was as though the Waldensians from the end of the seventeenth century had returned to an 'Italian' homeland. In those years they began to re-read their history, highlighting their impressive loyalty to the Savoy monarchy throughout the centuries. In 1889 the *Société d'histoire vaudoise* (Waldensian History Society) was

---

[22] P. Gnudi, 'Valdesi nella terza guerra d'indipendenza (1866)', *Bollettino della società di studi valdesi*, 141–2, (1977), 27–52.

formed, which was subsequently changed to *Società di studi valdesi* (Society for Waldensian Studies), and the Museum of Waldensian History was opened in Torre Pellice, a place for both the conservation and the reconstruction of the memory of the 'church-people' and an instrument for the dissemination of a certain image of Waldensian history to the outside world: the history of persecuted men and women, who never gave in, who were exiled but never uprooted, who were cast out but not beaten, and who were above all heroes of the recent Italian history.[23]

VII

From 27 February 1848 onwards, the date when they first came down from the valleys *en masse* to take part in the demonstration for the *Statuto*, the Waldensians took part in all of the monarchy's main festivals, especially in the Festival of the *Statuto*, which was officially turned into a national festival in 1851.[24] In 1851 Giuseppe Malan mentioned in Parliament how the Protestants placed particular emphasis on the Festival of the *Statuto* because it corresponded with their own celebrations of liberty. In Turin and the more important centres of the valleys festivals took place where, by mutual agreement, Protestants and Catholics went to their respective churches for the religious services and then joined forces for parades and other celebrations. In 1854 and 1861 the Waldensian synod timed the Festival of Emancipation, established in 1848, to coincide not with the date of the promulgation of the emancipation edict but with the national celebration of the Festival of the *Statuto*. The 'nationalisation' of their anniversary of emancipation was, for the Waldensians, a reaffirmation of their pact with the monarchy and of their belonging to a civil, subalpine and Italian society. Thus, at the very moment of affirming strongly their separate identity, the Waldensians brought about their full integration into liberal civilisation. It was only at the end of the century that 17 February came to be known as the 'Waldensians' national festival', celebrated first only in the valleys, with the traditional fires of thanksgiving, and then throughout the communities in the Diaspora as a religious festival with worship, prayers, songs and convivial banquets. The first 17 February celebrations to take place outside the valleys was in 1871, in Leghorn, followed by Naples in 1876 and Turin in 1879.[25] Apart from Easter and Christmas, the only two

[23] G. Bouchard, *I valdesi e l'Italia* (Turin, 1988).
[24] I. Porciani, *La festa della nazione. Rappresentazione dello Stato e spazi sociali nell'Italia unita* (Bologna, 1997).
[25] G. Tourn, B. Peyrot, *Breve storia della festa del 17 febbraio* (Torre Pellice, 1994).

Waldensian festivals are those of the 17 February and 15 August, the latter of which was a Protestant answer to the Catholic festival of the Assumption of the Blessed Virgin.[26] Of all the national festivals, apart from the Festival of the *Statuto*, the 'Taking of Rome', signifying the end of the pontifical state, enjoyed particular popularity. Delegates from Protestant Churches, Jewish communities and the masonic world participated in this festival.

VIII

With the evangelising push that followed the unification of Italy, Italian Protestantism began to change in nature and appearance. Up to that point, confined to the mountain and rural population of a few Piedmontese valleys and to a few scattered groups of foreigners, Protestantism had, effectively, remained outside the course of Italian history. After 1860, however, it became ever more involved in the vicissitudes of the nation's development. The new circumstances primarily affected the Piedmontese Waldensians who, in the decade following the emancipation, had consolidated their presence in Turin and extended their it to other localities within the Savoy state. The Waldensian Church, however, continued to be firmly rooted in its valley traditions – its peasant world, its French tongue (as well as its Franco-Provençal patois), its cult of historical memories focusing on its founder, the merchant Valdo, and his followers among the poor of Lyon, its adherence to the Genevese Reformation, its seventeenth-century heroes Janavel and Arnaud, its centuries-old relationship with England – which linked the Waldensian valleys to Protestant Europe but not to the rest of Italy. After 1848 only a minority of Waldensians thought of extending their Church's presence to the whole of the peninsula. Even the presence of pastor Giorgio Appia (1827–1910) in Garibaldi's *Mille* ('Thousand') was the result of an individual's initiative and not of the Church's official planning. The growth of the Protestant community in Turin after 1848, with the addition of Protestants of foreign origin, and the conversion of Piedmontese ex-Catholics or, more commonly, of exiles from other Italian states, soon began to concern the Waldensians of the 'old stock'. 'The Italians', as the Protestants not originating from the valleys came to be known, found it difficult to gain acceptance. They were denied the right to elect deputies to the synod and were placed instead in a confederate, but nonetheless separate, 'Italian congregation'. The adoption of the Italian language for religious services, even though it was only in the parishes outside the

---

[26] G. Tourn, *I Valdesi. Identità e storia di una minoranza* (Torre Pellice, 1993).

valleys, did not please the Francophone Waldensians. Even those who believed that the Waldensian Church should step outside the narrow confines of the valleys and Piedmont still thought that the identity of Italian Protestantism should remain tied to the Calvinist mould, to the authority of the synod and the 'Table', with its well-structured pastoral body, rather than embrace the 'anarchical' spirit of other Protestant groups that were appearing spontaneously in various parts of Italy.[27] The two factions clashed during the 1860 synod and the majority made the following resolutions: first, the theology faculty of Torre Pellice (founded in 1855) would be transferred to Florence; second, the 'Table' would continue to direct only the communities in the valleys and in Turin, while the new Protestant infrastructure that had sprung up throughout Italy would be directed by the newly-founded Evangelisation Board, which was elected by the Synod but was independent of the 'Table'.

If for the Piedmontese Waldensians the slow process of emancipation was still continuing after 1861, for the rest of Italian Protestants it had only just begun through the patient work of dozens of itinerant evangelisers who spread the news of a new way of living the Christian faith, based primarily on Bible readings and inspired by the fundamental principles of the Reformation, but not immediately identifiable with the theology of Luther or Calvin. To try to describe what constituted Italian evangelisation one can point to four symbolic groups. First there were the itinerant almanac sellers, who came from the Waldensian valleys or were delegated by the 'Bible Society' and who distributed the first Italian translation of the Bible throughout the peninsula. Second were the itinerant evangelists, for the most part self-taught, who were the first point of reference for small groups of followers. Third were the pastors, most of whom were Waldensians, Methodists or Baptists, who came in to give stability to the newly-built communities. Unlike the others, the pastors were either graduates of the theology faculties of Protestant Europe or converted ex-Catholic priests. The fourth and final group was that of the school teachers, working in overcrowded village or city schools, which were identified by the population as the real innovation brought about by the new faith.

IX

Let us now try to draw a map of Protestant Italy from the day after unification. The most numerous and best organised communities were

[27] P. Geymonat, 'Emancipazione ed evangelizzazione', *Bollettino della società di studi valdesi*, 15 (1898), 95–105.

those of Piedmont, which were situated not only in the Waldensian valleys and Turin but also in the rural province of Alessandria where, between 1850 and 1860, numerous little 'free' Protestant communities had sprung up. As early as 1849 there had been many Waldensian communities in Genoa, to which a 'liberated' community consisting mainly of the dockyard workers, had attached itself. Outside Piedmont, the only other region where there was a significant Protestant presence was Tuscany. Thanks to the relative tolerance of the grand-ducal governments, foreign Protestant communities were formed in Florence, Pisa and Leghorn, which included a few Tuscans. In Florence a Swiss Calvinist church opened in 1826. The first Italian-speaking Protestant community in Florence was centred around Pietro Guicciardini in the latter half of the 1830s, who was a friend of the Catholic priest Raffaello Lambruschini (1788–1873), a liberal agronomist and pedagogue who, having been close to Protestantism during the 1830s and 1840s, eventually returned to a liberal brand of Catholicism. Apart from a handful of intellectuals, the Florentine Protestant community included numerous members of the working classes, like the Madiai couple, who were sent to prison in 1851 for reading the Bible in Italian. Their condemnation provoked protests throughout Europe, until British, Prussian and French diplomatic pressure secured their release. After 1849 even Guicciardini was exiled to Britain, where he came into contact with the movement of the 'Plymouth Brethren'. Upon returning to Florence in 1860, he founded a Protestant community on the 'Plymouth' model, which had ties with many other communities in Tuscany, Liguria and Piedmont. The inauguration of the Waldensian Faculty of Theology in 1861 and the opening of a new Waldensian temple in 1863 brought the presence of 'historical' Protestantism to Florence. The figures from the 1861 census put the number of Protestants in the former grand duchy at 4,396. Following the Savoy troops, the first Waldensian missionaries reached Milan in 1859, founding an urban community with a working-class base but also with a significant number of members of the lower middle class. In the Po Valley, between Lombardy and Emilia, the first Protestant communities sprang up between 1859 and 1860, mostly linked to the 'Free Churches' and to Alessandro Gavazzi's preaching. In Emilia in particular, the 'Gavazzian' Protestant communities carried a strong democratic and republican political connotation. In some cases they were identified with masonic lodges or with the growing number of workers' societies.[28]

---

[28] G. Spini, *Risorgimento e protestanti* (Milan, 1989); G. Spini, *Studi sull'evangelismo italiano tra otto e novecento* (Turin, 1994).

In southern Italy the spread of Protestantism was likewise closely tied to the *Risorgimento* and, in particular, to Garibaldi's operations. The first evangelisers were followers of Garibaldi, such as the ex-Barnabite Alessandro Gavazzi, who had already been active in Rome in 1848–49 and was later exiled to England,[29] the ex-friar Luigi Pantaleo, who founded the 'National Primitive Catholic Society' in Sicily, and the ex-priest from Naples, Pietro Taglialatela, who was destined to become the philosopher of the 'Free Churches' in the south before becoming an adherent of the Methodist Church. In spite of difficulties, the diffusion of evangelical communities of various denominations, many of which refused to be defined as 'Protestant' in the territory of the former kingdom of Naples, was incredibly fast in the months immediately after Garibaldi's expedition. The 1861 census registered 2,708 Protestants in the Neapolitan provinces as compared to 9,522 in Naples and 6,755 in Sicily in 1871. The Waldensian missionaries were quick to follow. Their most well-known representative was pastor Giorgio Appia, founder of the Palermo, Catania and Messina Waldensian communities as well as of the Franco-Italian congregation in Naples and in the Sicilian community of Riesi, a mining village. In the far south the work of evangelical preachers met with the greatest difficulties, coming up against the hostilities of the Catholic population who were spurred on by intolerant parish priests.[30] One of the most serious cases was the riot that broke out in the small town of Barletta in Puglia on 19 March 1869 during the festival of San Giuseppe. As the 'Evangelical Society' had refused to participate, a few Catholic priests persuaded the faithful masses to attack the houses belonging to the 'heretics', which provoked a riot that resulted in the death of six evangelists. This episode provoked the army's intervention and had serious repercussions in Parliament, where the government tried to minimise the magnitude of the events. Those responsible for the massacre were arrested and given severe sentences.

The evangelisation of the Veneto, from which the Austrians were ousted only in 1866, came fairly late. While the countryside remained securely under the control of the Catholic clergy, Protestant centres were built in the main cities: in Verona and Venice by the Waldensians; in Padua by the Methodists; in Treviso and Udine by the Free Churches. Last came the city of Rome, capital of the Papal States, destined to become the capital of Italy, and finally occupied by Italian troops on 20 September 1870. Tradition has it that two members of the 'Bible

---

[29] L. Santini, *Allessandro Gavazzi. Aspetti del problema religioso del Risorgimento* (Modena, 1955).

[30] G. Gangale, *Revival. Saggio sulla storia del protestantismo in Italia dal Risorgimento ai tempi nostri* (Palermo, 1991); V. Vinay, *Storia dei Valdesi: Dal movimento evangelico italiano al movimento ecumenico (1848–1978)* (Torino, 1980); Spini, *Studi sull'evangelismo*.

Society' breached the barrier at the Porta Pia, carrying with them the first Italian translations of the Bible, which had been banned until the day before by the pontifical authorities. In the months following the conquest of Rome numerous Italian and foreign evangelical missionaries arrived in the capital: first the English 'Wesleyan' Methodists, then the American 'episcopalist' Methodists, followed by the English and American Baptists, and finally the missionaries from the Gavazzian Free Churches, who rejected any organisational structure, and the Waldensians. The work of the evangelists and missionaries was so effective that the second census carried out by the unified Italy at the end of 1871 registered 4,146 Protestants of different denominations resident in Rome.

X

The slow but constant growth of the Protestant presence in Italy is documented by the post-unification censuses: in 1861 Protestants accounted for 32,684 out of over twenty-two million inhabitants – excluding Rome and the Venetian territories – concentrated mainly in Piedmont. Fifty years later, in 1911, they accounted for 123,253 out of 34.6 million inhabitants throughout the entire peninsula.[31] As far as the Waldensians were concerned, integration into the national community was complete by the beginning of the twentieth century. Discrimination seemed to have diminished at all levels and Waldensians were to be found in public administration, schools and the army, as well as in the professions and the business world. It has to be said, though, that the Waldensian elite was numerically tiny and the majority of the valley population was linked to the agricultural world. In the rest of Italy, with a few exceptions, Protestants belonged mainly to the lower classes: workers or peasants, small-scale artisans or employees, with the occasional tradesman or entrepreneur to be found in northern Italy. It is not possible to talk of a 'Protestant middle class' as existed in other European countries. Halfway through the century a Protestant lower middle class began to emerge, clearly divided into two components. On the one hand were Protestants of Waldensian origin, present mostly in Piedmont, Liguria and Lombardy and made up of teachers, lawyers, tradesmen and small-scale entrepreneurs, who became substantially assimilated, even on an ideological level, into the liberal middle class, especially during the Giolittian era. On the other hand there was a Protestant lower middle class that had its origins in the evangelisation of Italy, made up of state employees, technicians, skilled autodidactic workers, often with Methodist inclinations, leaning towards democracy rather than liberalism and not devoid of

---

[31] V. Vinay, *Soria dei Valdesi* (Turin, 1980).

socialist sympathies. The first group was more conservative and closed, the second more dynamic and open.

In the multifarious world of 'Free Churches' which formed in Italy in the 1860s, two stand out as more important than the others: the 'Christian Church of Brethren', which was organised on the Plymouth model and was in terms of religion the more rigorous of the two, yet less active politically and socially, and the 'Free Christian Church', which was of a Garibaldinian mould, democratic and republican, and politically committed in a progressive sense. This latter changed its name in 1889 into 'Italian Evangelical Church' in order to underline its national character, as distinct from the Waldensians who were still closely associated with their valleys. The Italian Evangelical Church was not as successful as expected. By the beginning of the twentieth century it had disappeared, being absorbed by the other Protestant denominations, in particular by the Methodists.[32]

In the political class of the new Italy there was a small but significant number of Protestant names – none of them originating from the old Waldensian nucleus. One must mention first the physician and art critic Giovanni Morelli, who was Swiss in origin. Born in Bergamo and brought up in Germany, he was elected as a member of parliament in 1860 and was returned four times to the Conservative benches before his nomination for the senate in 1873. Undoubtedly more famous than Morelli was the philosopher and Puglian jurist Bonaventura Mazzarella, who had been educated in the Hegelian school in Naples, but later moved on to neo-Kantian beliefs. He was elected deputy in 1861 for the extreme republican Left and was returned to Parliament until 1880, where he was always fighting against corruption, for the development of the south of Italy and in favour of democratic decentralisation.[33] Different again was the figure of Baron Sidney Sonnino, the son of a Tuscan Jew who had turned Anglican and of an Englishwoman. He was returned to Parliament in 1880 for the moderate Left but later converted to the Conservatives. Several times a minister and for a brief spell Prime Minister in 1906 and 1909, Sonnino was one of the principal architects of a nationalist foreign policy between the First World War and the collapse of the liberal regime. With the nomination of a Protestant as head of government, all discrimination seemed to have come to an end, at least on a political level. Moreover, with the new penal code that came into force in 1889, all religions practised in Italy were given an equal status for the first time. Articles

---

[32] G. Spini, *L'Evangelo e il beretto frigio. Storia della Chiesa Cristiana Libera in Italia 1870–1904* (Turin, 1971).

[33] S. Mastrogiovanni, *Un riformatore religioso del Risorgimento. Bonaventura Mazzarella* (Torre Pellice, 1957).

140, 141 and 142 held out the prospect of severe punishment for anyone who offended or interrupted the religious practices of 'one of the religions allowed in the State'. On a more fundamental level, however, Protestants continued to be discriminated against by the Catholic population, especially in the rural areas. From the the conquest of Rome until the arrival of fascism the history of Italian Protestants is, therefore, linked with the history of a struggle for affirmation of full religious freedom in a country that was overwhelmingly Catholic. And if we observe the geography of the evangelical movements which developed predominantly in southern Italy between the end of the nineteenth and the beginning of the twentieth centuries, we can see that it corresponds, in general, to the geography of the social movements that struggled for the rights of labourers and peasants against the large landowning families. Between the nineteenth and the twentieth centuries one may observe an explosion of evangelical movements in southern Italy, from Molise to Calabria, from Puglia to Sicily. In the course of two decades tiny Protestant communities sprang up everywhere, founded sometimes as a result of evangelisation efforts and in other cases following the return of emigrant workers from the United States who had converted to Protestantism over there.[34] The great emigration wave which affected rural Italy at the end of the nineteenth century involved Protestants to a great extent: thousands of Waldensians from the valleys emigrated to France and to Canada, especially to Francophone Quebec; others found a particularly favourable atmosphere in the United States, since it was a Protestant country; still others emigrated towards Latin America, especially to Uruguay and Argentina, where they founded Waldensian agricultural colonies still in existence today, at present counting around 15,000 inhabitants.[35]

We can draw the following conclusions. First, in the course of the second half of the nineteenth century the Waldensians of Piedmont, emancipated in 1848, became slowly but progressively Italianised, even if their participation in national life remained extremely limited. Second, the process of integration of Italian Protestants into the national community seemed to be complete by the early twentieth century, owing to the diffusion of Protestantism throughout the peninsula. Third, the Waldensian Church and other Protestant denominations adapted to an Italian society that was sustained by the liberal movement and its institutions, while simultaneously keeping themselves strictly separate from the state and refusing any financial contributions or institutional support.

---

[34] Spini, *Studi sull'evangelismo*, 136.
[35] E. Tron, 'I Valdesi nella Regione Rioplatense', *Bollettino della società di studi valdesi*, 89 (1948), 46–76.

9

Italian Jews

Gadi Luzzatto Voghera

To write the history of Jewish emancipation in Italy on the assumption of a unified Jewish experience common to all Italian Jews is impossible. The political, economic and jurisdictional fragmentation of the peninsula does not allow it.[1] At the end of the eighteenth century Jewish communities existed in all Italian states with the exception of the kingdom of Naples, from where the Jews had been expelled in 1541, already before the Counter-Reformation. The Papal States included the large community of Rome (three- to four thousand Jews), but also the fairly large centres of Ancona, Sinigallia and Urbino in the Marches and, within Emilia-Romagna, that of Ferrara. The grand duchy of Tuscany counted two large settlements, one in Florence and the other, more important, in Leghorn, a great commercial centre in which a very active Sephardic community flourished. Smaller communities existed in Siena, Pisa, Arezzo and Pitigliano. The kingdom of Sardinia ruled over the numerous small Piedmontese communities, which in the course of the nineteenth century, became concentrated around Turin, Vercelli, Casale Monferrato and Alessandria. The Jewish *università* (corporate community) of the Veneto was ruled by the Republic of Venice, which alternated between a restrictive and a liberal Jewish policy. The communities in Gorizia, Gradisca d'Isonzo, Trieste and the large community of Mantua with its hinterland of small settlements in the Po Valley fell

---

[1] No comprehensive study on the emancipation of the Jews in Italy exists. One can only refer to the dated volume by A. Milano, *Storia degli ebrei in Italia* (Turin, 1963), and to a second volume, edited by C. Vivanti, *Storia d'Italia. Gli ebrei in Italia*, 2 vols (Turin, 1997). See now: G. Luzzatto Voghera, *Il prezzo dell'eguaglianza: il dibattito sull'emancipazione degli ebrei in Italia, 1781–1848* (Milan, 1998). For overviews in English, see Andrew M. Canepa, 'Emancipation and Jewish response in mid-nineteenth-century Italy', *European History Quarterly*, 16 (1986), 403–39; Dan V. Segre, 'The emancipation of Jews in Italy', in Pierre Birnbaum and Ira Katznelson (eds), *Paths of emancipation. Jews, states, and citizenship* (Princeton, 1995), pp. 205–37; L. M. Gunzberg, *Strangers at home. Jews in the Italian literary imagination* (Berkeley and Los Angeles, 1992).

under the direct jurisdiction of the Habsburgs. The duchies of Modena and Parma ruled over the remaining numerous small settlements in Emilia and over the two large communities in Modena and Reggio. This was evidently a rather fragmented picture overall, and even more so when one considers the specific role that each tiny community played in the restricted local areas in which it functioned. In addition, there were internal divisions, the consequences of which are sometimes difficult to interpret: there were 'ethnic' differences between the Jews of the Italian tradition, the Sephardim – who were in turn subdivided into Levantines and Ponentines (often reconverted Marranos) – and the Ashkenazim, who had their origins either directly in the German lands or, as in the case of the Piedmontese Jews, in Provence. But there were also significant social divisions. A small economic elite almost always dominated the administration as well as the cultural life of the individual community. It managed the benefit funds which were abundantly drawn upon to permit the survival of the vast majority of poor Jews.

On the eve of the so-called first emancipation, caused by the invasion of Italy by French armies in 1797, the Jewish population amounted to little more than thirty thousand, scattered over the whole peninsula. We are, therefore, not dealing with a particularly important community from a quantitative point of view. It is misleading, however, to use these statistics to establish a direct relationship between the number of Jews in Italy and the overall population of the peninsula and express it in terms of percentage. This kind of arithmetical exercise has produced serious distortions in the historiography of Italian Jewry and has often lent itself to political manipulations that have had serious consequences in recent history. It has been stated, for example, that the alleged absence of anti-Semitism and of a 'Jewish question' in Italy was due to the fact that Jews never exceeded one per thousand of the entire Italian population.[2] Other historians have concluded that the considerable presence of the Jews, in spite of their small number, and their commitment in the fields of culture, economics, public administration and the military (in particular during the wars of independence and the First World War but also in the Resistance) are proof of their perfect integration into Italian society.[3] Finally, the Fascists have claimed that it is precisely this 'over-representation'

---

[2] R. De Felice, *Storia degli ebrei italiani sotto il fascismo*, 4th edn (Turin, 1993), pp. 5–64. The remarks on the presumed inconsistency of anti-Semitism seem particularly fragile. The quantity of Jews does not, in itself, constitute a variable determining the degree of anti-Semitism within a population or culture.

[3] Milano, *Storia degli ebrei in Italia*, pp. 382–91.

which demonstrates that the Jews occupied posts which were not due to them and that their presence ought to be radically reduced.

An impartial reading ought to correct these assumptions, which are based on questionable arithmetic. First of all, from the vantage point of their geographical distribution, it becomes clear that the Jews had resided for almost half a millennium only in central and northern Italy. Therefore, the south should be excluded from any statistics. With regard to the 'over-representation' of Jews in prestigious positions, the brief initial description of the distribution of Italian Jewish communities has indicated the great and variegated divisions within the communities themselves. Each single group operated in an entirely autonomous manner. The existence of a group mentality or of a willingness to behave like a 'lobby' remains to be proven. If, for example, in 1919–20 Professor Ludovico Mortara, the son of the rabbi of Mantua, was Minister of Justice for a brief period, it was not because of his close relations with the numerous Jewish lawyers on the register. There naturally existed trends, which were often easily identifiable and explicable on a historical level, that pushed the Jews into a clearly defined range of occupations. The high percentage of Jewish traders who were dealing on the Roman market in the nineteenth and twentieth centuries has been noted. It is equally obvious, however, that for several decades neither were these individuals registered with, nor did they pay taxes to, a Jewish community, notwithstanding the fact that they entertained official and stable relations with their Jewish counterparts in other Italian regions. The dispersion and the lack of a unity of purpose between the different Jewish communities lasted throughout the nineteenth century. Until after the First World War no permanent body existed to administer and co-ordinate the various Jewish communities of the peninsula, and even afterwards relations between the different communities remained complicated when it came to political, cultural, legal and economic decisions.[4]

With regard to the claim of over-representation, there were those who, like the historian Salvatore Foà, strongly emphasised the presence of at least eight Jews among Garibaldi's 'Thousand' who in 1860 started the unification of Italy – a fact which hardly seems surprising.[5] The Thousand were an elite group drawn from the younger generation of the

---

[4] The first attempt to provide an overall regulation of the relation between Jewish communities and the state was the so-called 'Legge Rattazzi' of 1857. See I. Rignano, *Della ugualianza civile e della libertà dei culti secondo il diritto pubblico del regno d'Italia* (Livorno, 1857); G. Disegni, *Ebraismo e libertà religiosa in Italia* (Turin, 1983).

[5] S. Foà, *Gli ebrei nel Risorgimento italiano* (Rome, 1978), p. 67.

educated northern Italian bourgeoisie, precisely the milieu in which a new generation of Jewish citizens had grown up. This generation was educated in institutions where the 'first commandment' was integration into the liberal fatherland. What is rather more astonishing is that there were only eight Jews among them. But if, in the years of integration, the pages of the Piedmontese Jewish newspaper *Il Vessillo Israelitico* (*Jewish Standard*) exalted the high percentage of Jews in all of the most advanced areas of national development,[6] in the years of Fascist persecution (1938–45) these same percentages came to be used to denounce the excessive Jewish presence and their unjustified obtrusiveness. These reasonings, being both false and manipulative, are speculative and can be exploited for opposite political purposes, but in essence they do not differ. Arguments about percentages should not, therefore, be applied to the study of Italian Jewish history. It makes far more sense to concentrate on the demographic significance and the economic and cultural role performed by the individual Jewish communities in their respective areas of residence. And it would doubtless be of great interest to discuss the Jewish 'peculiarities' which pushed individual Jews or groups of Jews to act in a specific way. To facilitate this, however, it would be necessary to undertake numerous studies exploring the history of individuals and different regions. In this chapter we will closely follow the vicissitudes of the life of a Venetian Jew and thereby attempt to identify trends that, albeit with many variations, have dominated the complex process of the legal, economic and cultural emancipation of the different Italian Jewish communities.

The economic and social emancipation of the Italian Jewish communities during the nineteenth century was an agonising process that can be said to have come to a conclusion only in 1870 with the end of the Papal States and the fall of the walls of the Roman ghetto. From the very start of the century Jews from a specific social stratum began to transform their cultural characteristics and to redefine their economic activities, with the explicit intention of becoming part of Italian society as quickly as possible. The small elite of landowners,[7] shipowners and entrepreneurs, consisting of only a few dozen families throughout the whole

---

[6] The newspaper boasted of the Jewish identity of Luigi Luzzatti (Prime Minister in 1910–11), while the politician denied that he was a Jew, vehemently admitting it only when confronted with acts of anti-Semitism.

[7] A number of references to the existence of Jewish landowners can be found at the time of the first emancipation (after 1797) and in some cases also before. See P. Bernardini, *La sfida dell'uguaglianza* (Rome, 1996), p. 31; Luzzatto Voghera, *Il prezzo dell'eguaglianza*, pp. 13–17.

peninsula,[8] began a broad programme of re-education and acculturation of the great majority of the Jewish population in schools and through technical education for men and women.[9] Two of the programme's objectives are of particular interest. Its first aim was to prepare the great majority of the poor Jewish population for participation in the middle-class model of social and economic life, which meant moving away from such occupations as money-lending and trading in small goods and used clothes (paradigmatic for the ghetto economy) and retraining for artisanal occupations, urban commerce, small businesses and administrative work. The second objective concerned the sense of Jewish belonging. The programme aimed to turn this key element in the direction of a 'religiosisation' that was free from all those particular forms of social aggregation which, to some extent, could appear to conflict with a total participation in the new bourgeois society of the nineteenth century. Participation was meant in the sense of the model designed in 1807 by Napoleon's Great Sanhedrin.[10] The second part of the project envisaged, for example, the transformation of the Italian rabbinate into a kind of 'Jewish clergy', deprived of economic and administrative autonomy, relegated more and more to functions of a strictly religious nature and subordinated to the economic and political elite of the community.

I shall try to illustrate these various points by following the vicissitudes in the life of a single personality and of a single community: Moisè Soave, a Jew from the community of Venice.[11] Although this one person cannot be regarded as a prototypical Venetian or Italian Jew during the emancipatory period, his case-study can help us to understand this period of rapid and turbulent transformation.

---

[8] Among them the Treves de'Bonfil, the Franchetti, the Romanin Jacur, the Massarani, the Wollemborg, the Ravenna, the Malvano, the Alatri, the numerous branches of the Levi family, the Vivante, the Brunner and the Morpurgo.

[9] In Germany the process of *Bildung* in the definition of Wilhelm von Humboldt played a similar role in the emancipation of the Jews. See D. Sorkin, *The transformation of German Jewry, 1780–1840* (Oxford, 1987).

[10] The Great Sanhedrin, which convened in Paris in 1807 and in which many Jewish notables and rabbis from France, Alsace, Italy and other locations were represented, responded to a variety of questions the Napoleonic administration had directed at them in order to demonstrate that Jews could integrate into European society. See S. Schwarzfuchs, *Napoleon, the Jews and the Sanhedrin* (London, 1979).

[11] On Moisè Soave, see the meagre biographical notes and the rich and detailed bibliographical review in C. Musatti, 'Il Maestro Moisè Soave', *Archivio veneto*, 36 (1888), 383–97; 37 (1889), 381–419; for interesting aspects of his intellectual life see M. Berengo, 'Luigi Luzzatti e la tradizione ebraica', in P. L. Ballini and P. Pecorari (eds), *Luigi Luzzatti e il suo tempo. Atti del convegno internazionale di studio* (Venice, 1994), pp. 527–42, in particular pp. 532–4; G. Luzzatto Voghera, 'Cenni storici per una ricostruzione del dibattito sulla riforma religiosa nell'Italia ebraica', *Rassegna mensile di Israel*, 60 (1993), 47–70.

I

From the outset one should avoid comparing Moisè Soave to the most famous Venetian Jewish figure in world literature, Shylock. Soave, like all his Venetian co-religionists living in the nineteenth century, had almost nothing in common with the Shakespearean character, save his place of residence. The atmosphere into which Soave was born, on 20 April 1820, was a very degraded one, in stark contrast with the image generally put forward by the historiography on emancipated Jews in nineteenth century Western Europe. The ghetto of Venice had been formally abolished by the provisional government in the summer of 1797. It was, however, only from 1805 onwards, after the establishment of the kingdom of Italy, that Jews were granted complete emancipation – that is, the possibility of living as free citizens with equal rights and being subjected to the same obligations as the rest of the population. After the Restoration in 1815 the legal situation of the Jews in the Habsburg Lombardo-Venetian kingdom did not change in any radical way. Certain restrictions were reintroduced, but in essence, the formal conditions did not deteriorate particularly.[12] In other parts of Italy the Restoration had worse consequences. In the Papal States the gates of the ghetto were closed again, as in Piedmont, which had serious repercussions on the social and cultural conditions of large numbers of Italian Jews, not to mention the grave economic damage done to those enterprises which had previously had the resources to buy factories, mostly in the textile sector, and farmland. Having tasted civil equality for less than twenty years, the Jews once again found such activities forbidden to them, and they were therefore forced to fall back on petty trading, the sale of used clothes and money-lending, the traditional economic activities of the ghetto. The Jews of Tuscany were luckier. Some restrictions notwithstanding, they could consider themselves as practically emancipated. They lived in conditions that were more or less comparable to those of the Jews in Lombardy and the Veneto.

But in what sense were they emancipated? Does the image of Jews who (on attaining civil equality) were able to enter economic and social life with all speed, to change professions, to shed their cultural traditions and to take steps towards complete assimilation really correspond to reality? Did these Jews assume prestigious positions in politics, finance, public administration and the army and achieve instant and resounding success?

---

[12] See M. Berengo, 'Gli ebrei veneti nelle inchieste austriache della restaurazione', *Michael*, 1 (1972), 9–37; M. Berengo, 'Gli ebrei veneziani alla fine del Settecento', *Italia Judaica*, 3 (Rome, 1989), 9–30.

Or – and this is one of the questions that will be explored in this chapter – did only a tiny elite of Jewish families profit from civil emancipation in the nineteenth century, in contrast to the large majority of Italian Jews who struggled hard for the slightest improvement of their living conditions and for a social mobility that, for a long time, was very limited? On the other hand, if the first scenario were true, we would be confronted with no less than a social miracle: it appears to be a fairly unlikely proposition that – in an under-developed Italy with backward manufacturing, without a real entrepreneurial middle class of its own, with an enormous peasant population, an urban proletariat still limited in numbers and a commercial class that was in general impoverished and had limited hopes of social mobility – only the Jews should, from scratch and immediately, transform themselves from rag-and-bone men into well-to-do professionals and businessmen.

The reality was not like that, and Moisè Soave discovered this as a child. His family, living right in the middle of the emancipation years, was poor. His father, Salomon Raffael (nicknamed 'Momolo'), lived by his wits and did not really make sure that his children were properly fed. Sometimes he could buy them clothes, at other times he could not. They were used to worn and threadbare garments, well suited to people living in one of the poorest areas of Venice, the Ghetto. In 1820 the old Jewish quarter was still populated mostly by Jews. When the first signs of a slow transformation were beginning to show, it was a change for the worse. With the ending of the Venetian Republic, the Jewish community had in fact stopped concerning itself with the ordinary maintenance of the houses, roads, bridges and canals that constituted the Ghetto. The municipal authorities had for a long time shown little interest, so that the quarter was deteriorating progressively into a state of general neglect. Many houses, particularly in the New Ghetto, had been abandoned by families who preferred healthier living conditions and who tended to move to the Cannareggio quarter to be nearer to the synagogue. Those who continued to live in the Ghetto were either the poorest families or, as in the case of the Soaves, non-Venetians who had moved to the city in search of better economic opportunities.[13]

It is one thing to live in a house, even if it is rather modest and dilapidated, but quite another to procure the necessary means of living and maintaining a family. Someone like Salomon Raffael Soave always had access to numerous agencies for charitable aid. Such agencies continued

[13] Soave himself tells us that his father was 'originally from Parma'. Letter from Moisè Soave to S. D. Luzzatto, dated 29 June 1858, Centro Bibliografico U.C.E.I., Rome, Archive of Samuel David Luzzatto, faldone 7, cartella 2.

to exist even after the termination of the Jewish segregation in ghettos. State aid, by contrast, was still unavailable to Jews. However, the particularly effective Jewish welfare network seemed capable of satisfying the most immediate demands of the numerous poor families. But how many of these families were there? For the 1820s we have only approximate figures. However, if we move on only two decades, we can confirm that in 1840 Venice had 2,137 Jewish inhabitants or 434 families.[14] Of these, little more than a third – 149 families – were capable of contributing to the 'religious tax' of the Jewish community, and of these families, in turn, only eleven made up for more than fifty per cent of the entire balance.[15] These were the same wealthy families, the Treves de'Bonfils, the Vivantes, the Levis, the Erreras, who before the fall of the Venetian Republic had distinguished themselves by their entrepreneurial strength to the extent that they were considered 'separate' families who enjoyed, among other privileges, some exemption from the regime of segregation in the Ghetto. Into a different category from this small elite fell the large mass of 285 families who could not afford to pay one Austrian *lira* per month as a contribution to the community. Like the majority of Jewish families in other Italian communities they lived just above or below the poverty line. Among them was the family of Moisè Soave and his younger brother Marco.

In 1828, after years of tribulation, Salomon Raffael Soave decided to enrol his two children at the *Midrash reshit da'at*, the Jewish elementary school. There were at least three good reasons why he did so: first and foremost, because he had to comply with the law of 22 January 1820 on compulsory education; then, as we understand, because the school, in addition to instilling the children with culture, provided them with a substantial meal thanks to the generosity of the wealthier families; and lastly, because it was customary for a Jew, however poor, to be able to read at least the book of daily prayers (*Tefillah*) and to be fairly familiar with the basic elements of tradition. If the commonly held view of a total absence of illiteracy among Jews was wishful thinking rather than reality, it is nevertheless revealing that the figures for Venice show that in 1829 more than 325 Jewish children between the ages of three and sixteen were enrolled at the twenty-four family-run Jewish schools.[16] Twenty-five years earlier, in 1805, only 56 out of 315 children of school age had been

---

[14] Archivio Comunità Ebraica di Venezia (ACEV), b. 67 '*Anagrafe Civile*, fasc. 1840'.

[15] ACEV, b. 219 *Tassa Culto*, 'Fraterna Generale. Stato dei nuovi accordi coi contribuenti biennio 1835/36'.

[16] ACEV, b. 178 *Scuole morali*, lists of those registered at the Jewish schools.

pupils there.[17] Thus, there is evidence of a considerable degree of progress in achieving literacy among the Jewish population.

It was not easy, however, to register Moisè and Marco at school. First, a certificate had to be obtained from Chief Rabbi Elia Aron Lattes, confirming the children's good behaviour.[18] Then they had to go and see the physician, Doctor Giuseppe Ravenna, who had to issue a vaccination certificate. In the presence of the district health officer and representatives of the school authorities the physician examined all school applicants and would find a variety of diseases. Nearly twenty per cent of the children were reported to be suffering from ringworm, an infection of the scalp, probably as a result of the living conditions in the Ghetto.[19] On 31 March 1829 Moisè Soave, after passing through this bureaucratic procedure, was finally admitted to the first class of the primary school, at the house of the schoolmistress (Ester Padovani Scandiani), no. 1485 in the Old Ghetto. And there we encounter something which needs to be explained. It has been argued that the Jews under Austrian rule enjoyed more or less civil equality. Why then did they attend Jewish schools and not the state schools? In the first months of 1820 some Jewish families tried to enrol their children into state schools, in compliance with the newly-issued education laws. They met with resistance from the authorities, who issued an explicit order allowing Jewish children to attend the state schools but simultaneously put pressure on the Jewish community to set up a school of its own.[20] In the end the Jewish children were admitted to the state schools. For religious instruction, however, it was agreed that these children would have to attend the Jewish schools.[21] The situation was somewhat confused in practice. The children of the well-to-do families continued to be taught by private tutors at home. Many of the younger children attended only the first years of schooling at the Jewish schools, whereas only a few of the older children – 41 out of 325 in 1829 – went to the state schools.[22] Moisè Soave was nine years old when he first received instruction in religion as well as in reading and writing from

---

[17] Archivio Storico Comunale di Venezia (ASCV), *Anagrafe 1805*, alphabetical list of all Venetian inhabitants, listed with their religion and profession; some boys appear as 'students'.

[18] ACEV, b. 178, *'Suppliche per ammissione di alunni (1824–29)'*. Soave's date of birth given here differs from the date indicated by M. Coen Porto in the obituary that appeared in the periodicals *Vessillo Israelitico*, no. 31, 1883, *Corriere Israelitico*, no. 21, 1883 and *Mosè. Antologia Israelitica*, no. 6, 1883.

[19] ACEV, b. 176 *Scuole morali*.

[20] ASCV, 1820. *Scuole*, Prot. 5522, letters from Rabbi Jacob Recanati.

[21] Ibid., *Accettazione faniculli Ebrei alle Scuole pubbliche*, 27 July 1820.

[22] ACEV, b. 178, *Scuole Morali*.

the wife of a man who was to become his teacher for all his Hebrew studies: master Moisè Padovani.

II

Soave went on to a Jewish general school, at which the language, the culture and the traditions of the Jews were taught following a model in some ways similar to the *cheder* of the traditional Jewish community in Eastern Europe, but with some substantial differences.[23] Among these differences were the comparative paucity of Talmudic studies, the introduction of the Austrian catechism, *Bene' Zion,* and the presence of very young children in the lower grades, but in some cases also in the advanced grades. The most important difference, however, was that in contrast to the traditional schools in Eastern Europe, the language of instruction in Venice, as in all other Italian communities, was neither Yiddish nor Hebrew but the vernacular. In 1829 only one Jewish general school existed in Venice. In these years, however, vocational training schools that responded better to the demands of Jewish society were built throughout Europe. On the one hand, the children of the poor had, at least in theory, the opportunity of learning a trade there that was not necessarily linked to commerce. This gave them the hope of improving their occupational and social standing. On the other hand, the families of the elite of the community invested enormous financial resources into these vocational training schools: every effort had to be made to prove that the civil emancipation was being well received by the Jews who were committed to changing their occupational profile with the aim of becoming ever better subjects and model citizens.[24] The underlying cause was probably a paternalistic attitude, for it certainly contradicted the immediate interests of an upper middle class that, given its social ambitions, could not permit itself to be lumped together with a mass of underprivileged beggars who had no means of sustenance. A new generation of citizens was trained – one that was educated and well versed in every kind of 'productive' trade, that is to say a generation far removed from the anti-Semitic image of the Jew as parasite. With this perspective in mind numerous vocational training schools were founded in the Italian Jewish communities. Among them those of the greatest importance was the *Pie*

[23] *Cheder*, Hebr. lit. 'room'.
[24] In spite of the apparent contradiction in terms of 'subject' and 'citizen', the Jewish catechism *Bene' Zion* provides the inclusion of the two concepts in the Lombardo-Venetian kingdom, cf. *Bene' Zion. Libro d'istruzione religiose-morale per la gioventù del regno Lombardo-Veneto* (Venice, 1828), ch. 9, pp. 241–59.

case israelitiche di ricovero e d'industria (Jewish industrial school) in Mantova, founded in 1825 and visited three years later by Emperor Francis I. Venice had to wait a few more years. From 1822 a school existed which trained girls for domestic work, but only in 1843 did a vocational training school comparable to that in Mantova open its doors. It had not been particularly easy to bring about its establishment. Early on, the bellicose Rabbi Abraham Lattes, a graduate of the rabbinical college in Padova, had asked peremptorily whether the abandoned and jobless Jews, 'lazy youths', could go to the municipal *casa d'industria* (industrial school), maintaining that, as citizens Jews had the same duties but also the same rights as everyone else.[25] The director of the school gave a negative reply. Since his school formed part of the public benefit system, it constituted an exception from the general permission given to the Jews to attend state schools and universities.[26] The director, a member of the noble Querini family, appeared to be afflicted by nostalgia for a regime of segregation that had ceased to exist almost half a century earlier and seemed unable to come to terms with a society that had changed profoundly. Venetian Jews had, in certain cases, already gained access to public institutions. At the provincial hospital, for example, an entire section, complete with separate kitchen, warder and mortuary, was expressly dedicated to Jewish patients. However, resistance was such that in the end the Jewish community was obliged to open a separate branch of the *casa d'industria* in the Ghetto, with a modest contribution from the municipality. As is evident, resistance to the full emancipation of the Jews was still widespread in the very social fabric of the city and not just in the upper political echelons.

Moisè Soave only discovered this several years later. We do not know, whether his father, had he had the opportunity, would have steered him towards a vocational training school, but what is certain is that the young Soave was a good pupil. Throughout his studies he obtained the highest marks in all subjects in spite of the unfavourable atmosphere in which he had to study. His family belonged to that great majority of poor families who frequently turned to the *Fraterna di Culto e Beneficenza*, the community charity, for aid. Only perseverance and a great love of books can explain the continual progress which the young Moisè made in his studies. The school was a kind of shelter, and many efforts were made to keep the pupils away from what was surely an unhealthy and perhaps also a criminal atmosphere. A warder had the task of guarding the school

---

[25] ASCV, 1840–1844, VI, 7/11, 'Attivazione casa filiale d'industria israelitica', letter from A. Lattes of 27 June 1842.
[26] *Ibid.*, letter from Querini dated 7 July 1842.

gates, and if he did not want to remain outside for the whole day Moisè Soave had to arrive by eight o'clock in the morning. From 1835, a teenager by now, Soave was also enrolled at the ordinary state school, to which he and his fellow classmates were accompanied by the school warden, so they were not bothered along the way by ill-intentioned people who could lead them into 'depraved' ways.[27]

To continue his studies and thereby improve his social position held out little prospect of success for Soave. When he was due to sit the exams which he had to pass in order to be admitted to his final year of studies (which was, at the same time, the preparatory year for going on to the rabbinical college in Padova), his material situation was bordering on the desperate. A few weeks earlier the first cases of cholera had been registered in the Ghetto, which threatened to spread first of all to the poorest families who lived in unsanitary conditions. The name of Soave's father, Momolo, was put on the list of those entitled to receive some charitable funds from the community as well as the minimum necessary to sleep in a clean and healthy environment (as far as possible), which meant a straw mattress, one cover, two sheets and a basic bed.[28] In spite of this help Momolo was obliged to beg the school authorities for an outfit for Moisè so that he could turn up to his exam decently dressed.[29] We do not know whether or not Moisè's father worked and, if he did, what kind of work he might have done, but we do know that he never managed to earn enough money to provide his son with a decent shirt.

Nevertheless, the young Venetian Jew passed his exams brilliantly. After a further year of study he graduated and prepared himself for a job, full of hope. Besides the classical subjects, Bible classes, Hebrew grammar, religious precepts and also some *Mishnáh* and rabbinical literature, Moisè Soave had studied in some depth a text which, for the entire first half of the nineteenth century, was the moral and spiritual guide for any good Jewish citizen in the Lombardo-Venetian kingdom: the *Bene' Zion*.[30] The version he possessed was a translation and a partial revision of the German original which had been in use in Austria for some time. It consisted of nine chapters which were subdivided into 411 paragraphs. It discussed the fundamental principles of everyday life, paying great attention to the balance between an absolute faith in man's rational faculties and an equal trust in religion and faith in God. Whether it was man, with

---

[27] ACEV, b. 180 *Scuole Morali*, '1837 Istruzione', rules for the supervision of students, 18 January 1837.
[28] ACEV, b. 202 *Sanità*, '1835'.
[29] ACEV, b. 180 *Scuole Morali*, '1835 Scuole religiose morali'.
[30] See note 16.

his reason, or God, they naturally followed the same principles of virtue and morality. Any rebellious behaviour and disrespect for religion and civil laws was, therefore, regarded as a deviation from the laws of nature and the will of God. The young Jew who studied in the nineteenth century grew up with the conviction that he lived in a world that would eventually be free, where he could choose any profession or occupation, where he would be considered an equal citizen and governed by a just sovereign who issued just laws, because he was inspired directly by God. One has to understand that, now that the emancipation had been achieved the overall aim was to live in harmony with the majority society and to respect all the rules and laws of the state. The young Jews were, therefore, encouraged to take on professional careers that were different from their traditional commercial activities – for example, to train as artisans or to work in agriculture or navigation. Alongside these recommendations went the basic principles of bourgeois liberalism, which they took as their guide to correct social behaviour: 'everyone has the duty not to impede the development of the strengths of his fellow citizens, and not to disturb them in the possession and enjoyment of their property';[31] the free citizens were united in a 'civil society', which corresponded to a single state; all citizens were naturally obliged to love their state and to consider it their fatherland, for which they also had to be prepared to die. All this advice, the substance of which expressed the corner-stone of the manual of the good citizen living in a nineteenth-century nation state, was laid down in the *Bene' Zion*, getting its strongest justification from the Holy Scriptures. Thus, a connection was established between modern society and religious tradition. It was not the first time that such an operation had been proposed for Venetian and Italian Jews. As early as 1807 the Great Sanhedrin set up on the instigation of Napoleon – and in which among others the Venetian rabbi Jacob Cracovia participated – was expected to approve a whole series of rules that were intended to regulate the life of emancipated Jews in civil society. In this case too, it had been necessary to insist that Jews abandoned their traditional economic activities and at the same time to demonstrate that Jewish traditions were not in any conflict with modern society.

Let us now return to our Moisè Soave and the other young people of his generation. They were asked to abandon their traditional economic activities, but Moisè could have asked himself what activities were meant, since he and his father lived on charity.[32] Surely, he was so filled with

---

[31] *Bene' Zion*, p. 242.
[32] In 1840 Moisè Soave received a small charity donation, ACEV, b. 67 *Anagrafe Civile '1840'*, list of 20 July 1840.

love for his country that when the occasion arose he would not hesitate for a second to take up arms; but not exactly for the fatherland for which he had been taught to fight – that is to say, the Austrian Empire. In 1848 the twenty-eight year old Moisè Soave, having gained his teaching diploma,[33] abandoned his honourable profession to defend the fledgling Venetian Republic at Fort Marghera from the assaults of an army which, until a few months earlier, had been ruled by the sovereign whom God had chosen for him, according to what he had learnt from his study of the *Bene' Zion*. Soave must have realised a long time ago the hypocrisy that wound its way through the pages of the school catechism. He considered himself a free citizen, even if he was still incredibly poor. Perhaps he was less tolerant of the impositions of the established authorities, whether they were represented by His Majesty's government or the heads of the Jewish community, precisely because of his dreadful economic situation. As soon as he had obtained his teaching qualification he managed to get a three-year contract from the community to teach the lower grades. He was, however, continually trying to improve his situation. While teaching he cultivated his philological studies with great passion, to which he owed his friendship with Samuel David Luzzatto, a famous professor at rabbinical college in Padova. He could not bear the idea that any authority could prevent him from fulfilling his duties as he thought fit. Therefore, in the spring of 1842, he was suspended from teaching for ten days because he had refused to conform to the timetable.[34] After his contract had expired in late 1843, Soave found himself out of work, just as he was about to marry his cousin Dolcetta Calabi.[35] He decided to give up teaching for a while and took up a job at the Vivante firm.

III

From a certain point in his life Soave made tutoring for the wealthy Jewish families in Venice his main occupation, and so he signed his name 'Maestro Soave'. 'Master' is a title that in the Jewish tradition is not limited to teachers, but is also used to denote people of a certain level of education, men of culture, wise men who show the right path to those who listen. It corresponded in many ways to the image of the rabbi before the emancipation, who was more than a shepherd of the souls and was above all a judge and a learned cultivator of the Jewish tradition. In the

---

[33] ACEV, b. 181, *Scuole Morali*, '1839 Istruzione'.
[34] *Ibid.*, '1841 Istruzione', precautions of 29 March 1842.
[35] Soave had six children from the marriage, of which only Giacomo and Rosa outlived their father.

case of Soave, this notion turned into the image of the new, typically nineteenth-century, learned, non-practising Jew, with a very personal idea of the Jewish tradition. On the other hand, the very image of the rabbis in Italy had changed rapidly in the course of the nineteenth century, as the majority of the Jewish population gradually distanced itself from respect for traditional teachings. This was not only a question of religion but also a social matter. One has to remember that, with few exceptions, the large majority of rabbis, who were either educated directly in the minor communities or graduates from the rabbinical colleges in Padova, Leghorn and Piedmont (the last functioning only for a short time), came from extremely poor families. By taking on rabbinical duties these people became the indisputable religious authority and had, in theory, the same level of responsibility as the lay-leaders of the community, who were inevitably representatives of the middle-class economic elite. In some cases the rabbis assumed an even more important role.

In Venice, for example, the municipal authorities were not over-particular in distinguishing between the various internal ranks within the Jewish community, and they invariably directed their correspondence straight to the rabbi, who in this case would almost assume the function of political as well as religious representative of the Jews. This became such a source of controversy that during the nineteenth century all the community's new laws contained quite restrictive rules for the rabbinate. The rabbis thus came to be regarded as employees who could be dismissed whenever the communal authorities saw fit. They were expected to concern themselves with teaching and religion and not to interfere in politics and community administration.[36] The result was the creation of something which one can only call a 'Jewish clergy', relegating the rabbinate to a role which it had never had before. This, I suggest, is one of the principal causes of the substantial cultural impoverishment suffered by the Italian Jewish communities in the nineteenth century. The rabbis, who were once the 'masters', could no longer dedicate themselves freely to studying and teaching, for in a century of forceful secularisation they were held hostage by an increasingly uncertain professional situation and were subjected to continual economic blackmail. Moisè Soave who never became a rabbi, could, in this sense, still be regarded as a free 'master'.

Although instilling Judaism into the descendants of the wealthy families who were well on the way to a decisive secularisation was probably not his first choice, it nevertheless gave him the opportunity to continue

---

[36] The most incisive attempt to unhinge this situation was carried out by Lelio Cantoni, a leading Piedmontese rabbi, whose *New Order of the Jewish Religion in the Royal States* was rejected by a large part of the Piedmontese communities.

his studies, making the most of the well-equipped private Jewish libraries which were, by then, no longer being used. At the same time he developed his own autonomous concept of Judaism, which was motivated by an authentic desire for change. This he expressed in his writings, which, in my view, place him among those most explicitly in favour of a Jewish Reform inspired by Italian Judaism. Reform, incidentally, was never officially recognised in Italy in the same way that it later flourished in Germany, then in the United States of America and, to an extent, in Britain and France. The communities of the peninsula were occasionally tempted to introduce new ways of following the Jewish tradition, but no decisive initiative was ever taken.[37]

Some elements that were classified elsewhere as Reform were already in existence in Italy: sermons in the vernacular were an old tradition dating back as far as the Middle Ages, and music had been introduced into the synagogues during the Baroque period, even though the introduction of the organ did not pass without controversy. The habit of celebrating the *bar mizwah* (a boy's attaining the age of religious responsibility) with a public ceremony in the synagogues started in the nineteenth century. Numerous translations of the prayer books were introduced for the benefit of the large number of Jews who could by then read Hebrew only with difficulty and who could no longer understand the meaning of what they read. The first photographs appeared on tombstones, violating a centuries-old ban on the adoration of images. However, these changes touched only the external side of a religiousness that remained nevertheless, at least nominally, orthodox. Although some scholars argue that the official introduction of Reform in Italian Jewry would not have made sense, since by their actions Italian Jews showed only a moderate degree of respect for the religious precepts, nobody has in fact carried out any in-depth studies on the subject.

Soave, not being content with any halfway solutions, confronted the problem of Reform head-on. After consulting his friend Samuel David Luzzatto, who had, however, flatly refused to yield to Reform, he thought that the moment had arrived when he should put down in writing what appeared to him to be vital for the survival of a Judaism that was showing clear signs of crisis.[38] Accordingly, he wrote a short pamphlet and published it anonymously.[39] Taking an explicit stance against orthodoxy,

[37] Luzzatto Voghera, *Cenni storici*.
[38] Letters from S. D. Luzzatto to Soave dated 27 July and 5 September 1865 in *Epistolario italiano francese latino* (Padova, 1890), vol. 1, pp. 1066–7.
[39] [M. Soave], *L'Israelitismo moderno* (Venice 1865). In a letter directed to S. D. Luzzatto, Soave speaks of this booklet, which was originally supposed to be a work on the occasion of the wedding of his pupil Emma Treves, cf. Centro Bibliografico UCEI, Rome,

he sided with the Reformists, who wanted 'harmony between religion and the pressing needs of the time'. His pamphlet was about the delineation for the Venetian and the Italian public of what was left of Judaism that ought to be kept and valued and what ought to be abandoned as the inheritance of a dark past. Soave believed he could establish the essentials of Judaism in three dogmas: the existence of God, providence and Moses' prophetic mission. He derived his moral concepts from what he had read as a youth in the *Bene' Zion*, which taught love of one's neighbour, family and country and fraternal charity. These formed the foundations of the 'Israelite Religion', which, with the advent of emancipation, would have to undergo a profound revision. Soave proposed several reforms. Prayers should remain, but in smaller numbers and translated into Italian. The separation between men and women in the synagogues should be eliminated. Some obsolete aspects of religion which had become difficult to justify in modern times ought to be abolished, such as the splitting up of holidays in the Diaspora and the overabundance of days of fasting; it would be better to incorporate them all into one solemn day, Yom Kippur. With regard to the Sabbath, the work restrictions could be limited to the banning only of manual labour on Saturdays. As for kosher food, one should only refrain from eating those animals explicitly forbidden in the Bible.

Soave's position was a rather radical one, having its roots partly in his own personality and partly in the education which had been practised in Italian Jewish schools for decades. He was always restless and strongly against any principle of superior authority. This he had confirmed a short time earlier in a private letter to one of his pupils, the very Luigi Luzzatti who was soon to become one of the most renowned economists in the united Italy, several times a minister and, for a brief period, even Prime Minister. In this letter he described to him how an Anglican priest had tried to convert him by a totally inappropriate sermon, to which Soave had responded in a fairly impatient manner:

> he [the Anglican priest] raged, because since I was a Jew, and according to him a Talmudist, he wanted to catch me out. Poor fool! In order to show him that I do not take my hat off before any authority, be it the Gospel or the Talmud, I gave him my little book on the Tortosa conference.[40]

Archivio di S. D. Luzzatto, faldone 7, cartella 2, letter of 14 May 1865.
[40] Istituto Veneto di Scienze Lettere ed Arti, Archivio Luzzatti, b. 43, letter of 23 October 1863. In all, fourteen of Soave's letters are preserved in this archive. The 'little book' referred to is the *Controversia tenutasi a Tolosa alla presenza dell'antipapa Benedetto XIII fra Girolamo da Santa Fè e alcuni rabbini della Spagna* (Venice, 1862).

Soave displayed this tendency to reject any kind of authority throughout his whole life. His education had also played a part in his designs for reform. The study of the Talmud and rabbinical literature was almost entirely absent from the curriculum. First, this created an abyss between Italian Jews and the vast majority of other Jews scattered all over the world, especially in Eastern Europe, who based their Hebrew studies on the rabbinical tradition. Second, it pushed Italian Jews like Soave towards the belief that the guiding precepts for Jewish social behaviour, whose roots went back to the Talmudic commentaries and to the codification of laws ordered by medieval rabbis (and more recent rabbis like Maimonides and Josef Caro) were out-of-date and against the 'pressing needs of the time'.

This was not the only time that Soave threw himself into a public controversy. In 1863 he intervened in *L'Educatore Israelita* (*The Jewish Educator*) to rebut the criticisms which Elia Benamozegh, the great rabbinical authority and mystic, had raised against Samuel David Luzzatto's comments on the work of Maimonides.[41] It was again the clash between different approaches to Jewish thought which characterised and animated Italian Jewish life. These were last flashes of a vivacity that was becoming progressively less evident until it disappeared almost completely towards the end of the nineteenth century.

Soave spent the last twenty years of his life teaching young boys, to whom he tried to convey his love for the 'good', which he had learned at school.[42] He still held on to some political hopes, strongly believing in the unification of Italy, as did the vast majority of Jews. He saw the dream he had fought for as a young man come true in 1866 when the Veneto was annexed to the kingdom of Italy, and again in 1870, when the Italian army entered Rome after it had lost French protection and the gates of the last ghetto in Europe were knocked down. In the 1870s he dedicated himself to historical research, which brought him into close contact with prominent individuals in European culture, like the Hebraist Moritz Steinschneider and Ernst Renan.[43] Soave died on 27 November 1882.

When the journal of Venetian historical research, the *Archivio Veneto*, decided to celebrate the life of Moisè Soave in 1888, the editor, Bartolomeo Cecchetti, briefly exalted his scholarly talents but did not

---

[41] M. Soave, 'Breve riposta all'opuscolo: "Le missioni di Terra Santa" di E. Benamozegh', *L'Educatore Israelita*, 8 (1863).

[42] Archivio Luzzatti, letter of 12 November 1864.

[43] Numerous letters from Soave to Steinschneider are conserved at the Jewish Theological Seminary of America in New York. I would like to thank Dr Seth Jerchower for this invaluable information.

omit to highlight his critical attitude towards Jewish Orthodoxy. Speaking from a nationalist point of view, he reproached Jews for their tendency towards cultural separatism and admonished them: 'If there is anyone who needs to be forgiven for something, let him show a true desire for social equality which is morally worth very much more than material justice'. Soave would not have been happy with this obituary. He, who had struggled for national unity and fought in his own way for full emancipation, had to come up against another 'Anglican priest' even after his death – a secular, Italian priest this time, who disputed his Jewish character. The wind of modern anti-Semitism had begun to blow in Italy too, and new obstacles were erected to prevent full emancipation.[44]

---

[44] See G. Miccoli, 'Santa Sede, questione ebraica e antisemitismo fra Otto e Novecento', in Vivanti (ed.), *Storia d'Italia*, vol 2., pp. 1371–574.

10

Emancipation as path to national integration

Stephan Wendehorst

This concluding chapter begins with a brief survey of problems in the historiography on the emancipation of religious and religiously defined minorities. Without claiming to give an authoritative interpretation of the individual contributions, I shall then attempt to point out where the present volume has contributed to a better understanding, first, of the emancipatory experiences of Catholics, Jews and Protestants and, second, of the interaction between emancipation and nineteenth-century nation-building in Britain, France, Germany and Italy. The last paragraph contains suggestions for further research.

I

The study of a minority's experience is interesting not only for its own sake but also for what it reveals about the society which surrounds that minority. Although the perspective of a minority provides the historian with a vantage point from which many apparently well-known historical developments appear in a different, less familiar light, this approach has two potential drawbacks. First, there is a danger of regarding the minority's relations with society at large as being determined primarily by a dynamic intrinsic to that relationship rather than by developments that had their origins and purposes elsewhere; and, second, there is a risk of taking into consideration only parts of the surrounding society. How to incorporate the latter is a problem that any study of a minority faces. To relate the minority to major developments within the larger society – in particular, to those of the political spectrum, to public opinion or to the state, are the most common options for bringing the majority society into play.[1] Though legitimate and necessary, these options should not obscure the inevitable losses they entail. The reduction of the surrounding society to key elements, by which its attitudes and actions *vis-à-vis* a minority assume a degree of coherence and direction not necessarily reflected in reality, becomes the more questionable the more fragmented the society. The correlation of the history of a minority with political history is prone to undifferentiated generalisations, for example, the presentation of minorities as quasi-automatically gravitating to the Left or unanimously supporting liberal nation-building projects. As a result, counter-currents and ambivalent stances, such as members of minorities favouring the Right, combining allegiance to the political Left with conservative views on social, economic and religious issues or supporting the traditional order against liberal national movements, have mostly been eclipsed.[2] A potential danger of taking the state as the point of reference for the history of a minority lies in the temptation of taking the policy of the state towards a minority as representative of society as a whole.

By complementing our understanding of the emancipatory experience of religious minorities in two ways we may arrive at a more comprehensive and differentiated picture. First, only by comparing the emancipation of different religious minorities does it become possible to distinguish to what extent the relations of a minority with society at large were determined by a dynamic specific to that relationship or by factors that operated independently of it. With regard to the latter, one can further differentiate between, on the one hand, those factors which characterised majority–minority relations in general, and on the other hand, developments that, although affecting them, had their origins and purposes elsewhere. Second, by exploring the emancipation process of a religious minority as a 'path to national integration', one shifts the emphasis away from the impact of the state and of the factors intrinsic to a specific minority–majority relationship and towards the repercussions that nine-

---

[1] For studies taking political history as the point of reference for the history of minorities, see, for example: G. Spini, *Risorgimento e protestanti*, 2nd edn (Milan, 1989); P. Pulzer, *Jews and the German state* (Oxford, 1992); P. Birnbaum, *Les fous de la république. Histoire politique des juifs d'état, de Gambetta à Vichy* (Paris, 1992); P. Birnbaum and I. Katznelson (eds), *Paths of emancipation: Jews, states and citizenship* (Princeton, 1995), pp. 1–36, esp. pp. 20, 22, 36.

[2] For French right-wing Protestants, see G. Davie, 'Rightwing among French Protestants (1900–1944)', Ph.D. thesis, University of London (1975). For the decline of the Liberals' appeal for British Jews, see G. Alderman, *The Jewish community in British politics* (Oxford, 1983), pp. 31–46. For pro-Habsburg sympathies among Italian Jews, see P. Bernardini, 'The Jews in nineteenth-century Italy: Towards a reappraisal', *Journal of Modern Italian Studies*, 1:2 (1996), 296, 301.

teenth-century nation-building had on the emancipation of a religious minority. The shift to the nation as the point of reference for writing the history of a religious minority makes it possible to highlight the divisions within the European nation states, in particular, by borrowing from theories of nationalism as well as from concepts that question the homogeneity of national societies, such as internal nation-building, sub-culture, *milieu* or *verzuiling*.[3] The result is a picture of the nineteenth-century European nation state that is characterised by divisions along political, religious, social, linguistic and regional lines and by often competing nation-building projects. The study of the internal divisions and of the ongoing struggles for the definition of national societies has led to a more complex and dynamic understanding of society at large and has, in turn, heightened the awareness of the impact of these divisions and nation-building projects on the emancipation of religious minorities.

II

Several recent studies have placed the development of a minority squarely within the context of nineteenth-century nation-building.[4] Following this direction, the present volume has sought to make a further contribution by studying two subjects in parallel: the emancipatory experience of the Jewish minority and of one non-dominant Christian minority within the context of one nation state; and the experience of one minority under the conditions prevailing in different nation states.

Two ideas stood at the beginning of this project: first, to apply the comparative method to the study of the emancipation of religious minori-

---

[3] For internal nation-building, see, for example: E. Weber, *Peasants into Frenchmen* (London, 1979); S. Patriarca, *Numbers and nationhood. Writing statistics in nineteenth-century Italy* (Cambridge, 1996), pp. 1–2, 122–209. For the concept of *milieu*, see M. R. Lepsius, 'Parteiensysteme und Sozialstruktur: zum Problem der Demokratisierung der deutschen Gesellschaft', in G. A. Ritter (ed.), *Deutsche Parteien vor 1918* (Köln, 1973), pp. 56–80. For internal divisions, see T. Nairn, *The break-up of Britain* (London, 1977); P. Nora (ed.), *Conflits et partages, Les lieux de mémoire. Les France*, vol. 3: 1 (Paris, 1992). For *verzuiling*, literally 'pillarisation', meaning the segmentation of society, see A. Lijphart, *The politics of accommodation*, 2nd edn (Berkeley, 1975). For the incompleteness of nation-building, see A. Lyttelton, 'The national question in Italy', in M. Teich and R. Porter (eds), *The national question in Europe in national context* (Cambridge, 1993), pp. 63–105, esp. pp. 99–101.

[4] D. Feldman, *Englishmen and Jews. Social relations and political culture 1840–1914* (New Haven and London, 1994), pp. 1–47, 353–88; D. Blackbourn, *Marpingen. Apparitions of the Virgin Mary in Bismarckian Germany* (Oxford, 1993), pp. 96–120, 282–300; H. W. Smith, *German nationalism and religious conflict. Culture, ideology, politics, 1870–1914* (Princeton, 1995); H. Daalder, 'Dutch Jews in a segmented society', in Birnbaum and Katznelson (eds), *Paths of emancipation*, pp. 37–58.

ties, and second, to throw light on the impact of British, French, German and Italian nation-building on the emancipatory experience of religious minorities. In the present volume the advantages of the comparative approach could only be partially exploited, for the simple reason that scholars equally at home in the histories of different religious groups are a rare species. The extant comparative scholarship on religious minorities tends either to compare one minority in different contexts[5] or, when dealing with more than one religious group, to focus on a specific topic or geographical area.[6] The alternative was to ask historians to write contributions on the religious minorities of which they possessed expert knowledge. The result has been the juxtaposition of separate contributions on the various minorities in Britain, France, Germany and Italy, rather than a comparative study written by a single hand, which means that results are tentative and implicit, as far as the comparative aspect is concerned, and that it remains, by and large, for the readers to draw their own conclusions.

This volume has corroborated existing evidence, presented it from a new perspective, identified so-far neglected problem areas and raised new questions concerning both the concept of emancipation and the impact nation-building had on the emancipation of religious minorities. It is hardly surprising that all the contributors should have underscored the necessity of taking into account not only the formal but also the informal side of emancipation for a comprehensive understanding of emancipation.

---

[5] M. Brenner, R. Liedtke and D. Rechter (eds), *Two nations* (Tübingen, 1999); M. Breuer, 'Orthodox Judaism in Eastern and Western Europe', in D. Kerr (ed.), *Religion, state and ethnic groups. Comparative studies on governments and non-dominant ethnic groups in Europe, 1850–1940*, vol. 2 (New York and Aldershot, 1988), pp. 79–93; Birnbaum and Katznelson (eds), *Paths of emancipation*; J. Frankel and S. Zipperstein (eds), *Assimilation and community: The Jews in nineteenth-century Europe* (Cambridge, 1991); J. Katz (ed.), *Toward modernity: The European Jewish model* (New Brunswick and Oxford, 1987); F. Sofia and M. Toscano (eds), *Stato nazionale ed emancipazione ebraica: atti del convegno 'Stato nazionale, società civile e minoranze religiose: l'emancipazione degli ebrei in Francia, Germania e Italia tra rigenerazione morale e intolleranza'. Roma, 23–25 ottobre 1991* (Rome, 1992); T. Endelman (ed.), *Comparing Jewish societies* (Ann Arbor, 1997).

[6] See, for example: E. François, *Die unsichtbare Grenze: Protestanten und Katholiken in Augsburg 1648–1806* (Siegmaringen, 1991); D. Sorkin, 'Juden und Katholiken: Deutschjüdische Kultur im Vergleich, 1750–1850', in S. Volkov (ed.), *Deutsche Juden und die Moderne* (Munich, 1994), pp. 9–30; W. Altgeld, *Katholizismus, Protestantismus, Judentum. Über religiös begründete Gegensätze und nationalreligiöse Ideen in der Geschichte des deutschen Nationalismus* (Mainz, 1992); V. Caron and P. Hyman, 'The failed alliance: Jewish–Catholic relations in Alsace-Lorraine, 1871–1914', *Leo Baeck Institute Year Book*, 26 (1981), 3–21; for a critique of the failure to look across the confessional divide, see the review article of H. W. Smith, 'Priests, pastors: the transformation of the Christian clergy in nineteenth-century Germany', *Bulletin of the German Historical Institute London*, 18:1 (1996), 29–31.

More original, however, is the emphasis which they have placed on the 'collective' side of emancipation as being a decisive factor in the emancipation of a religious minority. With regard to the intersection of the emancipatory experience of a religious minority with the formation of the modern nation state, it would seem that some reassessment of the implications of nineteenth-century nation-building for religious minorities is called for.

In order to draw a comprehensive picture of the emancipatory experience of a minority, one has to take into account both its 'formal' and its 'informal' emancipation. Even formal emancipation was not unproblematic, despite the fact that by the end of the nineteenth century equality before the law, irrespective of religious affiliation, had been formally enshrined on the national level in Britain, France, Germany and Italy. As far as formal emancipation was concerned, it was the 'small print' of legislation, the tenacity of older legislation discriminating against minorities and the administrative practice which proved crucial for the success (or otherwise) of the emancipation of a religious minority rather than constitutional guarantees of equality before the law and of freedom of conscience.

Encrevé has shown that, after the Revolution the French central government as well as the political class tended, with brief interludes, to defend the rights of Protestants. On the local level, however, where the Catholic Church continued to wield considerable influence and where overlapping social and religious antagonisms were felt directly, Protestants continued to be discriminated against.[7] When it came to the access of Protestant ministers to military barracks and prisons and the erection of Protestant churches, administrative practice favoured Catholicism until well into the second half of the nineteenth century. While the example of the French Protestants illustrates the importance of the administrative practice as well as of the discrepancy between centre and periphery in the implementation of emancipation, in Germany it was also the 'small print' of legislation, a layer of remaining older legislation in the individual states, the difference between citizenship rights at municipal and at state level, as well as exceptional laws that worked to the detriment of religious minorities.[8] Article 14 of the Prussian Constitution of 1850, which, by denoting Prussia as a Christian state served to justify the exclusion of Jews from appointments in the civil service, the military and in teaching, demonstrated that the promise of equality held out by the constitution of the North German Federation and subsequently of the Wilhelmine

[7] See pp. 75–8.
[8] See pp. 104–5, 114–16, 127–9, 130–1.

Empire was not necessarily honoured at the level of individual German states.[9] As Altgeld has pointed out, Catholics continued to be discriminated against formally in a number of smaller German states until 1918. More serious for the deficiencies of the Catholic condition in Germany, however, was the legislation of the *Kulturkampf*, some of which, like the ban of the Jesuit order, continued to occupy a prominent place on the agenda of national politics. Although directed against a numerically small segment of German Catholics, it served as a constant reminder that Catholic participation in the national community remained controversial.

If the formal emancipation of Catholics, Protestants and Jews remained deficient in several respects by the end of the nineteenth century, the picture becomes more problematical when one turns to the informal side. On the social and cultural planes the reservations of the majority society towards members of religious minorities remained strong. In Germany elite groups which were recruited through co-option, such as in academia and the officer corps, remained by and large closed to Jews (and in the case of the former, also to Catholics) until 1914.[10] The example of the German Catholics, who, in contrast to the Jews, were not emancipated in a formal sense, highlights the importance of the concept of 'informal' emancipation: powerful social and cultural conventions, which acted as barriers to their integration, made them 'not only a quantitative, but also a qualitative minority'.[11]

Whereas it has already become standard practice to take into consideration the informal side of emancipation, the emphasis that all the contributors have given to its 'collective' side represents a significant shift in the understanding of what was crucial for the success of the emancipation of a religious minority. Although it is customary to talk about 'Catholic emancipation' or the 'emancipation of the Jews' – the implication being that one is referring to a group – scholarship on the emancipation of religious minorities has traditionally focused on the individual. At the centre of the debate were the struggle for equality before the law, enfranchisement and such topics as access to public office and the opening of career opportunities. Examinations of an emancipated minority as a 'collective' concentrated on its social and economic profile – for example, the embourgeoisement of German Jews. Otherwise, the collective side has been neglected.

Three closely related issues will, for lack of a better expression, be subsumed under the term 'collective emancipation': first, the question of the

[9] See pp. 138–9.
[10] See pp. 115–16, 118, 144.
[11] See p. 112.

conditionality of the emancipation of the individual on the dissolution of the collectivity; second, the parameters within which the state and society at large defined and recognised the collective character of a minority after the emancipation; and third, most important in the long run, whether (and if so, to what extent) the collective continuity of the minority was envisaged as legitimate and desirable in the respective nation state. Given that the emancipation of the individual Catholic, Protestant and Jew – in the sense of equality before the law – was achieved in Britain, France, Germany and Italy, with all necessary reservations and qualifications, by the end of the nineteenth century, one could argue that the real touchstone for the success of the emancipation of a religious minority was its collective emancipation.

The contributors to this collection have demonstrated that it was disagreement about the delimitation of the collective emancipation, rather than the emancipation of the individual, which strained the minorities' relations with the state and the larger society during the nineteenth century. With regard to the debate on the emancipation of Jews in France and Germany Malino and Clark have identified different assumptions about the extent to which regeneration necessitated an abandonment of the Jewish identity and a fusion with the non-Jewish community as an area of disagreement between Jews and non-Jews.[12] Cesarani has argued that it was the permissible behaviour of British Jews in the public sphere which was at issue.[13] More specifically, he has, among other examples, pointed to the debate over the provision of separate Jewish education on the occasion of the 1870 Education Act, where the hostility of Liberal universalism to Jewish particularism showed itself.[14] Apart from the debates over the provision of separate religious instruction and denominational schools, the question of public worship was one of the issues which served as a reminder of the collective quality of religious minorities. Since the opening of Protestant churches in areas without a traditional Protestant presence remained a matter of administrative discretion until the Third Republic, it was, as Encrevé has noted, the religious equality of Protestants that was at issue in nineteenth-century France, not their civil equality, which had been uncontested even during the Restoration era.[15]

When the emancipation of the individual is complemented by collective emancipation, not only does one arrive at a broader concept of eman-

---

[12] See pp. 91, 98, 132–5, 140.
[13] See pp. 49–50, 53–4.
[14] See pp. 47–8.
[15] See pp. 76–7.

cipation but the emphasis on the collective dimension of emancipation also throws into sharper focus the ambivalent relationship between the emancipatory experience of religious minorities and modernisation. The traditional view has been that the success of the emancipation of minorities depended on the emancipation of society as a whole.[16] This picture of emancipation as an intrinsic part of the modernisation process has been questioned.[17] The ensuing debate about the relationship between emancipation and modernity is also reflected in the contributions to this volume. The more radical the critique, the more pronounced the tendency to regard the emancipation of a religious minority and modernisation not as synonymous but rather as partially complementary and partially conflicting processes.

On the one hand modernisation undoubtedly facilitated the emancipation of religious minorities in several crucial respects. As Clark has pointed out with respect to German Jewry, the idea of legal emancipation and the concept of universal citizenship presupposed the transition from the religious and personal law of the *ancien régime* to a modern, abstract, formal and impersonal legal system.[18] A further characteristic of modern societies that was a necessary condition of emancipation was a degree of secularisation, in particular the divestment of the political and public sphere of exclusive religious or confessional attachments. Emancipation also presupposed the destruction of the corporate structure of the political and social order of the *ancien régime* with its estates, guilds and other privileged corporations, or at least the transformation of these bodies into voluntary organisations.

The argument that minority emancipation progressed in proportion to the modernisation of society retains its general validity as long as the focus is on the individual member of a religious minority and as long as one equates modernisation with the evolution of civil society and the emancipation of the individual from the corporate structures of the premodern political, religious and social order. Shifting the emphasis

[16] For expositions of the predication of the minority condition on a liberal state and society, see, for example, R. Rürup, 'German liberalism and the emancipation of the Jews', *Year Book of the Leo Baeck Institute*, 20 (1975), 59–68; Spini, *Risorgimento*; Pulzer, *Jews and the German state*, Birnbaum, *Les fous de la république*.

[17] For challenges of the argument of enlightenment and liberal benevolence towards the Jews, see A. Hertzberg, *French Enlightenment and the Jews* (New York, 1968); Bill Williams, 'The anti-Semitism of Tolerance', in A. J. Kidd and K. W. Roberts (eds), *City, class and culture: Studies of social policy and cultural production in Victorian Manchester* (Manchester, 1985), pp. 74–102; for further literature on the ambivalent liberal attitude towards Jews, see Birnbaum and Katznelson (eds), *Paths of emancipation*, pp. 3–36, 157–205.

[18] See p. 142.

from the individual to the collective and adopting a broader view of modernisation, however, reinforces the argument that the emancipation of a religious minority was not simply a corollary of modernisation but that it possessed a trajectory of its own, which modernisation enhanced in many respects and complicated in others. In order to assess the extent to which the emancipation of a religious minority has been successful or deficient, it seems, therefore, better to treat emancipation and modernisation not as two parallel processes (the success of the latter being automatically sufficient for the completion of the former) and to employ a broad concept of modernisation – one that includes not only the ascendancy of bourgeois society but also the widening of political participation, the birth of mass politics and the expansion of state intervention.

III

As many of the developments associated with modernisation can be subsumed under the heading of state- and nation-building, changing the perspective by studying the emancipation processes of Catholic, Jewish and Protestant minorities as paths to national integration promises to provide a more satisfactory access to the emancipatory experiences of religious minorities and to highlight the impact on them by the respective construction processes of the British, French, German and Italian nation states. The interpretation of minority emancipation as a corollary of a mono-linear, liberal modernisation process favours the bipolar classification of the determinants of the emancipation process as supportive or antagonistic and their equation with the supporters and opponents of modernisation. The examination of the emancipatory experience in the context of modern state- and nation-building, by contrast, shows not only a greater number of variables shaping the emancipation of a religious minority but also that their impact on the minority could be contradictory, depending on which particular aspect of the minority's experience is under scrutiny.

The constructions of the nineteenth-century British, French, German and Italian nation states were the result of different combinations of external and internal state- and nation-building processes. Their trajectories, reflecting national variations on the common theme of the modern nation state, differed significantly with regard to the timing of the emergence of nationally defined civil societies, their underpinning ideologies, the degree of political participation, the areas and the extent of state intervention or the relations between Church and state. Common trends notwithstanding, these differences had far-reaching implications for the emancipation processes of the religious minorities. The impact of selected elements of nineteenth-century state- and nation-building on the emancipatory experience of religious minorities will be discussed in the following. Whether a nation was defined in political, liberal terms, as a religious, cultural or racial community, or in terms of several competing or co-existing national projects was crucial for the chances of minorities to be included in the national community. Although the criteria for inclusion differed, nineteenth-century nation-building shared one characteristic: the demand for a homogeneous, rather than pluralistic, national community. The evolution of civil society in the countries under consideration meant not only the emancipation of the individual from the corporate ties of the pre-modern social and political order but also the formation of a single national body of, ideally, equal citizens and the establishment of an immediate relationship between the individual and the nation. Many of the disabilities and informal disadvantages that religious minorities encountered during the nineteenth century on account of their collective interests were, therefore, not the result of deviations from the modernisation process, but bound up with the emergence of the modern nation state, which presupposed a homogeneous body of citizens and the de-legitimisation of intermediary structures. The hostility towards collective manifestations of religious minorities was not necessarily directed against a particular community as such. Encrevé has pointed out that not only religious prejudice but also etatist considerations had a share in French anti-Protestantism and that it was the logic of the nineteenth-century nation state which went against the diversity of public worship as a potential source of disorder.[19] The aversion towards the collective continuity of religious minorities was not restricted to the state authorities but was shared by adherents of the Enlightenment and liberalism. In France it formed the background for Clermont-Tonnere's paradigmatic demand that: 'One must refuse everything to the Jews as a nation but one must give them everything as individuals; they must become citizens'.[20] As Clark and Malino have pointed out, non-Jewish liberal supporters of Jewish emancipation expected the eventual abandonment of Jewish distinctiveness.[21] Theodor Mommsen's defence of the Jews against Heinrich von Treitschke's diatribes and his simultaneous aversion to manifestations of Jewish collectivity – for example, the post-emancipationist continuation of distinct Jewish social work – was

[19] See pp. 69, 77–8.
[20] Quoted in Hertzberg, *French Enlightenment*, p. 360.
[21] See pp. 91 and 140–1.

characteristic of the liberal ambivalence towards the Jews.[22] Liberal hopes for the dissolution of the collective character of the Jewish minority were not confined to France and Germany but could be found in Britain as well, as Cesarani has argued. The 1870 Education Act, a step on the road to universal, compulsory and non-denominational popular education, which meant the end of autonomous Jewish schools, was met with criticism by parts of the Jewish community.[23] If Italian liberals had near-unanimously advocated Jewish emancipation this did not mean the absence of charges of particularism, as Luzzatto Voghera has noted.[24] The protagonists of the nineteenth-century liberal nation state reacted strongly not only against internal divisions of the nation along religious lines but also against trans-national links entertained by religious minorities. Disraeli's support of the Ottoman Empire in the Eastern Question and the pro-Turkish sympathies of British Jews during the Bulgarian agitation resulted in charges of dual-loyalty on the part of Gladstone and fellow Liberals.[25] In Britain and Germany Catholics were accused of forming a state within a state on the grounds of their allegiance to Rome.[26] In France Protestants faced charges of being German fellow-travellers.[27]

The homogenising efforts of nineteenth-century liberal nation states were not necessarily vehicles of exclusion: they could also serve as a powerful means of including religiously defined minorities, as the Republican French and the Italian national projects demonstrate. The predication of Protestant and Jewish emancipation on the success of a national movement was most evident in Italy, where the conquest of Rome meant not only the completion of the nation state but also the introduction of civic equality irrespective of religious belief.[28] *La nazionalizzazione parallela* – the parallel formation of an Italian national identity by Jews and non-Jews during the *Risorgimento* – has been advanced as an expla-

[22] H. Liebeschütz, 'Treitschke and Mommsen on Jewry and Judaism', *Leo Baeck Institute Year Book*, 7 (1962), 153–82, esp. p. 180.

[23] See pp. 47–8.

[24] Luzzatto Voghera, p. 142. For Italian liberal manifestations of anti-Semitism and demands for the Jews' fusion with society at large, see A. Canepa, 'Emancipation and the Jewish response in mid-nineteenth-century Italy', *European History Quarterly*, 16 (1986), 407–10, 413–15, 428–9; and 411–13, 431 for his assessment of their relative insignificance in comparison with both Italian Catholic opposition to and French and German liberal reservations about Jewish emancipation. See also M. Toscano, 'L'uguaglianza senza diversità: stato, società e questione ebraica nell'Italia liberale', *Studia Contemporanea*, 25:5 (1994), 685–712, esp. 687–95.

[25] See pp. 40, 50–3.

[26] See pp. 13, 113, 144.

[27] See p. 82.

[28] See pp.157–8, 165–6, 172, 186. However, the national unification of Italy brought no substantial improvement for Jews living in the Habsburg territories. See p. 174.

nation for the relatively solid post-emancipationist position of Italian Jews.[29] Even where nationalism was as divisive as in Germany, there was a counter-current, which demonstrated that nation-building could provide an avenue for the inclusion of minorities. The creation of the Borusso-German nation state and the simultaneous completion of formal Jewish emancipation through the constitution of the North German Federation of 1867, which was extended to the South German states in 1871, is a case in point.[30] One also finds examples where, given the opportunity, members of a minority joined the nationalist bandwagon. In Upper Silesia and among the Polish immigrants in the Ruhr area the Catholic clergy acted as agents of Germanicisation, and in the nationalist clashes in Posen German Catholics and Jews tended to side against the Poles.[31] Symptomatic of the success of the national integration of religious minorities was their festive culture. The lack of national identification among German Catholics can be deduced from their reluctance (particularly marked in the 1870s) to participate in the national festivals of the Wilhelmine Empire, the 'Day of Sedan' or the 'Emperor's Birthday' and their creation of an alternative festival culture.[32] The Waldensians, by contrast, deliberately fashioned their communal festivals so that they coincided with the festivals of the Italian nation state and, in part, in opposition to the dominant religion.[33]

An important strand of nineteenth-century internal nation-building, which did not necessarily work in tandem with the emancipation of minorities, was the expansion of political participation. Referring to several recent studies on German Jewry in the Restoration and pre-March era, Clark has pointed out that support for Jewish emancipation was largely restricted to the wealthy and mainly urban social stratum that dominated cameral politics and the liberal press, whereas the numerically stronger rural and lower middle-class constituency which lay outside the margins of the electorate opposed it.[34] Although there was no British parallel for the pre-1848 outbreaks of popular anti-Jewish violence in Germany, Cesarani has argued that modern mass politics raised new problems for minorities on the grounds that policies based on the

---

[29] A. Momigliano, 'A Review of Cecil Roth's *Gli Ebrei in Venezia*', in *idem*, *Essays on ancient and modern Judaism*, trans. by M. Masella-Gayley (Chicago and London, 1994), pp. 225–7.; A. Gramsci, *Il risorgimento* (Turin, 1948), pp. 166–8; for a critique of this argument, see A. Canepa, 'Emancipation', 431–2.

[30] See p. 139.

[31] Smith, *German nationalism and religious conflict*, pp. 167–205.

[32] See pp. 116–17.

[33] See pp. 161–2.

[34] See pp. 142–3.

utilitarian and majoritarian maxim of 'the greatest happiness for the greatest number' was implicitly inimical towards minorities.[35] Although Encrevé has seen no fundamental conflict between the enfranchisement of ever broader sectors of the population and the condition of French Jews and Protestants,[36] the relationship between the expansion of political participation and the emancipation of religious minorities seems to have been at least ambivalent. The situation in Italy – where, with less than two per cent of the population allowed to vote until the electoral reforms of 1882 and seven per cent until 1912 the discrepancy between *pays réèl* and *pays légal* ('real' versus 'legal' country) was extremely wide by comparison with Britain, France and Germany – appears to vindicate the argument that the absence of mass politics smoothed emancipation, whereas the expansion of political participation exacerbated the relations of religious minorities with the majority society.[37]

A further feature of nineteenth-century modernisation that presented dilemmas for religious minorities was state intervention. As Cesarani remarked, the tendency of the state to interfere in areas that were once deemed the domain of the individual increased from the middle of the nineteenth century. Several of the regulations enacted by the state had implications for British Jews, in two ways. First, the imposition of compulsory general regulations on matters ranging from factories, schools and slaughterhouses to Sunday observance meant that the state frequently came into conflict with the way of life of British Jews, and second, because the Jews required exemptions, they were marked out as being different from the majority.[38] While Cesarani has a point in identifying a trend towards greater state intervention as causing difficulties for minorities and although this characteristic was common to the British, German, French and Italian nation states, this should not obscure the fact that the boundaries of the state – the areas and extent of state intervention, the way in which it was exercised, as well as the legal system through which it operated – differed considerably from country to country. The differences in those boundaries were reflected in differences in the scope of the formal emancipation for each minority. In Britain, where the state was 'weak' the formal emancipation of the Jews revolved around their politico-legal status. In Germany, by contrast, where the

---

[35] See p. 39.
[36] See pp. 79, 81–2.
[37] C. Seton-Watson, *Italy from liberalism to Fascism, 1870–1925* (London, 1967), pp. 16, 50–1; D. Mack Smith, *Modern Italy: A political history* (New Haven and London, 1997), pp. 123–4.
[38] See pp. 39–40, 48–9.

presence of the boundaries of the state extended further into social, economic, educational and religious areas, the emancipation of the Jews was not only an issue of political reform but also one of social, economic, educational and mental changes, as Clark has demonstrated.[39] If in Germany, and to a certain extent also in France, it was primarily the state that sought to change the socio-economic structure of the Jewish minority, ideally on the model of the majority society, by active intervention, in Britain and Italy most of the initiative to refashion the Jewish communities to conform with the standards of the surrounding society appears to have come from the communal leadership.[40] As crucial as the extent of state intervention in the lives of the members of a religious minority was the manner in which it was executed. In Britain government measures that concerned religious minorities were usually negotiated, as Cesarani has admitted.[41] On the Continent, by contrast, they tended to be unilaterally imposed by the state, as demonstrated by the Napoleonic reorganisation of the French Protestant and Jewish communities.[42] The greater penetration of continental societies by the state was, however, not necessarily detrimental to minorities. The state-controlled Italian, French and German university systems, the latter at least on the student level, were open to the members of religious minorities in the nineteenth century, whereas the British universities of Cambridge and Oxford, as well as the independent public schools, discriminated against non-Anglicans.[43]

Another important aspect of the construction of the British, French, German and Italian nation states that had important repercussions on the emancipatory experience of religious minorities was the respective organisation of relations between the state and the Church – an area in which, as the present volume (if implicitly) suggests, there is scope for reassessment. The argument that religious minorities benefited from the separation of state and Church on the model of the United States has been echoed in the contributions on French Jews and Protestants.[44] Malino explicitly links the vindication of Dreyfus in 1906 to the separation of Church and state a year earlier.[45] While an attenuation of the exclusive position that the established Church enjoyed *vis-à-vis* the public sphere was a precondition for the emancipation of religious minorities,

[39] See pp. 132–7, 139–41.
[40] See pp. 54, 172–3, 178–9.
[41] See p. 40.
[42] See pp. 73, 89–90.
[43] See pp. 20, 47–8, 93, 139.
[44] See pp. 71–2, 82, 91.
[45] See p. 99.

the example of Britain demonstrates that the existence of established Churches was not *per se* detrimental. More important for the successes and deficiencies experienced by the religious minorities in their emancipation appears to have been the degree of national consensus on relations between the state and the Church, irrespective of whether it was based on strict separation, as in the United States of America, or the gradual co-option of religiously defined minorities into a nation state with an established Church, as in Britain.

Secularisation in general has come to be seen as a characteristic of nineteenth-century British, French, German and Italian history and, like the separation of Church and state, as beneficial to the emancipation of religious minorities. With the emphasis on the emergence of a secular public sphere as a precondition for such emancipation, two questions raised by secularisation have not figured prominently in the debate until recently. First, what impact did countervailing trends of secularisation have on religious minorities? Second, how did religious minority communities meet the challenge of a process that undermined their defining element *vis-à-vis* the state and society at large? The nineteenth century was characterised not only by secularisation but also by countervailing trends.[46] That the persistence or revival of the religious beliefs of the majority population and the ruling elites, both in traditional and modernised versions, was problematic for religious minorities, is reflected in the contributions to this volume.[47] By drawing attention to the concept of the 'Christian state' in the wake of Catholic emancipation, Cesarani underlined not only the place Christianity occupied in British politics but also its novelty. Only when Catholic emancipation had undermined the Protestant character of the British state was it redefined as Christian. This left British Jews in a comparatively worse position, as they had previously occupied a place which was similar to that of other non-Anglicans, without being singled out as Jews. It would be intriguing to apply Cesarani's interpretation of the nineteenth-century Christian (rather than exclusively

---

[46] See, for example, M. Anderson, 'The limits of secularisation', *Historisches Jahrbuch*, 38 (1995), 647–70, and H. McLeod (ed.), *European religion in the age of great cities (1830–1930)* (London, 1995). For the problems involved in developing adequate concepts for the assessment of the de-Christianisation and re-Christianisation, see H. Lehmann (ed.), *Säkularisierung, Dechristianisierung, Rechristianisierung im neuzeitlichen Europa: Bilanz und Perspektiven der Forschung* (Göttingen, 1997); Lehmann, 'The christianization of America and the dechristianization of Europe in the 19th and 20th centuries' and 'Zwischen Dechristianisierung und Rechristianisierung', *Kirchliche Zeitgeschichte*, 11:1 (1998), 8–20 and 158–9.

[47] See pp. 18–19, 31, 35–44, 63, 66, 74–81, 91, 104–5, 112–13, 118, 129–30, 138–9, 159, 168.

Protestant) definition of the British state, with its consequent marginalisation of the Jews, to the German scene. One could argue – probably with more justification than in the British case – that the Christian state, as opposed to the early modern confessional state, was a nineteenth-century novelty, an instrument to provide a coherent underpinning ideology to states with a mixed Catholic–Protestant population – a coherence that was based on the exclusion of the Jews.

With regard to the substitutes of traditional religion Cesarani has argued that Victorian mainstream mentalities characterised by a mixture of Protestantism, secularised forms of Protestantism, liberal and utilitarian beliefs were not only unwelcoming of British-Jewish particularity but also, because of their universalist claims, positively threatening to it.[48] Secularised German Protestantism was no more hospitable to Jewish distinctiveness.[49] Theodor Mommsen, for example, no longer believed in traditional Christian doctrines but in a Christian civilisation, which he thought Jews well advised to join by conversion, if for purely secular reasons.[50] In a similar vein, the majority of the proponents of cultural Protestantism intent on reconciling the Protestant religion with modernity and propagating a moral and cultural state – who in the political arena, as members of the *Verband zur Abwehr des Antisemitismus*, were staunch defenders of Jewish civil rights – insisted on a homogeneous German culture in which there was no place for either Jewish or Catholic distinctiveness.[51] Not only did religion differentiate religious minorities from the majority society and the state, it was also the criterion by which its place in the nineteenth-century British, French, German and Italian nation states was defined, however problematical this place was. One wonders how religious minority communities met the challenge of a process that undermined their defining element.

IV

If this collection of essays has corroborated existing evidence about the emancipatory experience of religious minorities in nineteenth-century Europe, provided a novel view on their development by examining them in parallel and paved the way for new insights, it has no less highlighted significant *lacunae*. Further areas where the comparative method could be employed include: the forms of post-emancipationist collective continuity,

---

[48] See pp. 39–40 42–3.
[49] See G. Hübinger, *Kulturprotestantismus und Politik* (Tübingen, 1994), pp. 263–75
[50] Liebeschütz, 'Treitschke', pp. 176–80.
[51] Hübinger, *Kulturprotestantismus und Politik*), pp. 263–75, 291–302.

inter-minority relations, the diversity within minorities, and the impact of the overall numerical weight of a minority or its share in specific socio-economic strata on its emancipatory experience. One could further compare the 'prizes' minorities had to pay for their emancipation and ascertain whether the scope of the changes demanded explicitly or implicitly of Jewish minorities by state and society at large had any kind of a parallel in the case of non-dominant Christian minorities.

The importance of the delimitation of the continuing collectivity of religious minorities after their emancipation has been underscored in the contributions to this volume. Following on from this, one could establish several criteria for comparison. First, how did the collective side of a religious minority manifest itself? Was the infrastructure maintained by a religious minority directed to purely religious ends or did it pertain to other areas, such as party politics, social work or social life? In which ways was the respective minority linked to members of the same group across the border?[52] Second, one has to identify those elements of the collective existence of a minority which caused controversy between the minority and the majority society.[53] Third, how did the minority defend its collective interests *vis-à-vis* the larger society? Was it possible to make demands as members of a particular group, or was there a need to present them in a universalist fashion in order to be successful in the political arena? The third question can be reversed: To what degree, if at all, did the state and the surrounding society recognise the collective existence of a religious minority? To what extent were they prepared to tolerate minority customs, allow separate schools, respect religious holidays or the dietary requirements of the adherents of a religious minority? Were religious minorities organised as private associations or were they recognised by the state?[54]

---

[52] D. Vital, 'European Jewry 1860–1919: Political organisation and trans-state political action', in P. Smith (ed.), *Ethnic groups in international relations. Comparative studies on governments and non-dominant ethnic groups in Europe, 1850–1940*, vol. 5 (New York and Aldershot, 1991), pp.39–57.

[53] The most convenient way of identifying the potential sources of friction between minority and majority that needed to be regulated is to look at the respective legislations and jurisdictions. For an account of the legal position of British Jews from the resettlement until the early twentieth century, see H. S. Q. Henriques, *The Jews and the English law* (London, 1908); for the legal position of Italian non-Catholics, see G. Peyrot, 'La legislazione sulle confessioni religiose diverse dalla cattolica' in P. A. D'Avack (ed.), *Atti del congresso celebrativo del centenario delle amministrative di unificazione. Firenze 10–12 ottobre 1965* (Vicenza, 1967), pp. 519–56; G. Fubini, *La condizione giuridica dell'ebraismo italiano. Dal periodo napoleonico alla Repubblica* (Florence, 1974) and C. Ghisalberti, 'Sulle condizione giuridica degli ebrei in Italia dall'emancipazione alla persecuzione: spunti per una riflessione', in *Italia judaica. Gli ebrei nell'Italia unita, 1870–1945. Atti del IV convegno internazionale. Siena, 12–16 giugno 1989* (Rome, 1993), pp. 19–31.

[54] See, for example, E. Capuzzo, 'Sull'ordinamento delle communità ebraiche dal Risorgimento al Fascismo', in *Italia judaica. Gli ebrei nell'Italia unita, 1870–1945. Atti del*

Apart from the methodological desirability of establishing the 'collective' side of emancipation as a category in its own right and of research concerned with a set of corresponding questions, several thematic areas deserve further attention. Comparatively little still is known about inter-minority relations. While there has been some interest in inter-minority relations within the context of the study of anti-Semitism and of attempts at co-operation in the political arena, everyday relations between members of religious minorities are largely unknown territory.[55] Although one would like to know more about the extent (or lack of) co-operation in national politics, a social history of inter-minority relations appears to be the major desideratum. When Count Beust, one-time Prime Minister of Saxony, remarked of his compatriots that their blood reached boiling point at the sight of a Jew or a Jesuit, one wonders what consequences discrimination, contempt and condescension by the majority society had for the attitudes of members of a minority *vis-à-vis* one another, whether they rather sought to establish links with the majority society, or whether the antipathy with which they were met by society at large resulted in the formation of a sphere of social interaction among themselves.[56] In *Doctor Faustus* Thomas Mann implies as much when he has Serenus Zeitbloom – a Catholic from the fictitious town Kaisersachern, located in the Protestant heartland of Germany – say: 'It was remarkable that besides our priest, Eccl. Councillor Zwilling, the rabbi of the place, Dr. Carlebach by name, used also to visit us in our home above the shop and laboratory, and that, in Protestant houses, would not have been easy.'[57] In order to establish whether such utterances may be taken as symptomatic of a significant social reality or must be dismissed as anecdotal curiosities one needs to examine inter-minority relations on a local level.

Apart from inter-minority relations the divisions within religious minorities deserve further study. The diverse components of religious minorities have attracted attention in their own right and as sources of

---

IV convegno internazionale. Siena, 12–16 giugno 1989 (Rome, 1993), pp. 186–205.

[55] See, for example: O. Blaschke, *Katholizismus und Antisemitismus im Deutschen Kaiserreich* (Göttingen, 1997); C. Nonn, 'Zwischenfall in Konitz', *Historische Zeitschrift*, 266:2 (1998), 387–418; V. Caron and P. Hyman, 'The failed alliance'; M. Breuer, *Jüdische Orthodoxie im Deutschen Reich, 1871–1918: Die Sozialgeschichte einer religiösen Minderheit* (Frankfurt, 1986), pp. 87, 89, 231, 281, 298–300; for the relations between German Catholics and Jews, see Clark, pp. 144–5.

[56] *Memoirs of Friedrich Ferdinand Count von Beust*, ed. by Baron H. de Worms (London, 1887), vol. 1, p. 129.

[57] Th. Mann, *Doctor Faustus: The life of the German composer Adrian Leverkühn as told by a friend*, trans. from the German by H. T. Lowe-Porter (London, 1949), p. 7.

intra-communal friction.[58] In this volume Machin has drawn attention to the differences between 'old Catholics' and Irish immigrants, as has Romagnani to the divisions between Waldensians and the more recent adherents of Protestantism in Italy.[59] Less is known about the divisions that resulted from the identification (or the lack of it) with the modern nation state than is known about the diversification of religious minorities for internal reasons. Whereas Birnbaum has been comprehensive in his portrayal of the *'juifs d'état'*, the French Jews who formed a close relationship with the Third Republic,[60] one would like to know more about the social and cultural background of the *Staatskatholiken*, those Catholics who sided with the State in the *Kulturkampf*, or about that segment of British Catholicism which formed the social matrix of the anti-ultramontane 'Cisalpine Club' of 1792 and later attempts to form a 'native British' form of Catholicism.[61]

A considerable body of scholarship exists on the demographic development of minorities and their share in specific socio-economic strata, such as the professions, academia, the military, commerce and industry or the political class. It is, however, only from a comparative angle that the impact that the weight of numbers, the economic role or the social standing of members of a minority had on minority–majority relations can be assessed. The fact that German Catholics constituted approximately a third of the population and played a corresponding role in national politics appears to be an important reason for the intensity of the *Kulturkampf*, for which there was no real parallel in Britain, although the anti-Catholic antipathies of the majority society were probably no less pronounced. The effect of the social composition of a minority on its emancipatory experience stands to gain from a comparison of, for example, the nineteenth-century *embourgeoisement* of German Jews with that of their British counterparts, which was by and large a twentieth-century phenomenon.

As can be gathered from the above observations and suggestions, there is ample scope for comparative studies of Catholic, Protestant and Jewish minorities promising a better understanding both of the emancipatory experience of the minorities themselves and of the nation states of which they formed part. It is hoped that this volume has highlighted the benefits to be gained from a comparative approach and that it will act as an incentive to undertake cross-minority comparisons.

---

[58] Breuer, *Jüdische Orthodoxie*; L. P. Gartner, *The Jewish immigrant in England, 1870–1914* (London, 1960); W. Loth, 'Soziale Bewegungen im Katholizsmus des Kaiserreichs', Geschichte und Gesellschaft, 17 (1991), 279–310.
[59] See pp. 16–17, 162–3.
[60] Birnbaum, *Les fous de la république*.
[61] See p.16.

Chronology of formal emancipation

British Catholics

1791	Freedom of worship for Catholics in England and Wales (1793 in Scotland)
1793	Catholics allowed to vote in Irish parliamentary elections
1829	Catholic Relief Bill, allowing Catholics to become members of the House of Commons
1836	Marriages among non-Anglicans officially recognised
1845	Maynooth Act. House of Commons voted for a much enlarged and regular subsidy to the central seminary of the Irish Roman Catholic Church
1871	Abolition of University Test Acts, enabling Catholics to take all degrees (except divinity) in Oxford, Cambridge and Durham

British Jews

1753	Parliament repealed Jewish naturalisation Act of the same year after popular agitation
1832	Jews permitted to obtain the Freedom of City of London
1833	Jews permitted to become barristers
1838	Moses Montefiore became the first Jew to hold a public office in England (Sheriff of London)
1858	First Jew to be admitted as Member of the House of Commons (Lionel de Rothschild)

1871	Abolition of University Test Acts, enabling Jews to take all degrees at the universities of Oxford, Cambridge and Durham
1885	First Jewish peer (Nathaniel de Rothschild)

French Protestants

1787	Edict of toleration for non-Catholics, relieving some of the civil disabilities of French Protestants
1789	Political emancipation
1802	Promulgation of the 'Organic Articles' for the Protestant cults
1905	Separation of Church and state

French Jews

1790	Emancipation of Sephardic Jews (28 January)
1791	Emancipation of Ashkenazic Jews (27 September)
1808	Promulgation of three edicts by Napoleon reorganising French Jewry (17 March). The third, the 'infamous' (*décret infâme*) imposed constraints on the economic activities of the Jews in the easternmost *départements;* it remained in force in France until 1818.
1831	Establishment of parity between Christians and Jews, whose rabbis are now paid by the public treasury, as were Catholic priests and Protestant pastors (8 February)

German Catholics

1803	Dissolution of the Imperial Church (*Reichsdeputations-hauptschluss*); millions of Catholics came under Protestant rule; monasteries and convents dissolved
1815	Federal German constitution guaranteed civic and political rights to Catholics, Lutherans and members of the Reformed Church

Chronology

1837	Cologne Disturbances following the arrest of Cologne's archbishop by the Prussian authorities
1850	Prussian constitution granted comparatively wide-ranging freedom to Catholic Church
1871–81	*Kulturkampf*
1871	Formation of 'Centre Party'
1872	Jesuits expelled from Germany
1873	'May Laws' drastically curtailing Church rights
1875	Most Catholic religious orders dissolved
1878–79	Negotiations with the papacy for the cessation of the *Kulturkampf*; piecemeal, though incomplete, abrogation of repressive laws during the following years
1918	Constitution of the Republic of Weimar

German Jews

1782	'Edict of Toleration' for Austrian Jews
1798–1814	Jews of several German territories occupied by the French obtained civic equality (revoked after liberation)
1807–13	Numerous German states passed 'Jew laws', partially enlarging, partially restricting Jewish rights
1812	Prussian 'Edict of Emancipation'
1848	Frankfurt National Assembly proclaimed civic rights regardless of religious creed (revoked in 1850)
1862	Jewish emancipation completed in the first German state (Baden)
1869	North German Confederation proclaimed complete emancipation of all religions
1871	Constitution of the German Empire adopted law of 1869
1918	Constitution of the Republic of Weimar

Italian Protestants

1798	Proclamation of legal equality irrespective of religious belief by the provisional Republican government in Turin, following French invasion
1815	Abolition of the civil and political emancipation of non-Catholics in Piedmont
1848	Granting of civil and political rights to non-Catholics in Piedmont and Tuscany; constitutional guarantee of the civil equality of all subjects through the *Statuto Albertino*
1870	Completion of Protestant emancipation following the Italian conquest of Rome

Italian Jews

1782	'Edict of Toleration' for Austrian Jews (including the Jews of the Lombardo-Venetian kingdom)
1798	'First Emancipation' following the invasion of Italy by French troops
1805	Complete emancipation following the establishment of the Kingdom of Italy
1815	Abolition of emancipation (with the exception of the Hapsburg Lombardo-Venetian kingdom and Tuscany, where it remained in place *de facto*)
1848	Granting of civil and political rights to 'non-Catholics' in Piedmont and Tuscany; constitutional guarantee of the civil equality of all subjects through the *Statuto Albertino*
1870	Completion of Jewish emancipation following the Italian conquest of Rome

Select English-language bibliography

British Catholics

D. Hempton, *Religion and political culture in Britain and Ireland: From the Glorious Revolution to the decline of empire* (Cambridge, 1996).

W. Hinde, *Catholic emancipation: A shake to men's minds* (Oxford, 1992).

R. W. Linker, 'The English Roman Catholics and emancipation: The politics of persuasion', *Journal of Ecclesiastical History*, 27 (1976), 151–80.

G. I. T. Machin, *The Catholic question in English politics, 1820 to 1830* (Oxford, 1964).

E. Norman, *The English Catholic Church in the nineteenth century* (Oxford, 1984).

D. G. Paz, *Popular anti-Catholicism in mid-Victorian England* (Stanford, 1992).

D. Quinn, *Patronage and piety: The politics of English Roman Catholicism, 1850–1900* (Basingstoke, 1993).

British Jews

G. Alderman, 'English Jews or Jews of the English persuasion? Reflections on the emancipation of Anglo-Jewry', in P. Birnbaum and I. Katznelson (eds), *Paths of emancipation: Jews, states and citizenship* (Princeton, 1995).

I. Finestein, 'Anglo-Jewish opinion during the struggle for emancipation (1828–1858)', *Transactions of the Jewish Historical Society of England*, 20 (1964), 113–34.

U. R. Q. Henriques, 'The Jewish emancipation controversy in nineteenth century Britain', *Past and Present*, 40 (1968), 126–46.

M. C. N. Salbstein, *The emancipation of the Jews in Britain. The question of the admission of the Jews to Parliament* (East Brunswick, N. J., 1982).

French Protestants

E. Berensen, *Populist religion and left-wing politics in France 1830–1852* (Princeton, 1984).

E. Leonard, *A history of Protestantism* (transl. from the French) (Indianapolis, 1968).

G. Lewis, *The Second Vendée: The continuity of counterrevolution in the Department of the Gard, 1789–1815* (Oxford, 1978).

T. Margadant, *French peasants in revolt: The insurrection of 1851* (Princeton, 1979).

B. Poland, *French Protestantism and the French Revolution: A study in Church and state, thought and religion, 1685–1815* (Princeton, 1957).

S. Schram, *Protestantism and politics in France* (Alençon, 1954).

T. Tackett, *Religion, revolution and regional culture in eighteenth-century France: The ecclesiastical oath of 1791* (Princeton, 1986).

French Jews

P. Birnbaum, *Anti-Semitism in France: A political history from Léon Bloom to the present* (Oxford, 1992).

V. Caron, *Between France and Germany: The Jews of Alsace-Lorraine, 1871–1918* (Stanford, 1988).

P. Hyman, *The emancipation of the Jews of Alsace* (New Haven, 1991).

P. Hyman, *From Dreyfus to Vichy: The remaking of French Jewry, 1906–1939* (New York, 1979).

F. Malino, *The Sephardic Jews of Bordeaux: Assimilation and emancipation in Revolutionary and Napoleonic France* (Tuscaloosa, 1978).

M. Marrus, *The politics of assimilation: A study of the French Jewish community at the Dreyfus Affair* (Oxford, 1971).

M. Marrus and B. Wasserstein (eds), *The Jews in modern France* (Hanover, N.H., 1985).

German Catholics

M. L. Anderson, 'The Kulturkampf and the course of German history', *Central European History*, 19 (1986), 82–115.

D. Blackbourn, 'Catholics and politics in Imperial Germany: The Centre Party and its constituency', in David Blackbourn, *Populists and Patricians: Essays in modern German history* (London, 1987), pp. 188–214.

D. Blackbourn, *Marpingen: Apparitions of the Virgin Mary in Bismarckian Germany* (Oxford, 1993).
R. J. Ross, 'Enforcing the Kulturkampf in the Bismarckian state and the limit of coercion in Imperial Germany', *Journal of Modern History*, 56 (1984), 456–82.
J. Sperber, *Popular Catholicism in nineteenth century Germany* (Princeton, 1984).
H. Walser Smith, *German nationalism and religious conflict: Culture, ideology, politics, 1870–1914* (Princeton, 1995).

German Jews

J. Katz, 'The term "Jewish Emancipation". Its origin and historical impact', in J. Katz, *Zur Assimilation und Emanzipation der Juden: Ausgewählte Schriften* (Darmstadt, 1982), pp. 99–123.
W. E. Mosse, 'From "Schutzjuden" to "Deutsche Staatsbürger jüdischen Glaubens". The long and bumpy road of Jewish emancipation in Germany', in P. Birnbaum and I. Katznelson (eds), *Paths of emancipation: Jews, states and citizenship* (Princeton, 1995), pp. 59–93.
Reinhard Rürup, 'The tortuous and thorny path to legal equality: "Jew laws" and emancipatory legislation in Germany from the late eighteenth century', *Leo Baeck Institute Yearbook*, 31 (1986), 3–33.
David Sorkin, 'The impact of emancipation on German Jewry: A reconsideration', in J. Frankel and S. Zipperstein (eds), *Assimilation and community. The Jews in nineteenth-century Europe* (Cambridge, 1992), pp. 177–98.

Italian Protestants

P. Stephens, *The Waldensian story: A study in faith, intolerance and survival* (Lewes, 1998).
G. Tourn, *You are my witnesses: The Waldensians across 800 years* (Turin, 1989).

Italian Jews

Y. L. Batto, 'Italian Jewry', *Leo Baeck Institute Year Book*, 3 (1958), 333–43.
A. Canepa, 'Emancipation and Jewish response in mid-nineteenth-century Italy', *European History Quarterly*, 16 (1986), 403–39.
L. Dubin, 'Trieste and Berlin. The Italian role in the cultural politics of

the Haskalah', in J. Katz (ed.), *Towards modernity: The European Jewish Model* (New York and Oxford, 1989), pp. 189–224.

L. M. Gunzberg, *Strangers at home: Jews in the Italian literary imagination* (Berkeley and Los Angeles, 1992).

H. Stuart Hughes, *Prisoners of hope: The silver age of the Italian Jews, 1924–1974* (Cambridge, M.A., 1982).

C. Roth, *The history of the Jews in Italy* (Philadelphia, 1946).

D. Segre, 'The emancipation of Jews in Italy', in P. Birnbaum and I. Katznelson (eds), *Paths of emancipation: Jews, states and citizenship* (Princeton, 1995) pp. 206–37.

Index

Note: 'n.' after a page number refers to a note on that page.

Aachen 106
Achili, Father 27
Acton, Sir John 30
Acts of Supremacy and Uniformity 20
d'Aguilar Samuda, Joseph 46
Airdrie 27
Alba-Lasource, Marc David 68
Albi (Tarn) 56
Alessandria 164, 169
Algeria 99
Allgemeine Zeitung des Judentums 145
Alliance Israélite Universelle 95–7, 99
Alsace 8, 57–60, 67, 69–70, 84, 88, 93–4, 99
Altenstein, Karl von 105
Amicis, Edmondo de 160
anti-Semitism 7–9, 34, 41, 54, 97–9, 114, 143, 145–7, 170, 172n.6, 178, 187, 195n.17, 198n.24
Appia, Giorgo 160, 162, 165
Archives israélites 93
Archivio Veneto 186
Arezzo 169

Arnaud 162
Ashkenazim 8, 84, 86, 170
Austria 102, 104, 105n.14, 106n.16, 138
Azeglio, Roberto d' 153, 155

Bachem, Julius 120–1
Baden 103–4, 106n.16, 110, 125, 130–1, 136, 138, 141
Bagdad 97
Balbo, Cesare 154
Baptists 78, 163, 166
Barbaroux, Giuseppe 153
Barletta 165
Barruel, Abbot 71
Bavaria 106n.16, 124, 127, 134, 136, 138, 143
Bayonne, 91
Beckwith, Charles 152
Belgium 106
Benamozegh, Elia 186
Bene' Zion 178, 180–2, 185
Benisch, Abraham 44–5, 50–2
Berg 129
Bergamo 150, 152, 167
Berlin 106, 129, 136, 139–40
Berr, Berr Isaac 90

[215]

Bert, Amedeo 154–6
Bertin, Henri Léonard 84
Beust, Friedrich Ferdinand, count 205
Biez, Jacques 99
Bigart, Jacques 97
Birkenhead 27
Birmingham 25
Bismarck, Otto von 21, 113, 144–5
Bleichröder, Gerson von 97
Bonaparte, Jérôme, king of Westphalia 125
Bonn 133
Bordeaux 91, 95n.25
Bosnia 50
Bourbon, Lucca Carlo Ludovico, duke 153
Brandenburg 128
Brighouse 28
Brissot, Jacques-Pierre 95
British and Foreign Bible Society 151, 163, 165
Broglie, Victor de 87
Brotkorbgesetz 115
Brunswick Clubs 18
Bulgarian agitation 40, 50–5, 198
La Buona Novella 160
Burials Act (1880) 20
Bursa 97
Bute, marquess of 18

cahiers de doléances 64
Calabi, Dolcetta 182
Calabria 168
Calvin, John 69, 75, 163
Camborne 28
Cambridge University 20, 46, 201
Capuchins 59, 96
Carfin 31
Carlo Alberto, king of Sardinia-Piedmont 153, 155–6
Carlyle, Thomas 24
Caro, Joseph 186
Casale Monferreto 169
Castlereagh, Robert 49
Catania 165
Catholic Association (Ireland) 14
Catholic Defence Association of Great Britain and Ireland 19
Catholic Institute of Great Britain 19
Catholic Relief Act (1829) 12, 31
Cavour, Camillo 154, 158, 160
Cechetti, Bartolomeo 186
Centre Party 111–14
Cévennes 58n.7, 61, 67, 74–5
Chamberlain, Joseph 48
Charles X, king of France 76
Charles XI, king of France 67n.30
cheder 178
Chisone, Val del 148
Christian monarchy 61, 72
Christian state 7, 39, 43–4, 61, 130, 138, 142, 192, 202–3
Church of Brethren 159, 167
Clarendon, George Villiers, earl of 80
Clermont Tonnere, Stanislas de, count 83, 197
Cobbett, William 41
Code Napoléon 129
Cologne 106
    Cathedral 107n.20
concordat (1801) 72, 82, 90, 150
Conrad, Valentin 58
Constant, Benjamin 73
Contemporary Review 53
conversion
    Catholic 17, 24, 27, 153, 168
    Jewish 42–3, 91, 94, 129–30, 137, 167, 185

Index

Protestant 18, 57–8, 76, 158
Le Courrier de Gorsas 86
Le Courrier de Provence 87
Cracovia, Jacob 181
Crémieux, Adolphe 92, 97
La Croix 99

Daily News 50–1
Damascus Blood Libel 96
Daudet, Léon 71
Dauphiné 61
décret infâme (1808) 90–1, 126, 128
Derby, Edward Stanley, earl of 39
Deutsche Bundesakte 8, 103
Dickens, Charles 41
Disraeli, Benjamin 18, 46, 49, 51–2, 54
Dissenters *see* Nonconformists
Dohm, Christian Wilhelm 132, 136
dragonnade 57
Dreyfus affair 8, 99, 201
Dreyfus family 95
Drumont, Edouard 98–9
Dublin 12
Dundee 25, 27
Duport, Adrien 87
Duquesne, Abraham 58
Durham 20

East Prussia 128
Ecclesiastical Titles Act (1851) 19, 22
L'Echo della Verità 160
L'Echo des Vallées 159
Edict of Nantes 57–8, 60–2, 64
Edict of Tolerance (1787) 56, 62, 71
Edinburgh 25
education *see* schools

Education Act (1870) 47–8, 194, 198
Education Acts (1902) 29
L'Educatore Israelita 186
Emancipation Act (1829) 7
'emancipation contract' 34, 53
emigration
    French Jews 94
    Italian Protestants 168
Emilia 164, 169–70
Engels, Friedrich 24
Erzberger, Matthias 120
Eton 48
Evangelischer Bund 118
Eynard, Jean-Gabriel 151

Factory (Extension) Act (1867) 49
Fauchet, Claude 68
Ferrara 169
First Empire 85, 88–9
Florence 151–2, 163–4, 169
Fontane, Theodor 147
Fould, Achille 93
franchise 12, 78–9, 82, 89, 138, 142–3, 158, 196, 199–200
Francis I, emperor of Austria 179
Frankfurt 18, 138
Frankfurter Zeitung 145
Frederick-William II, king of Prussia 124
Frederick-William III, king of Prussia 127, 129
Frederick-William IV, king of Prussia 107, 137
Free Christian Church 159, 164–6
Free Churches 165, 167
Freeman, A. E. 51–2
Freiburg 118
French Revolution 7–8, 14, 42, 63, 68–72, 74–5, 81, 83–6, 88, 96, 98, 103, 124, 126

[217]

Index

Freytag, Gustav 147
Fritsch, Theodor 147
Froude, James 54

galériens pour la foi 61
Gard 75
Garibaldi, Giuseppe 159–60, 162, 165, 167, 171
Gavazzi, Alessandro 27, 164–6
Gay, Enrico 160
Gazetta Piemontese 155
Geneva 75
Genoa 164
Genossenschaft für die Reform im Judentum 140
George III, king of England 11
George IV, king of England 11
Germanasca 148
German Confederation 103, 127
Geymet, Pietro 149–51
Giolitti, Giovanni 166
Gladstone, William Ewart 28, 30, 39, 47, 49, 51–3
Glasgow 25–7
Glorioso Rimpatrio 160
Gluckstein, Leopold 51
Goriza 169
Görres, Joseph 106
Gorsas, Antoine-Joseph 95
Goudchaux, Michel 93
Gradisca d'Isonzo 169
Greece 97
Greene, J. R. 54
Greenock 27
Grégoire, Henri, abbé 83, 85–6
Gregory XVI, pope 77, 106
Guiccardini, Pietro, count 153, 164
Guizot, François 56, 77

Halévy, Léon 91

Hamburg 131
Hanover 104, 112n.34, 138
Hardenberg, Karl August von 125, 127–8
Harrow 48
Heine, Heinrich 94
Helvetic Republic 88
Henry, Michael 47–9
Henry IV, king of France 58, 77
Hertling, Georg von 120–1
Herzegovina 50
Hesse 136
Hesse-Cassel 104, 130, 133, 138
Hesse-Darmstadt 104, 127n.10, 133
Hochland 120
Hoensbroech, Paul von 118
Holy Coat pilgrimages 107
Holy Roman Empire 59, 102
Hourwitz, Zalkind 85–6
Hoym, Karl von 136

immigration
    Irish 14–17, 23–6, 28–30, 32
    Eastern European Jewish 34, 36, 54, 97
infamous decree *see décret infâme*
Inglis, Sir Robert 39, 43
Ireland 7, 11–16, 18–22, 24, 26, 37
    Home Rule 29–30
Irish Church Temporalities Act (1833) 18, 21
Itzig, Daniel 124

Janavel 162
Janssens, Johannes 117
Jaucourt, Arnail François, marquis 75
Jesuits 59, 115, 145, 193, 205
'Jew Bill' (1753) 41

Jewish Chronicle 44–51
Jewish Historical Society of
    England 41
Jewish Quarterly Review 41
'Jewish Question' 9, 37, 55, 123,
    145, 147
Joseph II, emperor of the Holy
    Roman Empire 124

Ketteler, Wilhelm Emanuel von,
    bishop 117
Killowan, Lord Russel of 30
Kölner Wirren 106, 108
Krauß, Anton Edler von 130
Kulturkampf 8, 102, 109,
    110n.29, 111–19, 121,
    144–5, 193, 206

Lambruschini, Raffaello 156, 164
Lattes, Elia Aron, chief rabbi 177
Lattes, Abraham, rabbi 179
Leghorn 150, 152, 161, 164, 183
Lenoir, Jean, 84
Leopoldo II, grand duke of
    Tuscany 156
Lévi, Sylvain 97
La Libre Parole 99
Lieber, Ernst 120
Liguria 164, 166
Lisle, Ambrose Phillips de 18
Liverpool 26–8, 32
Llandaff, Lord 30
Lombardo-Venetian kingdom 174,
    178n.24, 180, 198n.28
Lombardy 164, 166, 174
London 15, 20, 25–7, 31
    City of 46, 49
London Society for the Promotion
    of Christianity among the
    Jews 137
Lord's Day Observance Act
(1873), 49
Lorraine 94
Louis XIV, king of France 62, 65,
    73
Louis XVI, king of France 62
Louis XVIII, king of France 76
Louis-Philippe, king of the French
    77, 92
Luserna San Giovanni 150
Luther, Martin 78, 113, 117, 163
Luzzatti, Luigi 185
Luzzatto, Samuel David 182, 184,
    186
Lyon 162

Macaulay, Thomas 43
Maimonides 186
Maistre, Joseph de 71
Malan, Giuseppe 158, 161
Malesherbes, Chrétien Lamoignon
    de 84–5
Mallet du Pan, Jacques 62
Manchester 24–7
Mann, Thomas 205
Manning, Henry Edward 17, 29,
    31
Mantova 169, 171, 179
Marpingen 115
Marriages Act (1898) 20
Marseille 95n.25
Mauras, Charles 71, 82
Mayer, Rupert 118
Maynooth College 12, 19, 21, 28
Mazzarella, Bonaventura 167
Mazzini, Giuseppe 159
Mecklenburg 139
Mecklenburg-Schwerin 127
Mendelssohn, Moses 132
Merk, Joseph 140
Messina 165
Methodists 78, 159, 163, 165–7

Index

Metz 84, 92–3
  Academy of Arts and Sciences 84–5, 88
Meyer, Rabbi Félix 83, 92, 99
Midi 70
Milan 164
Miquel, Johannes 147
Mirabeau, Honoré-Gabriel Riqueti, count 67, 69, 83, 87, 95
Mommsen, Theodor 197, 203
Modena 170
Montauban 69
Montpellier 57, 70
Morelli, Giovanni 167
Mortara, Edgar 46, 96
Mortara, Ludovico 171
Mugdan Affair 47n.40
Mulhouse 95
Munk, Salomon 94
Murphy, William 27
Muth, Karl 120

Nancy 85, 95n.25
Naples 161, 165, 167, 169
Napoleon III, emperor of France 8, 78, 80–1, 89
Napoleon Bonaparte 3, 8–9, 72–5, 89–90, 95, 124–9, 150, 152, 173, 181, 201–2
Nassau 104, 128
National Catholic Conservative Association 29
National Primitive Catholic Society 155
Naumann, Friedrich 119
Necker, Jacques 64
Netherlands 127n.10
Nevers 81
Newdegate, C. N. 21
Newman, John Henry 17, 31, 78

Nièvre 81
Nîmes 69, 73, 75
Nineteenth Century 53
Nonconformists 15–16, 19–20, 29, 42–3, 45–6, 48, 53
Norfolk 16
North German Confederation 104, 139

O'Connell, Daniel 14
Orangeism 18, 26
Organic Articles (1802) 72, 78, 90, 150
Der Orient 130
Ottoman Empire 96–7
'Oxford Movement' 17
Oxford University 20, 46, 51, 53, 201

Padova 165, 179–80, 182–3
Padovani, Moisè 178
Palermo 165
Palmerston, Henry John Temple, viscount 42
Pan-German League 118
Pantaleo, Luigi, 165
papacy 17–18, 27, 113 *see also* pope
Parandier, Jacques 155
Paris 57–8, 66–9, 75, 78, 80, 86, 89, 91, 93, 95n.25, 96–7, 149–50
Parliamentary Reform Acts (1867–68) 20, 28
Parma 170
Parnell, Charles Stewart 30
Peel, Robert 21
Peyrot, Giulio 159–60
Piedmont 9, 148–9, 151, 153, 162–4, 166, 168–70, 172, 174, 183

Index

Pignan 57
Pinerolo 149–50
Pisa 152, 164, 169
Pitigliano 169
Pitt, William 11–12
Pius IX, pope 117
Plymouth Brethren 164
Poitou 67, 74
Poland 113, 136–7
political participation *see* franchise
Pomaretto, 152
Pomerania 128
pope 13, 16, 22–3, 30, 107–8, 117
    see also papacy
Posen 137, 199
Poujol, Louis 89
Po Valley 164, 169
Presbyterians 28
Protestant Alliance 19
Protestant Operative Societies 18
Prugnon, Louis Pièrre Joseph 87
Prussia 104–6, 110–11, 113, 115–16, 118, 120, 124–9, 131, 133, 136, 138, 144–5
    Allgemeines Landrecht 104
    Rhine Provinces 121n.60, 128, 137, 142

Rabaut Saint-Etienne, Jean Paul 62–3, 65
Rathsamhausen, Christophe-Philippe, baron 67
Ravensburg 118
regeneration 5, 86, 90–1, 95, 132–5, 140–1, 173, 194
Reichsdeputationshauptschluß 102
Reggio 170
Renan, Ernest 186
rentrée 160
Reubell, Jean-François 88
Revolution (1848) 9, 109, 138, 143

Rheinische Zeitung 138
Rhineland 101, 107n.18, 133, 146
Richelieu, Jean Armand du Plessis, cardinal 58
Riesi 165
riots *see* violence
Ripon, George Robinson, marquess 18, 30
Risorgimento 159, 165, 199
Il Risorgimento 156
Rochette, Franois 61
Romania 97
Rome 10, 162, 165–6, 168–9, 171–2, 186, 198
Rost, Hans 121
Rothschild, Lionel de 44n.32, 46
Rousseau, Jean-Jacques 149
Rugby 48
Russel, Lord 22

Sachsenhausen 118n.51
St Bartholomew's Eve 62, 67, 75
    see also violence, anti-Protestant
Saint Martin 160
Sandwich 46
Sanhedrin (1807) 89, 90n.12, 173, 181
Scandiani, Ester Padovani 177
Saxony 124, 138
schools 94, 151, 155, 166, 173, 177, 179, 186, 201
    Catholic 21, 23, 29, 112
    Jewish 48, 84, 92–3, 95–7, 135–8, 143, 173, 176, 178–9, 198
    Protestant 150, 152
Scotland 14–15, 17, 19–20, 23, 28–9, 32, 37–8
    Church of 13
    Episcopal Church of 22
Scottish Reformation Society 19

[221]

Index

Second Empire 93
Second Republic 93
Sedan 117
Seeley, Sir John 54
Sephardim 8, 84, 169–70
Sicily 168
Siena 169
Silesia 106n.16, 128, 136
Sinigallia 169
Sinn Fein Clubs 32
slavery 38
Smith, Goldwin 53
Soave, Moisé 9, 173–7, 179–86
Soave, Salomon Raffael 175
Società di studi valdesi 161
Société d'histoire vaudoise 160
Société des sciences, agriculture et arts de Strasbourg 92
Sombart, Werner 146
Sonnino, Giorgio Sidney, baron 167
Soulier, Enrico 159
South Prussia 136
Spahn, Martin 118
Staël, Germaine de 73
Stahl, Friedrich Julius 130
Statuto 155–8, 161–2
Steinschneider, Moritz 186
Stockhausen, Georg Konrad 133
Stockport Riots 27
Strasbourg 60n.12, 78, 89, 92, 126
Stuttgart 118
suffrage *see* franchise
Sulamith 139
Sully, Maximilien de Béthune, duc de 58
Switzerland 97
Sybel, Heinrich von 116

Taglialatela, Pietro 165
Le Témoin 159

Test and Corporation Acts repeal of (1828) 13, 15–16
Tetuan 97
Thiéry, Claude-Antoine 85–6
Third Republic 74, 81–2, 97–9, 194, 198
Thile, Ludwig von 144
Times, The 51
Tories 49
Torre Pellice 150–4, 161, 163
Tower Hamlets 46
Tredegar 28
Treitschke, Heinrich von 197
Trier 107
Trieste 169
Turkey 50–3
Turin 148, 150, 152, 154–5, 161–2, 164, 169
  Academy of Sciences 149
Tuscany 164, 169, 174

ultramontanism 16, 18, 119n.29, 118, 121
Umberto I, king of Italy 160
Unger, David 129
United Irish League of Great Britain 32
United States of America 15, 71n.41, 96, 168, 184, 202
Univers Israélite 93
university 20, 93, 116, 118, 121, 139, 155, 179, 201
University Tests Act (1871) 20, 47
Urbino 169

Valdo 162
Vatican Council (1870) 28
Vaughan, Bishop Herbert 29
Venice 10, 165, 169, 172–6, 178–80, 182–3, 185–6

[222]

Vercelli 169
Verona 165
Il Vesillio Israelitico 172
Vichy 82, 99
Victor Emmanuel II, king of Italy 160
Victoria, queen of England 30
Vienna 130
  Congress of 102, 127
Vivarais 61
violence
  anti-Catholic 7, 15, 23, 25–8, 32, 115, 117
  anti-Jewish 8, 131–2, 143, 199
  anti-Protestant 57, 60–1, 69, 75, 117, 165
Virchow, Rudolf 116
Voluntary Schools Association (1884) 29
Vormärz 104, 106, 128, 134–5, 141

Waldburg-Truchsess, Friedrich Ludwig von 152–3
Wales 37–8
Weber, Max 119
Wellington, duke of 12, 18
Westphalia 101, 107n.18, 125, 129, 146
Wetzlar 128
Whigs 16, 18, 35
Whitehaven 28
Wigan 27
Windthorst, Ludwig 100n.1, 112n.32, 114
Wolf, Lucien 97
Wolffe, John 35
Worms, Henry de 46, 48, 205n.56
Württemberg 104, 136, 138

Yiddish 139

Zentrum see Centre Party